THE PRINCE OF THE MARSHES

ALSO BY RORY STEWART

The Places in Between

RORY STEWART

THE PRINCE

OF THE

MARSHES

AND OTHER OCCUPATIONAL
HAZARDS OF A YEAR IN IRAQ

HARCOURT, INC.

Orlando   Austin   New York   San Diego   Toronto   London www.HarcourtBooks.com

Library of Congress Cataloging-in-Publication Data
Stewart, Rory.
The prince of the marshes: and other occupational hazards of a year in Iraq/
Rory Stewart.—1st ed.
p.   cm.
1. Iraq—Description and travel.   2. Iraq—Social life and customs—20th century.
3. Stewart, Rory—Travel.   4. British—Iraq.   I. Title.
DS70.65.S74   2006
956.7044'31—dc22   2006006905
ISBN-13: 978-0-15-101235-0   ISBN-10: 0-15-101235-0

Text set in Baskerville MT
Designed by April Ward

Printed in the United States of America

First edition
A C E G I K J H F D B

To my father,
A great man, a fierce ally,
and most constant friend.

CONTENTS

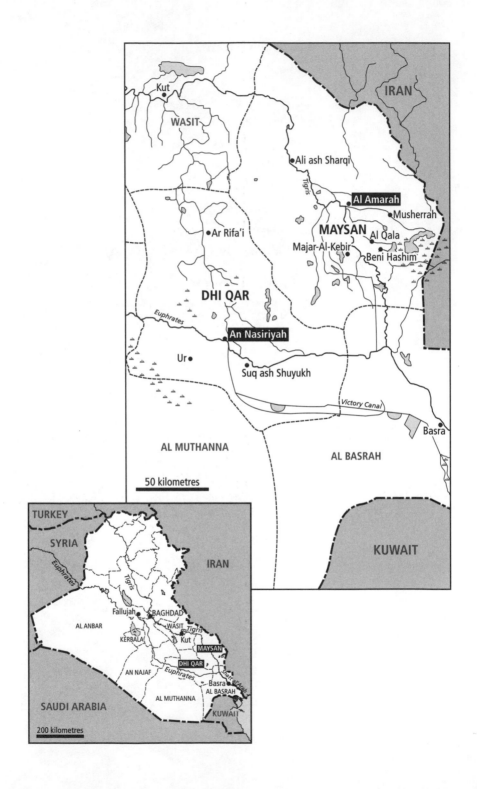

FOREWORD

This book is a record of my personal experience in two provinces of Iraq. It is not a history of the Coalition Provisional Authority. Even as a description of my own experience, it is limited. We worked long days and it seemed a luxury to keep a diary, when there was much else to be done. I took notes in every meeting but there are few complete transcripts of conversations and some notebooks were lost after the siege in Nasiriyah. Much, therefore, depends on memory. Iraq remains a dangerous place and occasionally I have felt it necessary to conceal identities; it is also a confusing place and, while I want to reflect that, I have also occasionally simplified a protracted story.

Because it is a personal memoir, it also focuses—unfairly to my colleagues—on my own work. There were many others in Iraq, whose work was often much more significant than mine. In particular, Molly Phee in Maysan and Barbara Contini in Dhi Qar. They were my superiors and I acted under their authority. Other civilian advisers and military civil affairs teams implemented the development projects, and the British military played a large part not just in security but in politics. Stephen Anderson, Dominic Asquith, Andy Bearpark, Harry Boyle, Toby Bradley, Bruce Brearly, Antonio Burti, George Butler, France Corbani, Tash Coxen, Rachid Elbardi, Mark Etherington, Jeremy Greenstock, Eric Gudenius, Ahmed Harazi, Samantha Jennings, Dick Jones, General Lamb, Kyle Lang, Jay Lucas, Edward Melotte, Ginnie Mottram, Jeremy Nathan, Stefano Nigri, Patrick Nixon, Roberto Pedrale, David Richmond, General Stewart, Hilary Synnott, and Peter Williams, among many others, could each write accounts of the occupation that would be very different from mine. A couple already have.

Just as I have passed over many simple achievements in Iraq, so I have not catalogued the national failures in planning, policy, and administration. This is because I believe it was not grand policy but rather the meetings between individual Iraqis and foreigners that ultimately determined the result of the occupation. I have therefore focused on difficult interactions, in which both sides may often appear combative, comical, bewildered, and grasping. In other contexts, the same people could be patient, wise, clear-sighted, and generous, and I regret that less space has been given to their virtues. I have emphasized the negative because it was the mutual suspicions, not the harmonies, that were decisive.

Finally, I have recorded the politics, the individuals, and histories of the provinces as I understood them as a foreigner. Iraqi friends have already pointed out many errors and omissions. There must be many more.

With the caveats above, to paraphrase Rousseau, while I may not always have recorded what is true, I have tried not to record what I know to be false.

DRAMATIS PERSONAE

MAYSAN

COALITION PROVISIONAL AUTHORITY
Molly Phee—governorate coordinator, Maysan

CIVIL AFFAIRS TEAM
Major Edward Melotte—CPA representative
Major George Butler—head of the civil affairs team
A.J.—finance officer
Charlotte "Charlie" Morris—social affairs officer

IRAQI POLICE
Abu Rashid—police chief, Maysan
Brigadier General Sabih—acting police chief
Seyyed Faqr—police chaplain
Nadhem—police chief, Amara

MARSH ARABS
Seyyed Issa—head of the district council of Beni Hashim

The "progressive classes"
Ali—a young activist
Asad—a middle-aged poet
Hussein—director of the Finance Ministry

POLITICAL PARTIES
"The Prince's Party"
Rural/tribal and relatively secular
Karim Mahood Hattab—"Abu Hatim," "The Prince of the Marshes"

Riyadh Mahood Hattab—brother of the Prince—head of the regeneration committee and candidate for governor

Shia parties

All derived from the original Dawa Party, founded in the late fifties and led by Ayatollah Muhammad Bakr al-Sadr (Sadr I), martyred in 1980

The "Iranian-linked groups"

Supreme Committee for the Islamic Revolution in Iraq (SCIRI)
Formed by the Marytr Ayatollah Muhammed Bakr Al-Hakim
Militia—Badr Brigades and Party of God
Abu Ahmed—SCIRI central, candidate for governor
Abu Miriam—Movement of the Party of God
Abu Maytham—Badr brigades, candidate for police chief

Dawa

Formed by the Martyr Ayatollah Muhammad Bakr al-Sadr (Sadr I)
Abu Muslim—ex-cleric from Dawa movement
Abu Akil—national head of Dawa Iraq tendency
Abu Mustafa—cleric—independent Dawa
Sheikh Rahim—cleric—independent Dawa

The Sadrists (Office of the Martyr Sadr and Fodala)
Formed by the Martyr Ayatollah Muhammad Sadeq al-Sadr (Sadr II)
and led now by his son Muqtada (Sadr III)
and Chief of Staff Al-Yakubi
Militia—Army of the Imam Mehdi
Seyyed Hassan—head of the Sadr Party
Seyyed Sattar—head of the Majar branch of Sadr
Hassan—head of the "alternative councils"

TRIBES
Albu Muhammad
Beni Lam

Al-Azerj

Suwaad

Beni Kaab

Albu Deraaj

Abu Ali

Sudan

Saada

Bahadil

DHI QAR

COALITION PROVISIONAL AUTHORITY

John Bourne—governorate coordinator, Dhi Qar

Barbara Contini—governorate coordinator, Dhi Qar

Jeremy Nathan—deputy governorate coordinator, Dhi Qar

Toby Bradley—political officer, Dhi Qar

Franco Corbani—special projects, Dhi Qar

Sabri Badr Rumaiath—governor of Dhi Qar

Abbas—deputy governor, a Danish citizen

Adnan Sherife—assistant governor

Abdul Amir Al-Hamdani—Director of Archaeology

SADRISTS

Sheikh Aws Al-Khafagi—head of the office

Sheikh Ali Zeidi—Al Rafai leader

Sheikh Muwayad—Nasiriyah leader

Asad Al-Ghuzzi—associate and ally

AL RAFAI TRIBES

Shweilat, Sheikh Arkan Hairullah

Beni Rikaab, Shlage

Yunus, son of Shlage

Ismail

Taleb

TIMELINE

3000 B.C.—Foundation of first Sumerian civilizations on the lower Euphrates

c. 2600 B.C.—Burial of Puabi, a "ruler," at Ur on the lower Euphrates near modern Nasiriyah

2113 B.C.—Ur-Nammu founds Second Dynasty of Ur and with his son Sulgi builds the ziggurat

c. 2000 B.C.—Destruction of Ur by Elamite invasion from the territory of modern Iran

c. 600 B.C.—Final building in Ur under Nebuchadnezzar II of Babylon and his successors

539 B.C.—Capture of Babylon and Mesopotamia by Persian Empire

331 B.C.—Alexander the Great takes Babylon from the Persians

c. 129 B.C.—Parthians (Persians) take Babylon from Alexander's successors

A.D. 224—Sassanians (Persians) in Mesopotamia

637—Muslim/Arab conquest of Mesopotamia

762—Foundation of Baghdad as capital of Abbasid dynasty

869–883—Zinj rebellion, led by African slaves centered in the Marshes

1258—Baghdad sacked by the Mongols

1534–1918—Ottoman (Turkish) rule of the three provinces of Mosul, Baghdad and Basra (modern Iraq)

1916—Britain fights Ottomans for Southern Iraq, takes Amara and Nasiriyah, captures and then loses Kut under General Townsend. Philby and Leachman serve as political officers in Amara, Dixon and Thomas in Nasiriyah and Shatra

1920–1936—Period of British mandate in Iraq

1920—Shia uprising against British

1936–1956—Iraq under Sunni monarchy

1952—British travelers Thesiger, Maxwell, and Young visit and write about the marshes around Amara and Nasiriyah

1958—Coup of Abdul Qarim Qasim (July 14); king killed. Formation of Dawa Party under M. Bakr al-Sadr (Sadr I) in the late 1950s

1963—First Baathist coup, Qasim killed

1968—Second Baathist coup (July 17) makes Ahmad Hassan al-Bakr president and Saddam vice president

1979—Saddam becomes president

1980—Membership in Dawa a capital offense, M. Bakr al-Sadr (Sadr I) executed

1981—Foundation of SCIRI in Iran

1980–1988—Iran-Iraq War

1990—Iraqi invasion of Kuwait

1991—First Gulf War, Shia uprising in south, brutally repressed by Saddam

1991–2003—Sanctions

1998—Assassination of Ayatollah M. Sadeq al-Sadr (Sadr II)

MARCH 2003—Coalition invades Iraq advancing on Baghdad through Nasiriyah; Amara "liberates itself" under the command of the Prince of the Marshes

APRIL 7, 2003—Coalition troops enter center of Baghdad. Widespread looting. Assassination of Ayatollah al-Khoi, possibly orchestrated by Muqtada al-Sadr (Sadr III)

END OF APRIL 2003—Full Coalition control over Amara

MAY 2003—Establishment of Coalition Provisional Authority under Paul Bremer

AUGUST 2003—UN headquarters bombed, assassination of SCIRI founder Ayatollah M. Bakr al-Hakim (Rory Stewart visits Baghdad)

SEPTEMBER 2003—Rory Stewart to Iraq initially as acting governorate coordinator in Maysan

NOVEMBER 2003—Molly Phee arrives as governorate coordinator in Maysan; Rory Stewart becomes her deputy

MARCH 2004—Rory Stewart posted as senior adviser to Dhi Qar

APRIL 2004—Release of transitional administrative law

APRIL–SEPTEMBER 2004—Insurgency against Coalition under Muqtada al-Sadr (Sadr III)

JUNE 28, 2004—Handover of sovereignty from CPA to interim Iraqi government

JANUARY 30, 2005—Elections for transitional government and provincial councils

DECEMBER 15, 2005—Election of constitutional parliament

INTRODUCTION

Res dura et regni novitas me talia cogunt/moliri.
The hardness of reality and the newness of my kingdom force me thus to act.
—*Virgil,* The Aeneid

CAPITALIST-IMPERIALIST-CRUSADER

*Baghdad was a veritable city of palaces . . . and the scene on the river
was animated by thousands of gondolas, decked with little flags, dancing
like sunbeams on the water, and carrying the pleasure-seeking Baghdad
citizens from one part of the city to the other. There were also in Baghdad numerous colleges of learning, hospitals, infirmaries for both sexes,
and lunatic asylums.*

—*Yaqut ibn 'Abdallah ur-Rumi,*
Geographical Encyclopedia, *c. 1224*

In April 2002, after twenty months traveling in Asia, I returned from
Afghanistan to my home in the Highlands of Scotland, a mile from
the nearest town on the edge of a wood. There I wrote and planted
trees: four hundred gean, rowan, Scots pine, oak, box, and Simla de-
odar. I had resigned from the Foreign Office. But when the invasion
of Iraq began in March 2003, I sent in my resume. No one replied.
In August, I took a taxi from Jordan to Baghdad to ask for a job from
the director of operations.

I traveled around the city guided by a pamphlet I had found at
a book stall, lodged between a 1950s English chemistry textbook
and the third volume of a French almanac from 1983. There was a
strong smell of kebabs and stagnant river water, and the lanes were
choked with carts selling clothes and electronic goods. Satellite dishes,
banned by the old regime, were now, judging by the skyline, owned
by half the households in the city. I walked alone through groups of
men who wore the shiny western clothes and sunglasses I had seen in

the Balkans—I guessed the suits had probably been made in the Balkans. Everyone laughed and gestured in a way that to me, a newcomer, seemed theatrical.

I visited a family of eight living in a single tenement room behind the illegal weapons market in Sadr City. The father, a postal clerk, worked in the oil ministry, and the Coalition had just raised his salary from five dollars a month to sixty, fifty-five of which he was spending to rent the thirty-inch television that sat in the corner of the room. Beside the screen, on a torn blanket, lay his youngest child, three months old and weighing seven pounds. The infant had not been able to feed for three days, and he and his wife thought their child would soon die.

The pamphlet guided me past narrow houses with wooden balconies that had once belonged to Jewish merchants—a third of Baghdadis had been Jews, there were now none. In the corner of a parking lot I found the slender arch of a demolished mosque, decorated with stars, octagons, and Koranic script in fourteenth-century terra-cotta. Between these monuments to "the greatest city in the medieval world, the capital of a civilization that extended from Spain to India," were mosques decorated in ordinary bathroom tiles and underground arcades lit by strip lights, swinging from bare electric wires.

A few entrepreneurs had attempted a tourist industry. An Egyptian had converted a caravanserai into a restaurant, dressed his waiters in fezes, and offered an "Ali Baba banquet" complete with water-pipes. In the covered market, shops displayed piles of new Afghani carpets, fake amber beads, imitation muskets and suits of Mameluke armor. On the walls were Polaroids of Western women, smiling self-consciously in baggy shirts and striped hiking socks, their headscarves falling back on their heads. Their business cards, pasted to the ledger marked "visitors' book," revealed a collection of UN officials, embassy staff, and French oil workers. No one seemed, however, to have been to the shop in a month.

A few people spat or jostled me as I passed. In the old café where the painters sat, a poet lectured me on what he called the "capitalist-imperialist-crusader-occupation of Iraq." At a saint's shrine by the ruined city wall, an old man insisted I enter his car because he thought the crowd of men approaching had noticed that I was a foreigner and were coming to kill me. He may have been overcautious, but he dropped me safely back at the central Sunni mosque, and I went inside. When I left, the door-keeper requested a donation to support young Iraqis in the jihad against American soldiers, and when I refused, he presented me with a booklet detailing U.S. atrocities, illustrated with photographs of minarets that had been shattered by American bombs. Nevertheless, by my third night in Baghdad, in my small apartment in the south of the city, I felt happier than I had for a long time.

On my return to Britain, the Foreign Office asked me to be the deputy governorate coordinator of Maysan, which lay in the marshes just north of the Garden of Eden. Or rather just north of the dead date palm and visitors' parking lot that Iraqis claimed marked the site of paradise. Western travelers had often described the marshes of Maysan as though they preserved something of that pre-Fall innocence, with flocks of rare birds in the sky over the waterland and reed halls built to a design more than five thousand years old. The inhabitants, the Marsh Arabs, living in wicker huts on floating reed beds with their buffalo, contrasted dramatically with their neighbors in the tents of desert Arabia. The British explorers of the 1950s photographed these naked men standing with tridents against a flat marsh sky, making them appear, perhaps deliberately, to be Neolithic Polynesians in a changeless Eden. Meanwhile the traditional values of the Marsh Arabs were crumbling, young men left for low-paying jobs in the cities, the power of the tribes declined, government intruded, villagers grew healthier. In the 1980s, the marshes became the front line of the Iran-Iraq war; tens of thousands fled to Iran or were taken there as prisoners; trenches, minefields, and unexploded shells were scattered over the eastern side of the territory; the reeds hid deserters and Iranian-backed guerrillas. The population were almost all Shia Muslims and many joined the Shia uprising against Saddam in 1991.

In response, Saddam Hussein drained the marshes and scattered the inhabitants. A thousand square miles of water was run off into a ditch known as the Victory Canal, three kilometers wide and eighty kilometers long. Saddam denied Marsh Arabs medical treatment, bombed villages, burned houses, killed thousands of religious and tribal leaders and littered with water mines the small patches of marsh that remained. Much of the province was reduced to desert. More than a hundred thousand people became homeless. Small pockets of smugglers and resistance fighters continued to evade central control, but the marshes would never again shelter many of Saddam's enemies. The old structures of society had been shattered and replaced with the apparatus of the Baath party. Everything began in Baghdad, passing through the hands of the President's corrupt family and his security service.

Now, the U.S.-led invasion had destroyed the old regime. Those who had been in charge fled, afraid of retribution, taking or buying whatever files had not already been destroyed by the bombing and the looting. Middle-aged junior officials now found themselves directors of offices carpeted with charred documents and stripped of desks, ceiling tiles, and electrical wires. The sheikhs tried to reassert their power, but the young urban elites rejected them. Islamic militia groups began to gather weapons and occupy buildings; lawyers appointed themselves judges; the traffic police stood back and watched in horror as new cars poured into the streets and people began to drive at three times the normal speed. In the chasms between these fragile powers, gangsters and terrorists thrived.

Jay Garner, the first American administrator, had advocated keeping a "light footprint," transfering immediately to an Iraqi government and leaving quickly. He did not want the occupation to get bogged down like the UN in Kosovo, micromanaging everything for years, irritating local nationalists and preventing the local government from taking responsibility. But the first few weeks had been so anarchic, the newly improvised Iraqi government so unable to restore order, that the Coalition decided, perhaps on the orders of Secretary of Defense Rumsfeld, to take a more active role. Garner had been replaced by Paul Bremer on May 15, the 400,000-strong Iraqi army was disbanded, and some 40,000 Baath officials were sacked. The next day, the Coalition Provisional Authority was formed. Some time later, a decision was made to place Coalition "governorate coordinators" in each province. The governor of Maysan, who was a cousin of Saddam and a senior general, had run away. Until another Coalition officer arrived or an Iraqi governor was appointed, I was to be his replacement, exercising, as a representative of the U.S. administrator in Baghdad, all executive, legislative, and judicial authority in the province.

The Foreign Office said that I had been given the job because of my experience working in other post-conflict environments, because I spoke some Farsi and could, therefore, speak to Iranian refugees, and because the five hundred village houses in which I had stayed during my walk through Asia gave me an insight into rural Islamic culture. Someone joked about the fact that my grandfather had moved to India in the late nineteenth century and that my father had been a civil servant in British Malaya and had worked in Asia for fifty years.

I spoke little Arabic, and had never managed a shattered, unstable, and undeveloped province of eight hundred and fifty thousand people. I suspected that I was really given the job because most people in the Foreign Office were tied up in jobs already and because those with families were reluctant to go to Iraq, whereas I was keen and available.

I was a Scot, born in Hong Kong and brought up in Malaysia. I had briefly been an infantry officer before joining the Foreign Office and I had served in the embassies in Indonesia and in Yugoslavia. In

2000 I decided to take off twenty months to cross Iran, Afghanistan, Pakistan, India, and Nepal. I had written about rural life in Afghanistan and had briefly worked on the reconstruction of Afghanistan after the invasion.

Ten years in the Islamic world and in other places that had recently emerged from conflict had left me very suspicious of theories produced in seminars in Western capitals and of foreigners in a hurry. The best kind of international development seemed to be done by people who directly absorbed themselves into rural culture and politics, focused on traditional structures, and understood that change would always be very slow. I believed that politicians often misled others and themselves when they started wars and that there were dubious reasons for our invasions of Bosnia, Kosovo, and Afghanistan. But, because I had lived in police states, I felt I could sense how much Iraqis wanted to be rid of Saddam and how difficult it was to depose him.

Our mission was to create "a democratic Iraq at peace with itself and with its neighbors"—or in the jargon popular in Baghdad, "a multi-ethnic, decentralized, prosperous state, based on human rights, a just constitution, a vibrant civil society, and the rule of law." This language seemed overambitious but I thought we could still help to create a better society, the kind of society that many Iraqis wanted. I hoped to apply what I had learned in Afghanistan, to spend as much time as possible in rural areas and to work with moderate leaders. I thought there was a real limit to what I, as a foreigner, would be able to achieve, and that Iraqi society would remain, for some time, chaotic, corrupt and confusing. But I didn't think it would be too difficult to outperform Saddam.

WAKING UP DEAD

It has always been no less dangerous to discover new methods and institutions than to explore unknown oceans and lands since men are quicker to criticize than praise the deeds of others.
                              —*Machiavelli,* Discourses, *Introduction*

At the end of September, I flew to take up my post in Maysan on a Tri-Star chartered by the military, because passenger airliners were not yet prepared to land there. All of the seats had been turned around, because the Royal Air Force had determined that, in a crash landing, we'd be safer if we sat facing the rear of the plane. In the terminal I met a Special Forces soldier with whom I had worked in the Balkans, but he had forgotten his passport and was not allowed to board, so the only person I knew was Mark Etherington, who was to be the Coalition governorate coordinator of the city of Kut, upstream from Maysan. We had met on the same predeployment course run by the army in Britain, where we had been issued with body armor, helmets, and skimpy green towels; medically examined; and watched as we crawled, prodding every inch of the soil, through improvised minefields. On day three, a large warrant officer had given us some ideas on how to behave when taken hostage by Islamist extremists. He recommended attempting some conversation with one's captors—"You know, 'How are the negotiations, guys?' or 'Can I have some water?'"—but cautioned against angering them or drawing

9

attention to oneself. "Since you will be taken hostage by Arabs it is likely that they will male-rape you. Remember that in seventy-five percent of cases when you are male raped, you will get an erection or ejaculate. Do not worry about that," he said, enjoying the shock of the civilian audience and adding in his best drill sergeant voice, "It does not mean that you are gay."

The plane came down fast into Basra, with the wing-tip lights switched off because an insurgent had just shot a DHL plane with a surface-to-air missile. In the darkness I felt the accelerating smoothness of the long dive, suddenly brought up sharp, and then the kick of the runway between the wheels. We emerged into what had recently been a civilian airport but the immigration and customs desks were now unmanned. We lined up with soldiers and were given a PowerPoint presentation explaining that giving sweets to Iraqi children would encourage them to chase cars and be run over, and warning us of heat exhaustion. "One man, last week, who went to sleep in his cot having not paid attention during this briefing, woke up dead." It was 2:30 in the morning.

It was 5:30 before I was assigned to a bunkroom down the corridor from the general's headquarters, which occupied what had been the duty-free lounge and cafeteria. Soldiers came in and out of the room, turning the lights on and off, and three hours later I was woken by a man who told me to get dressed immediately because I was late for a meeting in Basra. I rushed out into the bright sun, where there were two armored land-cruisers, each of them with two men in the front of each vehicle, armed with automatic rifles and Glock pistols. I was placed in the rear of the front vehicle. Two armored vehicles and a bodyguard team of four was now the minimum requirement for moving a civilian safely from the airport. The vehicles cost about a hundred seventy thousand dollars apiece, and the men were paid about five hundred dollars a day.

This time there would be no sightseeing. The air-conditioning in the vehicle was cold and loud, and there was static from the radio. I could smell nothing and hear almost nothing outside, and the dark armored glass, an inch thick, distorted the view. As we came into the outskirts of Basra, I could make out people on the street, but it was impossible to guess their mood.

The leader of the close-protection team in the passenger seat, a thick-set Scot in his late fifties who introduced himself as Willy, began to swear at the second car through his various radios. "Block, block, block, Jesus Christ, you look at this guy. Turn here." We swerved up a side street and the heavy vehicle behind lurched after us. We were stuck behind a donkey cart. We sat there for about five seconds while Willy glanced at his map and looked quickly around him. "Right. Get over the other side of the road." The driver attempted to cross the central reservation but couldn't manage it. "Back. Back. Try again. Go." This time at a more acute angle, with a grind and a spurt of exhaust, until we had bumped back down and were driving against traffic. People shouted and hit their horns and then swerved out of our way. We passed the donkey cart. "Okay. Back across." We lurched over again and turned, but the rear vehicle, which was supposed to come around our left flank to block traffic for us, didn't make it. "Can he not see? Get in front of him. Put your foot down. Cut him off. Jesus, your fucking vehicle weighs two tons, you didn't need to be worried about some fucker on his motorbike. Block, block, block. One o'clock, car coming fast. He's past."

Then we were through the difficult patch and Willy relapsed into silence.

"Have you done this kind of work recently?" I asked.

"No."

"And how long have you been in Iraq?"

"Six weeks."

"Do the Iraqis seem happy here in Basra?"

"Can't say I've really had much contact with the local people."

"Is the electricity working?"

"Can't say I know the answer to that."

To me, Willy seemed to confirm the theory put about in Baghdad, that the bodyguard teams were undertrained and overpaid. As it turned out, I was wrong, at least about Willy. He had done twenty-two years in the military, had been a legendary instructor on one of the British Army's toughest courses, the Sergeant's course in Brecon, and had the respect of everyone who had ever worked with him. He was very sharp and had learned a great deal about Iraq. But he wasn't going to share it with me, an unknown civilian.

The headquarters in Basra was the old electricity department, protected now by high blast walls and a winding approach designed to frustrate truck bombs, and guarded by Gurkhas. I piled out into the dusty courtyard and walked in. After knocking on three doors, I discovered that the admin officer had brought me down because he'd been told to find me a bed for the night. I wasn't sure why he had waited six hours after my plane landed to send someone to pick me up, especially when I had a meeting back at the aiport at two. He, however, was the angry one. "I told them to give me seventy-two hours' notice before they sent someone in. Do you know how lucky you are that I have found you a bed here?"

I explained that I had a bed at the airport and needed to be back there by two. Impossible, he said. All the transport was booked up. I'd have to stay until tomorrow. Finally it was sorted out, and an hour later, I repeated the long, expensive drive back to the airport.

There I met with Major Melotte, a tall, sandy-haired officer in the Irish guards who had been running the province before my arrival. "Welcome, mufti of Maysan," he said. He seemed very relaxed. We were in the airport lounge, which was now the divisional headquarters. There were hundreds of soldiers, and I was one of the only civilians. Men in camouflage uniforms sat behind desks marked "SO2G3" or "SO2 Legal." The general could be seen writing at his desk through the long window of what must once have been a souvenir shop. A Japanese diplomat passed, setting off down the corridor with a towel round his waist. I hoped he would find his shower.

Major Melotte was planning to take some leave and cross the "Empty Quarter," the uninhabited desert of Saudi Arabia. He was carrying the diaries of his great-grandfather, who had been in Maysan in 1916. He gave me a PowerPoint presentation, with a lengthy description of each slide:

"Maysan liberated itself before the Coalition arrived. Local militia groups took it from the Baath. . . . We have currently got seventy-two border guards to cover a two-hundred-mile-long Iranian border. We should have four hundred and forty-four. We have appointed a supervisory committee of local leaders." He showed me photographs of twenty Iraqi men. There was a fat man in a safari suit who had been an anti-Saddam guerrilla commander, and three clerics in long robes and large turbans, who had spent much of the last twenty years in Iran. One was pushing for a gas station franchise, another wanted treatment for impotency. It was not clear how the "local leaders" had been selected. Each had been made, for the photograph, to hold a placard bearing his name in front of his chest. This made them look like convicts.

Amara, with a population of about four hundred thousand, was the largest town in Maysan. The population were almost all Shia Muslims. For the first month after the fall of Saddam there had been no Coalition control in the province, but there were currently more than a thousand British troops; they were due to be replaced by another battle group in a month's time. Alternative town councils had sprung up, which would cause problems unless we dealt with them. Major Melotte seemed to have enjoyed his job.

He brought up a slide with the word *Agricultural* highlighted in yellow. "It is basically an agricultural province. Our water situation is ruined by the lack of electricity to power the pumps. Sewage: sewage is at about 60 percent."

Did he mean it reached 60 percent of the population? That it worked 60 percent of the time? But before I could ask, Major Melotte thrust onwards. "Schools," he continued, bringing up the next screen, "were destroyed in the looting orgy after the liberation. We have given five hundred dollars to every school. There is a shortage of milk, sugar, and rice, which you must address. Communications costs us between thirty and fifty thousand dollars a month."

And so it went on, for two hours, until he flashed up a photograph he had taken of dusk on the Tigris. A crescent of aubergine light curved up from the black bank. A Marsh Arab stood in a canoe, reaching for a net. Against this sentimental backdrop, Major Melotte began to describe conversations with local officials. In each anecdote he was energetic, purposeful, and self-confident.

"I told the supervisory committee they were not to meet till I got back . . . I sat down all the ministry directors, ignored the finance briefing, and just said, 'Right, what do you want—what do you want?'" His hand chopped the air as he mimed it out. "Squared away—'Okay, these are the allocations . . . Why don't you do something for yourselves? Why are you expecting me to fix everything?'" He smiled. "Then there is the Prince of the Marshes . . ."

MORDOR

As for reforming these institutions all at once, when everyone realizes that they are not good, let me say that this uselessness which is easily recognized is corrected only with great difficulty; for to do this, it is not enough to employ lawful means, for lawful methods are now useless: it is necessary to have recourse to extraordinary measures, such as violence and arms, and to become above all else prince of that city in order to be able to deal with it in one's own way.

—*Machiavelli,* Discourses, *Book I, Chapter 18*

The Prince of the Marshes. When I first arrived in Iraq, this was a famous name, even to the chino-wearing U.S. Republican appointees, fresh from the West Wing and trapped sufficiently deep within the Green Zone not to have heard of the province from which he came. Provincial sheikhs tended to be elderly men who attended public meetings as a nervous proclamation of status and sat in silence, trussed in their formal robes and staring coldly at the new political class through gold-rimmed, tinted spectacles. Of the few young, active chiefs in public life, none had the looks of that more rugged Valentino, the tall leader of the province of Maysan: "Abu Hatim"; Karim, son of Mahood son of Hattab, of the Albu Muhammad.

The Prince of the Marshes had been waging guerrilla war in Maysan against Saddam for seventeen years, and he was now prepared to fight for the Coalition's new Iraq. Little wonder then that he was immediately made a member of the new governing council in Baghdad. And when journalists said the new Iraqi government lacked political appeal and included Baathists, Islamists, criminals, and millionaires who had not been in Iraq for twenty years, they were reminded of the love and respect Iraqis felt for this rebellious, secular peasant leader who had never deserted his country. And whenever, over the Formica tabletops of the mess halls, administrators were tempted to curse all Iraqi politicians as corrupt, politically suspect, and feckless, someone would always raise the Prince of the Marshes.

His cult flourished, I think, because of the doubt that was beginning to infect the occupation. The creed of the Prince of the Marshes gave some solace to officials who sensed support ebbing at home and who were beginning in their trailers at night to question whether they had the faith, the skills, or the resources to create a new Iraq, and whether Iraqis wanted them at all.

The Prince of the Marshes, then: one of only twenty-five members of the new governing council, murderer of the murderer of his father, Islamic not Islamist, Iraqi not Iranian, a nationalist not a foreign agent. He was of the Albu Muhammed, the great marsh tribe of southern Iraq; for the sake of the Iraqi people and their battle for freedom he had deserted from Saddam's army and trained with the Kurdish guerrillas in the north, and fought alongside them. He had been captured and imprisoned at Abu Ghraib, where he endured torture and was sentenced to death, but after six years he escaped and fled to the marshes, where he raised his own guerrilla force and led it against Saddam—and emerged, a month before the Coalition forces arrived, to liberate the people of the province of Maysan.

The very title we had given this man reflected our desperation. Some claimed Bremer was the first to dub him "Prince of the Marshes." But it seemed curious that our chief administrator, with his MBA from Harvard Business School, would wish to conjure an image of a monarch of a deceptive blend of earth and water crossed by smuggling tracks and the flickering lights of will-o-the-wisp. And indeed, later, when the Prince's fall began, Bremer denied that he had ever used the title. More probably it came from the pirated Kuwaiti

DVDs of *The Lord of the Rings* that civilians and soldiers watched on laptops after mess-hall dinners: a sobriquet for an ally in our war against Mordor. The journalists embraced the creed, with even the worldly-wise *Le Monde* running the July headline *"Le Seigneur des marais, héros de la résistance contre Saddam, aspire à la paix."* But no one quite agreed whether he was in fact the King, the Prince or, like a breed of Australian frog, the Lord of the Marshes.

In truth, of course, Iraq didn't have princes anymore, and it hardly had marshes. The last princes were murdered on the kitchen steps of the palace in 1958 and disemboweled and mutilated in the streets, where the mob used the Regent's intestines as necklaces. And the marshes, since 1992, had been a thousand square miles of dry desert. The Prince was not even chief of his own tribe, the Albu Muhammed. This may have been why most Iraqis preferred to call this noncommissioned officer from the city Abu Hatim, "father of Hatim." Though he did not have a son called Hatim either.

PART ONE

THE PRINCE OF THE MARSHES

THE BRITISH CAMP

A Prince cannot avoid ingratitude.
                    —*Machiavelli,* Discourses, *Book I, Chapter 29*

Pursuant to my authority as Administrator of the Coalition Provisional Authority (CPA), relevant UN Security Council resolutions, including Resolution 1483 (2003), and the laws and usages of war, I hereby promulgate the following: The CPA is vested with all executive, legislative, and judicial authority necessary to achieve its objectives . . . This authority shall be exercised by the CPA Administrator.
                    Coalition Provisional Authority (Iraq)
                    Regulation Number 1

MONDAY, OCTOBER 6, 2003

On the three-hour drive north from Basra to take up my post in Maysan, I passed through the territory the Prince of the Marshes claimed to control. I saw the canal Saddam had dug: some reeds, a few fishermen in tin boats and some water birds. Long parallel lines stretched for miles across the drab earth. There were very few people to be seen: most Marsh Arabs now lived in slums on the edge of cities. Boats were no longer the standard method of transport and the buffalo herds had gone. The thicket of six-foot reeds in chest-deep water that once covered thousands of square miles had become parched and barren mud.

We turned off the highway down an avenue guarded by two rusting Iranian tanks kept as souvenirs, one with a drunken turret. We passed buildings whose roofs had collapsed under the impact of American J-Dam explosives, came up along the edge of a bastion wall serving as protection against car bombs and stopped at the guard house of Camp Abu Naji. Six months earlier it had been the base of the semi-mystical Saddam-funded terrorist group, the Mujahaddin-el-Halq.

A private from the King's Own Scottish Borderers approached the car, recognized the driver, saluted, and lifted the drop bar for us. On either side were low, shabby concrete buildings, rolls of barbed wire, and corrugated iron. There were soldiers on the roofs, presumably sleeping outside because there was no air-conditioning in the tents. I dragged my bags out of the Land Rover and was shown to a room.

Pushing back the heavy black curtain that served as a door, I lifted the nylon mosquito net and put my sleeping bag on the camp bed and brushed some sand off the tin trunk. The window frames were lined with duct tape and the curtain-door stretched to the floor but, as I was to find over my next six months in the camp, nothing was able to exclude the sand, which accumulated in a thick yellow film across the cement floor and the canvas chair.

We ate at six-thirty. At the entrance to the cook-house an Iraqi in a blue boiler suit was pouring bottled water into a large tea urn. A private stood next to it, making sure that everyone, officer and civilian alike, washed their hands from the urn to prevent the spread of diarrhea.

I sat with a group of young officers and the regimental padre. A subaltern barked, "Red or green?" and returned with plastic cups filled with juice of the relevant and astonishingly intense chemical color.

I was, it seemed, the first civilian to live in the camp. The officer on my left glanced at me and asked, "Do you work at the airport?" He assumed I was a soldier from the divisional headquarters.

"No, I'm the civilian who is setting up the Coalition Provisional Authority office in the province," I replied.

"What's that?"

"It's the new civilian administration."

"Thank God you've arrived at last and we can all go home," he said, pushing his chair back. "Cake in a box, anyone?"

To shower after dinner I walked around the accommodation block, across the edge of the runway and behind the hangars. There was a roar from the diesel-powered generators, and the beat of the rotor-blade of a Chinook helicopter on the landing zone. I had to use a flashlight to avoid the rubble on the uneven sand. Above, I could see stars in a clear sky and imagine something of the desert just beyond the perimeter fence.

The showers were well-lit. There was a thick slurry of brown mud on the floor from combat boots and camouflage uniforms piled on the wooden benches. While someone cursed the lack of hot water, men dried themselves ostentatiously in the center of the room, talking about the day's patrols, apparently oblivious to the two female officers brushing their teeth with mineral water at the sink.

The next morning at eight, I called on the colonel of the battle group. He was a slender man in his early forties, with gray hair scraped severely back from his head, dressed, like everyone, in desert camouflage. His office was decorated with the Leslie tartan of his regiment. He introduced me to the province with another PowerPoint presentation; one he seemed to have given many times before. He did not encourage questions.

"Maysan," he began, "is the size of Northern Ireland, and we are running it with only a thousand men." He explained that it was a very volatile place, and the battle group were short of equipment and development money. The regional corps headquarters of the Iraqi army had been looted, and all the weapons were now in the hands of the local population. The two key arteries of the province were Route 6, the highway that connected Basra and Baghdad, and the Tigris River.

"As for you, Rory—" I looked up, midway through my sixth packet of crackers "there are very high expectations here that the British will achieve things. If things don't happen they believe it is because we are deliberately trying to suppress their economic and political future. There is no possibility of a Baathist revival here. It is a small place and the Baathists would not be able to move here. There is a potential for Shia opposition here, connected to Iran and criminal gangs. I believe that the supervisory committee we have appointed here is relatively representative."

He brought up a new screen on the monitor: "Vital Ground: Our vital ground is 'the concept of regeneration.'"

The colonel seemed confident that he could keep order. He had been in command of his regiment for nearly three years and was a month from the end of his time in Maysan. He answered to no one nearer than a brigadier, two hundred miles away in Basra, had absolute control over his men and weaponry, and traveled incessantly. He knew the district well enough to answer the detailed complaints of local mayors. He had become close to the Beni Lam, an "aristocratic" tribe that had once been famous for their horses. But his strongest relationship was with Abu Hatim, whom the colonel described as "our local Robin Hood, sometimes known as the Prince of the Marshes." The two of them ran the province together.

I had no opportunity to discuss the briefings I had been given in London, and I left without a clear idea of our relationship. I had been told in Baghdad that, as the deputy governorate coordinator, I was to be "the deputy and alter ego of the governorate coordinator," in charge of a civilian team of eight that would include a political officer, a development projects officer, and others. But there was as yet no governorate coordinator; a U.S. State Department officer was supposed to be arriving in that role in a few weeks' time. Nor was there yet a political officer, a projects officer, or an Iraqi governor in Maysan. For the time being, I was a team of one, responsible for overseeing development projects and setting up Iraqi political structures.

I had been told to act as something like the de facto governor of the province.

The colonel had been ordered by the commander-in-chief to support our office. But he had little interest in the constitutional relationship between the CPA and the military. He was critical of the CPA, which had so far done little. He was doubtful that I would be able to do much. But, he said, the military were forced to perform political and economic roles that were better done by civilians, and it was about time civilians took up their responsibility. He suggested I could start by getting money. He referred to himself as the de facto governor of the province.

Outside the colonel's office, I was introduced to a tall man with a mane of black hair who was wearing dark glasses and a cream linen jacket over a crisp checked shirt with cufflinks, suede trousers, and suede boots. This was A.J., currently in charge of CPA finances. He was a territorial cavalry officer and the only man in the camp, apart from me, who wore civilian clothes. He offered one of his collection of exotic confiscated weapons for the ride into town. I took a chrome-plated Kalashnikov because it was the only one of the weapons I thought I could remember how to use. The bodyguard team I had been promised by the Foreign Office had not yet arrived.

I sat in the front passenger seat with the rifle between my legs as we drove north from the camp. After about ten miles, we reached the outskirts of Amara, where there were jerry-built brick houses with fancy new concrete columns. We turned past half-decaying apartment blocks, villas, an old covered souk, and an avenue of mature willows and clanked across a pontoon bridge over the Tigris. On the main road was the pink tiled façade of the building that would have housed the Iraqi provincial council and governor, had either existed. We stopped across the road, facing heavy metal gates set in a high concrete wall. They swung back, revealing British soldiers and men in Iraqi police uniform, a dusty yard the size of a soccer field, an empty swimming pool, and the white villa that housed the new CPA office. The Tigris, sluggish and brown, rolled past two sides of the compound. Across the water was a date-palm grove and a small white mosque. This tiny CPA compound on a peninsula in the heart of the old Ottoman city of Amara, fifteen miles from the British military base, was surrounded by three hundred thousand Iraqis and protected by a guard force of thirty.

At the door stood a man with neat pressed desert camouflage, a dark blue engineer's beret, gray hair, dark brows, and a huge smile. The badge on his chest said Butler. Major George Butler was the commanding officer of the civil affairs team, had set up the office and had been in Iraq for four months. He was a reserve officer, a senior water engineer in normal life and had worked in Egypt. He was friendly, explained that he already had my office prepared and guided me round the compound.

The villa had originally been the home of the young and newest wife of the great Albu Muhammed Sheikh, Majid Bin Khalife. She had been murdered here in the early 1950s by her stepson, who had in turn been murdered in the date palm grove across the river, probably by his father. It had then become the residence of the Iraqi governor, who had added the glass-fronted bungalow on the waterfront. There was no longer any electricity or furniture in the villa—it had been looted before our arrival—and there were only two cramped bathrooms. Major Butler had been saving money to paint the walls, install a generator, and provide some hot water. There were offices like these in the capitals of every province in Iraq, established by military civil affairs teams. During the first five months of the CPA's existence it had not deployed officials to the provinces. In Maysan, Butler's team had taken on the role of the CPA and grown from managing small popular engineering projects into providing support for twenty Iraqi ministries.

I was the first civilian administrator in Amara and part of the first group of British CPA administrators across the country: as I arrived in Amara, Mark Etherington, who had traveled into Iraq with me, was arriving upstream in Kut, and a veterinarian who spoke fluent Arabic had just settled into our twin province of Nasiriyah on the Tigris.

I was led to a large meeting room filled with heavy yellow and purple cushioned sofas and decorated with garish local paintings of Marsh Arabs. On the sofas sat the dozen heavily tanned young men and women of the British military civil affairs team. The electricity had failed, and the air conditioning with it, and there were sweat patches on their desert camouflage.

Most were reservists who had been called out of civilian jobs to serve six months in Iraq. Major A.J., the linen-jacketed finance officer, was a banker; Private Charlotte Morris, the social affairs officer, was a twenty-five-year-old who had been running a project for street children in Egypt. They had only one week's leave in a six-month tour in Iraq, and they slept in dormitories. Their lavatories at camp were unlit green plastic Porta-Johns. This was an innovation. Previously there had been long benches without partitions where the men could chat Roman-style as they did their business. The women were forced to wait until late at night and to cover themselves with sheets of newspaper. Flies were everywhere. The female captain who dealt with walk-in inquiries had just tested positive for malaria and, despite the enforced hand-washing, many soldiers from the colonel down had diarrhea and were vomiting much of the time, which made the privies unpleasant, especially during the heat of the day. There was a rumor that one soldier had died of heat exhaustion while sitting inside. Civilian contractors in Basra could earn a thousand dollars a day; Private Morris was managing projects worth hundreds of thousands of dollars and earning less than fifty dollars a day.

Although I was impatient to appoint a new provincial government, to develop key relationships with Iraqis and with the Coalition, and to acquire new funds and implement new projects, I spent the first couple of days learning from the civil affairs team. Every time I walked through the open-plan space on the ground floor of our villa office, I passed groups huddled in different corners, each consisting of a civil affairs officer, who often appeared to be striving for patience, a young Iraqi interpreter struggling to translate technical terms, and a couple of Iraqi civil servants nodding politely. Strewn across the tables were databases of the four hundred schools in the province, plans, tender documents, and bundles from the local kebab shop, waiting to be opened for lunch. Nearly fifty projects were waiting for money from Basra, and each officer continued to produce a flood of proposals and ideas. In addition to the half million dollars' worth of wheat and barley seed requested by the director of agriculture, the prison specialist sought four hundred thousand dollars for a new prison, and another civil affairs officer wanted to refurbish the souk. They had already repaired about a quarter of the schools in the province and most of the key ministry buildings. They did many of these projects by providing money to one of the half dozen international non-governmental organizations (NGOs) in the province, who managed and monitored the projects for them.

The civil affairs officers showed a sharp, ironic grasp of Amara's needs and seemed tough and sympathetic in the right measure. The health officer had concluded after a survey that there was no need to build new hospitals and clinics: the real priority was training and hygiene in the existing facilities. Some were learning Arabic, and all liked dealing with Iraqis.

And yet, despite the energy and competence of the civil affairs team and the hundreds of productive projects, they were failing to communicate their achievements to Iraqis. This may have been due to the soldiers' modesty or a distaste for politics or a lack of understanding of Iraqi expectations. Whatever the explanation, Iraqis were suspicious of our motives, disappointed by our performance, and often contemptuous.

Each morning, the convoy left for the office at eight, the civil affairs team gathered for our daily meeting at 8:30, and the rest of the day I found myself either talking to Iraqi officials or dealing with office problems and politics. Each evening, I drove back to the base and went for a run, shirtless in the astonishing heat. After supper, I saw the colonel. I went to sleep with fragments of Arabic in my mind, no longer hearing the roar of the generators, and woke often repeating the same fragments.

From one perspective, I had acquired near-absolute authority over eight hundred and fifty thousand people. A CPA governorate coordinator ranked theoretically as a one-star general, and the main mission of the lieutenant colonel who commanded the battle group was to support the CPA by keeping security. From another perspective, I was almost powerless. The Iraqi state was large and functioning, however poorly. I was constrained by the Geneva Convention and occupation law. The battle group did not take their orders from me. Even the newest private was part of an army with 150,000 men and clear lines of command. I was a lone foreigner who commanded nobody. If the Iraqis or the British chose to ignore me there was very little that I could do.

REGENERATION

Everyone knows how praiseworthy it is for a ruler to keep his promises . . . Nevertheless experience shows in our times the rulers who have done great things are those who have set little store by keeping their word, being skillful rather in cunningly deceiving men.

—*Machiavelli,* The Prince, *Chapter 18*

Thursday, October 9, 2003

On the morning of the third day, there was a knock at my office door and a tall man with heavy-rimmed glasses, a balding head, and a two-day stubble appeared.

"Hello, I am your chief interpreter," he said, emphasizing the "chief."

I asked him to sit down.

"It is not appropriate for me to sit in the governor's office," he replied. He explained that he had been an English teacher under the old regime. I asked him what he thought of the situation.

"Uneducated people, tribal people, without reading and writing, are now in the city. This is very bad. These men have no culture. They do not understand what is government. Because they do not understand what is religion. Let me ask you, what is the religion?"

I said I didn't know.

"You don't know?" he asked with great surprise. "Religion is about the respect for the other human being. Each of us is created by

one God. Each of us is respected. This is religion. Even the Jewish religion. But these men do not respect one another. Things are very
bad now."

"And what should we do?"

"You know already. We are not stupid. We know what games
your government is playing here with oil and with Israel. But please
remember only one thing. We Iraqis, we admire strong men. We have
tough heads. You must be a strong leader. Yes, like Abdul Karim
Qasim. You know Abdul Karim Qasim?" I nodded, although I did
not know much about the man who had led the 1958 coup. "The
British soldiers here," he continued, "they are weak. They are too
cautious. They make no promises. They are not keeping security,
they are dealing with the wrong people, they must use the educated
people. If not, there is much corruption, nothing is happening in development. You must make the Iraqi people believe that things will
get better."

I thanked him.

"There is no need to thank me. It is you who must be thanked."

As the translator left, I joined the civil affairs team mustered outside my office. Everyone but A.J. was in full desert camouflage with
weapons and body armor, which in their case was a small Kevlar
breast and back plate. A.J. was wearing his body armor above a pair
of yellow trousers, but he had put aside his chrome-plated Kalashnikov. Charlie Morris, I noticed, had managed to tuck most of her
blonde fringe under her helmet. We were on our way to the central
event of their week: the meeting with the ministry directors. It would
be my first public appearance as acting governor.

"Do not make any promises," Major Butler warned me as we
gathered.

"Show them you are the boss," whispered the interpreter. "You
are young and you must show them you are strong. Tell them you are
going to bring change."

We marched down the path beside the river to the compound wall. The policemen swung back the metal gates and we stepped out into the bright sun and crossed the main road, returning smiles from Iraqi men. We marched past the sentry at the gate of the pink-tiled provincial council building and the crowd of petitioners in the courtyard and up the cool dark stairs and into a dark room, where the ministry directors stood to greet us.

I walked the lines, shaking hands and returning embraces.

"A salaam aleikum." (Peace be with you.)

"Waleikum a salaam." (And also with you.)

"Ahlan wa sahlan." (Welcome.)

"Ahlan."

"Shlon hadartak?" (How is the respected one?)

"Al hamdulillah." (God be praised.) *"Shlon hadartak?"*

"Al hamdulillah."

Almost all the British governorate coordinators spoke fluent Arabic or Kurdish, and dozens of Foreign Office Arabists had been deployed in Iraq. But the little Arabic I knew I had picked up from other Islamic languages. There were decorative flourishes—arabesques—used across the Muslim world, such as *yanni, methelan,* and *taqriban,* which were the equivalent of "I mean," "you know, roughly" and "for example." There were some common theological ideas, pious references to God, words from Islamic law or from medieval cities: *haram, mash-allah, hokum, hamam.* Other Arabic—*dunia* (world) and *istirihat* (rest), for example—had entered unrelated languages which I spoke such as Farsi, Turkish, and Indonesian. With these and a few lessons, it was possible for me to be polite, but for serious work I needed an interpreter.

I sat at the head of the room beside the man I knew to be the brother of the Prince of the Marshes. Riyadh Mahood Hattab was stocky, with a thick black mustache and big hair. As I sat beside him he gave a weary smile and shrugged his shoulders. Many foreigners had sat beside him in the months since the invasion, and I guessed he was tired of them. His baggy black suit seemed to reflect his identity as an Arab modernist who had spent twenty years as an engineer at the ministry of roads and bridges. He was now coordinating chair of the "regeneration committee," which was supposed to iron out problems between ministries.

In front of us were more than eighty other directors: mostly middle-aged men, some in safari suits, some in business suits. Most had gold pens in their breast pockets and wore shiny watches and strong colognes. They belonged to twenty-six different ministries that dealt with everything from electricity to health. Since the invasion, communications with Baghdad had faltered and ministry offices had been looted. Many of these men were new to their jobs because their predecessors had been sacked as Baathists.

George Butler sat slightly behind me to my left; the translator stood on my right. Riyadh began without preamble. "This meeting begins at ten o'clock, not ten past. I would ask you all to be on time in future. And I note that the agricultural director and the director of electricity generation have failed to attend. They should come to explain their absences this afternoon." He continued, "Security has degenerated in the province and I will be taking steps to solve the situation," even though his job had nothing to do with security. Then he asked the director of the paper pulp factory why the factory was not running. The director said that the water supply had been cut off. The water director said that this was because there was insufficient electricity. Riyadh secured an undertaking from the director of electricity distribution to provide a set amount of power to the water department and then invited questions from the floor.

First to stand was a short middle-aged man in the front row. "Mr. Laith, the education director," whispered George.

"Seyyed Rory, welcome," he began. "Now that you have arrived I will ask you to do what the Coalition has promised and failed to do, which is to evict the political parties from the main school sports facility in Amara." He sat down.

A younger man stood up. "Director of agricultural seed provision," whispered George.

"Seyyed Rory, welcome. Why do we have no wheat and barley seed when the planting season is beginning?"

As each man spoke, George whispered the background of the case. The ration card manager asked whether we had managed to get infant formula, and the director of the pensions office wanted to know why his office had not yet been renovated. Some directors complained that the Coalition was making decisions without consulting them. Others protested that it had promised a great deal of construction but had so far delivered no money.

These men expected me to do a great deal. I did not want us to run independent parallel structures. I was determined to support and strengthen the ministries, and to involve the directors and citizens in deciding how money was spent. I knew that promises were risky, budgets were uncertain, Baghdad policy could change, and programs could be derailed by insurgency.

But in an ad hoc organization in a war zone, most power is the theater of power. It is not enough to do things, you must be seen to do things. I needed to promise change to give Iraqis some belief in us and in the future. I needed to claim authority and bluff people into falling in step. I would need to answer questions about programs I had only just heard of, raise expectations, and then take the risk that I might disappoint.

I told the education director I would have the parties evicted for him from the gym; I said we would acquire the seed and look into the milk ration. I did not promise to renovate the pensions office but I told the director he was welcome to discuss the matter with the relevant member of the civil affairs team. I said how pleased I was to be there and that I planned to unblock all the contracting delays and return that weekend with a half million dollars, to be followed by much more. I announced that there would be a new process for tenders and contracts, where the ministries would decide how to spend CPA money; that our budgets would now be open; that there would be weekly meetings between the ministries and the town councils where citizens could present complaints.

Beside me, I could sense George wincing. I knew that, as a cautious engineer and civil servant, he thought I was behaving like a politician and promising more than we could deliver.

That afternoon, I first slipped out of the compound. It was surprisingly easy. I had expected to be stopped by the guards at the gate, but it was clear from their easy smiles that their job extended only to preventing people from getting in. There had been no attacks or kidnappings yet in Amara, and although it was a breach of security regulations, many people slipped out to shop in the souk. I wanted to see the city before people recognized me as the deputy governor and before I was imprisoned by my bodyguard team, which was due to arrive the next day.

It was a warm afternoon and I blinked for a moment in the bright sun. I was wearing a white shirt, dark trousers, and leather shoes, and with my black hair I thought I could look reasonably Iraqi—at least from a distance. It was surprisingly quiet. There were very few cars; a group of women on the other side of the street in full black *abayas* dawdled, holding the hands of bright-clothed toddlers. Beneath the omnipresent layer of yellow sand, the pavement was a mosaic of pink tiles. The buildings on either side of Tigris Street were of plain cement block, their plastic signs unilluminated because the electricity had failed. People were having an afternoon sleep.

I came to a wooden cart, beside which was a generator powering a black and white television. The cart was piled with CDs and posters of Islamic clerics, and on the screen, the martyred Ayatollah Sadr II was shouting from a pulpit to a large crowd. A small knot of young men stood round the cart, their hands behind their backs. They wore plastic sandals and their trousers were dusty and frayed.

They seemed absorbed in the television and did not glance at me. The preacher on the television shouted something angrily about "America" and "Britain."

A little farther on, I caught the eye of a small boy and smiled. He was with a large group of boys who recognized me as a foreigner. They screamed "Englan wellygood," and then ran off down the street. A crowd gathered quickly and I smiled and shook some hands. The men smiled broadly back, and some of them invited me to their shops for tea. I apologized that I did not have the time to take up their invitations. To my surprise no one followed me and I continued, trying to imitate the slow, shambling gait of the shoppers around me.

I came round an abandoned warehouse onto a mud street scarred with deep ruts. The children on the corner seemed thinner and poorer than those I had just seen, and there was sewage overflowing from an open drain. Through a courtyard door I saw a small garden, a plain, high-walled building, and a grotto of round stones with a statue of the Virgin Mary. A young man walked across to greet me. "Christian?" he asked, and when I nodded he led me through the large wooden door. There were pews, a calendar depicting Moses in the reeds, and a picture of Christ in glory behind the altar; otherwise, the walls were bare and the plaster was peeling.

"How many Christians in this town?" I asked.

"Fifteen families," he said.

"What kind of Christians are you?"

An older man appeared beside him and said very precisely in English, "We are Chaldean Catholic—our services are in Aramaic," and then, having paused, continued in the traditional Islamic fashion, *"A salaam aleikum, ahlan wa sahlan,"* and invited me into a small office adjoining the church. He fetched some water and some boiled sweets for me, speaking in fast, colloquial Arabic to the other man.

"Our traditional work as Christian people, you know, was selling alcohol," he said, returning to English. "There was no problem under Saddam. But now the fundamentalists come from Iran and they are attacking anyone who sells alcohol and the police do not defend us. And they threaten our children. We now have to veil our daughters when we send them to school. Many people have already moved to Baghdad. Eventually all of us will. Then this church will be as abandoned as that other one across the wall."

He pointed to the large building with high broken windows that I had mistaken for an abandoned warehouse.

On my way back through the covered souk, I saw four bearded young men in black clothes, one of whom was carrying a weapon. They stiffened as I approached and said something. I smiled at them but they stared at me, expressionless. The passage was narrow but they made no move to step out of my way. As I squeezed past, one spat. Then they walked off together. I turned round and realized that many in the souk had been watching the scene. A shopkeeper beckoned me over and said, "These men are from the Iranian militia. They are paid by the Iranian government. They do not like foreigners. Also they do not like people like me." He pointed at his shop sign. He was a barber. "Or this," and stroked his clean-shaven cheeks.

A giant poster of Ayatollah al-Sadr II, whom I had seen on the street-stall television, was mounted on a concrete frame at a main junction. Followers of the Ayatollah's son Muqtada had probably plastered it over an image of Saddam. Farther down the street I could see two more pictures of the Ayatollah, and I had counted a dozen of them on the road between the office and the camp. Anything that had been named after Saddam was now named after Sadr. Amara had, I was told, more pictures of him than any other place in Iraq, barring perhaps Sadr City itself. But whereas Saddam was depicted in suits, sheikhly costume, or military uniform, holding rosary beads, a trilby, a Cuban cigar, or a hunting rifle, Ayatollah al-Sadr was always depicted in his black robes, preaching.

The Sadrists who had put up these posters also formed militias and parties in the name of the dead Ayatollah and refused to deal with the occupation forces, whom they perceived as infidel colonialists.

They were demanding our immediate withdrawal and threatened armed resistance. How many people supported the Sadrists?

As I turned back toward the compound gate, I noticed how vulnerable we were to missile attack from the street. The gate swung open. I stopped on the threshold and greeted a group of young men that was approaching. "Peace be with you," I said. They said nothing until they were almost abreast of me, then one replied gravely, "And also with you. And may the grace of Allah go with you."

THE GENERAL

I do not want to fail to remind any ruler who has recently gained power . . . that he should be well aware of the reasons why those who helped him to gain power acted as they did. If it was not out of any natural affection for him, but only because they were discontented with the previous government . . . he will not be able to satisfy them.

—*Machiavelli*, The Prince, *Chapter 20*

FRIDAY, OCTOBER 10, 2003

The weather was beginning to cool and, despite the flies that infested my new office and the kitchen, I was beginning to see why Alexander the Great chose to retire to Iraq. The skies had been a clear blue since my arrival. I was sitting on the terrace outside my office, in a plastic bucket chair with a broken back, watching the Tigris flow past and the date palms on the far bank moving in the dry wind. A man and a boy floated past, leaning over the side of their wooden boat with wires attached to an old car battery to electrocute the fish.

Summer in the marsh regions is so hot that you feel almost as though you are in the atmosphere of an alien planet in which every sound is distorted by the heat, but the winter is more moderate there than in the mountains, and the late autumn is dry, cool, and sunny. The ancient Persian court spent the winters in Susa, a hundred miles east of Amara, nearer than Basra. Alexander wintered there in 331 B.C., and again seven years later, after his return from India, when he organized a marriage ceremony between ten thousand of his companions and ten thousand Persians, intending to breed the new hybrid rulers of his empire. He then proceeded to Babylon, on a route that took him near modern Amara, and he died a year later of a marsh fever, perhaps contracted on this spot.

Someone came down from the office to the terrace to tell me that the general had arrived and we would be going to see the Prince of the Marshes. Since I was trying to involve Iraqis more in choosing contractors and projects and overseeing their implementation, on the grounds that these were schemes that the Iraqis would have to maintain, I had begun to meet local leaders. But I had not yet seen the Prince.

The general had been in a Scottish Highland regiment and commanded the British troops in Basra. I had also served briefly in a Highland regiment, and the general epitomized what I admired about Highlanders. Other generals tended to play the part of senior bureaucrats; they spoke gently and wore neatly pressed camouflage uniforms because they were not expecting to fight, and they often looked as though they had enjoyed too many mess dinners. But this man was wiry, strong, and tanned and was wearing a desert camouflage jacket that had faded to a pale purple. He had spent most of his career in the Special Forces, and I suspected his jacket dated from his time in the first Gulf War. His long, narrow desert boots were American, not British issue. His manner was direct, although I would discover that in political meetings he was polite and deftly diplomatic.

"Good morning, good morning," said the general. "Good to see you. Don't expect me to remember your name, though. How long are you here for?"

"A year, sir."

"A year?" He grinned. "Thank Christ for that. Every other diplomat is coming for six weeks at a time. What can you achieve in six weeks? Fuck all."

Silence for a moment, then he continued, "What were you doing before?"

I muttered something about having spent ten years in Islamic countries and then asked him whether he was enjoying his job.

"I'm enjoying rollerblading anyway." Every afternoon he rollerbladed round Basra airport in Lycra shorts and no shirt. "Tell you what, though. You've got the plum job. Most fun province in Iraq. Have you read Gavin Maxwell and Gavin Young about the marshes here? Better than Thesiger."

I said I had just tried to discuss the books with one of the most senior civilians in Baghdad, but he had had no idea what I was talking about. I asked him what he thought of the official.

"If I could get anywhere near with a rifle, I'd drop him from two hundred yards."

He insisted I ride with him in the convoy of Land Rovers, and we continued our conversation en route. "The fact is we want to get the fuck out of here as soon as we can. Our job is fighting wars. Now it's the civilians' turn—so anything I can give you, anything in the way of support, that will get you up to speed and help us extract, have it. Just ask."

I said I needed to keep half a platoon of troops to provide close protection to the civil affairs team so that we could support the ministries more.

"Jesus, you don't hang around, do you. A fucking multiple of troops? I'll see what we can do."

The Prince's large white villa on the Tigris had until a few months been, like all its neighbors, the house or office of a very senior Baath party official. No one now questioned how the Prince of the Marshes had come to possess the building. Until now, our policy had been to support him against his enemies, arrest the people he wanted arrested, employ his tribesmen, and follow his advice.

The Prince was standing on the front doorstep. He was over six feet tall, broad-shouldered, and dark, and looked strong and younger than his forty-five years. His slightly receding chin was hidden by a neatly trimmed beard. Although he was one of the few people there who might have seen as much action as the general, there was no sign of it in his dress. He wore dark brown robes and a light brown cloak, whose gold braid was in the Kuwaiti style, with red thread worked into the six-band design. He had a plain white head-dress under a black band, and highly polished slip-on shoes with gold buckles. He smiled broadly and shook the general's hand and launched through the interpreter into greetings. I stuck out my hand too, and he shook it briefly and then turned his back on me. He was clearly not interested in me, the brigadier, the colonel, the company commanders, or the policy advisors. He walked on into his office and invited the general to sit next to him. We arranged ourselves in the other chairs.

"How are you, General?" asked the Prince.

"Just fine, and how are you, Abu Hatim? Keeping everyone in line?"

"God be praised. I have just come back from pig shooting."

"Where?"

The Prince stepped forward to a map, which he had looted from the wall of Saddam's Fourth Army corps base and which showed now nonexistent regiments of the republican guard scattered all over the province. He pointed to an area in the southeast.

"Very fast. Very angry. Very dangerous," he said.

"We love pig shooting. Wilfred Thesiger, whom you remember, used to go pig shooting here fifty years ago. When are you going to take us with you?"

One of the other British officers who had been in the cavalry leaned forward and said, "You know, Abu Hatim, we used to hunt them on horses with lances. Pig sticking, it was called."

"No. No. You cannot do that. They are very fast. Very dangerous," the Prince replied.

"Yes, I understand but—"

I interrupted, "I think, Abu Hatim, the brigadier is saying they used to do it in the past, in history, not anymore."

"No," the Prince said again, "you should use a helicopter. Shoot from the helicopter."

"Well, I suppose that's an idea," muttered the general and then turned to his ADC. "Any problem in taking him up in a helicopter?"

"No sir."

"Why don't you come up with me in a helicopter, Abu Hatim, and we'll have a go together?"

The Prince nodded vaguely.

"Next week suit, Wednesday all right?" Again he turned to his aide, who nodded.

"Inshallah," said Abu Hatim, who didn't seem that interested.

"You going to take any of the rest of us, General?" asked the cavalry officer.

"Absolutely not. You're much too busy to be arsing around on a thing like that. Now for me it would be a different thing—important aerial reconnaissance work. Might take Major Johnny, though—can't keep the cavalry away from the pigs."

"And me, General?" I asked.

"What the hell is this becoming, Rory, an effing busman's holiday? Who's supposed to be running this place? Abu Hatim, I want you to meet this man here." He pointed to me. "This is Mr. Stewart. He's been all over the shop and he's going to be here for a year, so I want you to look after him for me."

Abu Hatim glanced at me and then looked away. "You are very welcome," he said. I wondered if he thought I was too young, a civilian, and not even an American—in short, not worth taking the time over. Smiling broadly at the general, he said, "Well, now, shall we all go through and meet the sheikhs?"

My sympathies and those of most of my colleagues extended barely beyond the provincial boundary. I regarded the two great Maysan tribes, the Beni Lam and the Albu Muhammad, as the most famous and powerful tribes in all of Iraq; I believed that ours was the poorest, most remote, and unruly area of the country, the most persecuted by Saddam and most threatened by Iran and the Sadrists. I had little sense of the sophisticated urban culture of Baghdad; no idea that the Prince of the Rabia in Kut was a much grander national figure than our sheikhs; that Samawah was poorer, or Anbar more dangerous. It took months to realize that many Iraqis saw Maysan either as a den of dirty, superstitious illiterates or, in the view of a friend in Baghdad, a tedious non-event. "I went to Amara once," he said. "There is nothing there. The only thing I did was play in the pool halls, waiting for the next bus home."

In terms of geography, Maysan was almost the twin of its neighbor, the province of Dhi Qar. They were adjoining areas of flat silt in the delta between the Tigris and the Euphrates, the north of which was farm and pastureland while the south, nearer the confluence of both rivers, had once been marshes. Amara was on the eastern, Tigris arm, Nasiriyah lay on the western, Euphrates arm.

In the nineteenth century there were almost no towns in the delta. The Muntafiq tribal confederation on the Euphrates was governed by the Saadun family. The Tigris areas of our province were controlled by the wheat-growing and horse-rearing Beni Lam of the northern prairie and the rice-growing, buffalo-rearing Albu Muhammad of the southern marshes, and these two tribes were at war with each other. In both provinces, the tribes supplemented their income by raiding river traffic, bound from the coastal town of Basra up the Tigris for Baghdad and up the Euphrates with corpses and pilgrims for the Shia shrine cities of Najaf and Karbala.

Almost all the inhabitants of these provinces, like the majority of people in Iran, were Shia Muslims. But the ruling class in Baghdad was from the Sunni minority, and they saw the Shia as backward and superstitious at best and, at worst, heretics. They believed that the wailing and self-flagellation in their processions, and the small clay discs they placed beneath their foreheads when they prayed, were signs of superstition. They thought that the Shia reverence for saints' shrines and pictures of the Prophet's family, and their respect for the twelve Imams, or leaders, was close to idol worship.

The Ottomans finally turned their attention to both provinces in the second half of the nineteenth century, building the city of Amara on the Tigris, at the frontier between the Beni Lam and the Albu Muhammad, and on the Euphrates, having defeated and exiled the Saadun family, the city of Nasiriyah. They made the tribal sheikhs into landlords, obliged them to pay tax, and settled small garrisons and governors in the new cities.

The British captured the provinces from the Ottomans by 1916 and initially posted political officers to administer the district towns. Amara acquired a British club and a weekly hockey match between the British and Indian soldiers. But in 1919, when Iraq became a mandate of the League of Nations, most of the political officers were withdrawn from the provinces to become advisers in Baghdad. The British, like the Ottomans and like Saddam, continued to rely on the Sunni minority—which was better-educated and wealthier—as the ruling class. In 1920, partly because of this, there was a serious uprising against the British centerd in the Shia areas, and many British and Iraqis were killed. In 1932, in accordance with their League of Nations obligations, the British transferred power to a government presided over by the new Sunni king and left. The monarchy failed to satisfy Arab nationalists, and in particular the military, and in 1958 the king and his senior officials were killed in a successful coup led by a nationalist general. In 1968, another coup brought the Baath to power, with the twenty-eight-year-old Saddam as vice president. He became the de facto power, and in 1979 the president.

When the invasion happened in April 2000, most of the Baathists fled Amara, abandoning their riverfront villas in one desperate night.

Not a single former judge remained in Maysan. A new political class emerged. In the political meetings, ties and safari jackets were replaced by robes and turbans. The old heads of the police and various ministries vanished. The political parties, militias, and refugees quickly occupied their empty villas. Within a week the guest rooms were piled with filing cabinets, ammunition boxes, and the kerosene stoves of families just back from Iran; plumbing ceased to function; and, without gardeners, the bougainvillea wilted.

The Ottomans, the British, and the Baath believed that in Amara they had built a modern state out of tribal chaos. Only a few pottery shards on marsh islands revealed that this area had once been the very center of world civilization, the heartland of the fertile crescent of Sumeria.

Commentators abroad complained that the Coalition did not remember any of this history. They believed we had ignored important lessons from post-war Germany and Japan and 1920s Iraq. But history has few unambiguous lessons. Many of my colleagues were well respected Arabists with extensive experience in post-war reconstruction, but none of them could guess the exact effect of a foreign invasion, the toppling of the President, and a society turned on its head. No library could tell you about the Prince of the Marshes; there were no polls that would reveal his popularity, now that events tested his strength. I continued to study Iraqi history; I visited neighboring governorate coordinators in four Shia provinces. But what mattered most were local details, daily encounters with men of which we knew little and of whom Iraqis knew little more.

The afternoon of my meeting with the Prince for example, I watched an elderly visitor enter the compound. He did not offer a bribe or an official letter at the gate, so he must have been known by the guard. The Iraqi police searched him and then a British sentry searched him. In exchange for a receipt he handed over his pistol. This indicated that he was not a policeman or a member of the supervisory committee. They were allowed to bring weapons into the building—loaded if they were policemen. Then he was made to sit for ten minutes on a decrepit wicker chair on the sidewalk. Some Iraqi sheikhs who were passing greeted him. It was probably embarrassing to be seen waiting in the sun, but they embraced each other warmly. The man smiled politely when a translator came out to greet him and, after a brief discussion, escorted him up the path to the reception.

There, in the waiting room, on purple and yellow sofas, were eight other Iraqi men: two in baggy suits carrying files; three in torn and mud-caked flannel trousers, gazing at Arabic posters that, judging by their vacant expressions, they were unable to read; two in sheikhly tribal costume; and a young cleric in a black turban. The sheikhs immediately stood to greet the new man, the laborers quickly followed, and even the men in suits got up, although they were hot and fat. The cleric raised a hand and rose slightly from his chair. The visitor returned the greeting of the cleric; embraced the men in tribal robes and kissed them, asking them in a tone of great tenderness how they were; shook hands with the men in suits; and, putting his hand to his chest, wished the laborers peace. Space was made for him on the sofa and after politely suggesting someone else might sit there, he took the place and began running his rosary through his fingers. The group sat in silence for half an hour until a translator entered and guided the new visitor to my office. He said: *Ya Allah* as he entered. I kissed him on each cheek—he used a cologne that smelled of roses—and said:

"*A salaam aleikum.*" (Peace be with you.)

"*Waleikum a salaam wa rahmatullah wa barakatu.*" (And unto you be peace and the grace and mercy of God be upon you.) He said this with a smile, as though teasing me for attempting the Islamic greeting.

"*Ahlan wa sahlan.*" (Be welcome.)

"*Ahlan wa sahlan bik.*" (Be welcome, honorable one.)

"*Shlon hadartak?*" (How is the respected one?)

"Al hamdulillah. Shlon hadartak?" (God be praised.)

"Al hamdullilah. Shlonak? Shlon saha?" (How are you? How is your health?)

"Al hamdullialh. Shlonak?"

"Al hamdullilah. Shlon umur?" (How is your life?)

"Al hamdulliah. Wa enta?" (And yours?)

"Al hamdullilah. Min fadhlak." (You, please.)

"Min fadhlak."

I gestured toward a chair.

"La, la, habibi enta min fadhlak." (No, no, my beloved, after you.)

"Tfadle." (You, first.) I smiled.

"Shukran." (Thank you.)

My guest made to stand up. I took his arm and made him sit down again. We smiled. This was the first time we had met, and I had no idea who this man was.

I stood to ask for coffee. My one clear innovation so far had been to introduce more hospitality for visitors. The civil affairs team had been reluctant to spend on entertainment; there was no budget for it and I suspect they didn't think such flummeries mattered. But no Iraqi official would receive a guest without offering him a drink. The ritual greetings and hospitality were a social necessity that seemed almost an obligation. A cup of coffee delivered in the right way could win more friends than a new high school, and no amount of money could wipe clean an insult. I hoped by treating people with elaborate courtesy to win consent for what would be unpopular decisions. So I paid Karim, who made traditional Arabic coffee by balancing a coffee pot on the toaster.

This man was in a short-sleeved shirt, his hair was scraped back, and his mustache curled slightly at the tips in the style of a World War I Turkish general. I knew he was not the leader of an Islamist party because they were usually bearded and Iranians wanted men to cover their arms. From the way he carried himself and had been greeted he could have been a professor, or a successful businessman. But whereas most such men dressed in khaki safari jackets or plain shirts, his was made of a shiny chiffon and caught the light in patches of dove-gray and gun-metal blue. He wore a thin leather watch strap when most people wore a heavy gold chain. And he had allowed his hair to go gray rather than dyeing it jet-black.

I returned with Ali, the translator. Karim came in with a handleless porcelain Chinese teacup rattling against a long-spouted brass coffee pot. The guest did not stand up but drank the half-inch of syrupy coffee, held out his cup for a refill, drank again, and then shook the cup to indicate he had finished.

"Seyyed Rory," said my guest, in English, "My name is Hussein Suwaadi." He then settled back into Arabic. He said he was in charge of the finance ministry for the province, or at least that was what the translator said. But the translator was ignorant of the ministry structure, and the man used Arabic words that were vague, perhaps deliberately so. I had heard him say he was a "mudhir"—a director. What exactly did this mean?

"Ali, please ask His Excellency Hussein whether he is a director of a section, the head of a department, or the provincial director-general of the ministry, controlling all departments."

"He is the director-general of the ministry, controlling all departments," said Ali.

"Ali, I didn't ask you, I wanted you to ask him."

"Are you the mudhir of the ministry of finance?" asked Ali.

"Yes, I am the mudhir of the ministry of finance," Hussein said, smiling patiently and clarifying nothing.

"And what is happening?" I asked, choosing a suitably general question as a cue for us to move on to the substance. It was rude to ask directly why someone had come, and I winced to hear Ali translate, "What is your problem?"

"I have come to get your help in accessing our operating budget this month. The treasurer will not release it." Pause. "Because he says he does not have the correct paperwork or permission. We can do nothing without our operating budget. My office is falling to pieces, we need to try to repair things and get staff back." This was a very common problem. The treasurer almost never paid out budgets, whatever kind of paperwork Baghdad sent. "I think he is a Baathist," continued the director. "That is why he will not release the money: he is trying to sabotage the ministries."

I nodded politely and pretend to scribble this down. I guessed that most people who were accused of being sabotaging Baathists were no more Baathist than their accusers: the accusation was just a convenient way of getting rid of rivals. "And what is your allocation for this month?"

"For this month we have been allocated two hundred million Iraqi dinars."

"Two hundred million Iraqi dinars?" It seemed an incredible amount of money—about 150,000 dollars.

"Yes."

"For all budgets: salary, capital budget, and operating budget?"

"No, just operational," he leaned forward so that I caught another whiff of cologne, mingled with what smelled like a big fish lunch, and produced a spreadsheet.

"But how much did you get last year in your operating budget?"

"That was under the old regime system."

I nodded and chose another tack. "How much was in the budget for this July?"

"One million three hundred thousand dinars." About a thousand dollars.

"Why have they increased it two hundred times?"

"Why have they increased it twenty times?" the translator asked. I corrected him.

"It is the new system," Hussein replied.

"But what is the justification?"

"I don't know," he said and smiled.

I took a guess. "Is this perhaps not just for you but for all the ten departments in your ministry?"

"Of course," he said. "And I have gathered them all together and we have agreed to split it equally, twenty million dinars for each of us."

"But what are you going to do with that kind of money?"

"Computers, air conditioners, sofas, and cars—none of us have office cars. Just sign this piece of paper and we will do the rest."

My telephone rang, the gate warning me that a senior visitor had arrived. I stood up, thanked Hussein for coming, and told him we would talk about it tomorrow when I had checked with Baghdad. He smiled. As I walked him out Hussein told me that he was the paramount sheikh of the Suwaad and that he should be the governor of the province; he knew everybody. We would be good friends, he could sense it, and he would help me with anything I needed.

As he walked through the waiting room everyone stood to greet him again except the cleric, and I reflected that these feudal lords and petty contractors understood my visitor's public life and private character in a way I never could. They had watched him at weddings and funerals and in the tribal meeting halls; they had a sense of whether he was funny or pompous, arch or considerate, wise or merely sly. They knew what kind of obligations he could be expected to fulfill; when a promise was sincere; when he would go out of his way and when he wouldn't.

These men also knew, I found out later, that Hussein's father was called Saad and that his grandfather Sehud was the brother of one of the paramount sheikhs of the Suwaad but that the most powerful sheikh of the Suwaad at the moment was Sheikh Muhajjer Ali Shiah, not Hussein. They knew that Hussein's two brothers and uncle had been killed by Saddam because of their part in the 1991 uprising; that Hussein had tried to take control of the province in the few weeks after the liberation but was beaten by the Prince of the Marshes; that he had a grand house, partially financed by corruption; that the contractor he favored was Hassan Ahmed, who had overcharged a thousand percent on a school complex in a northern province. I knew none of this. Only perhaps the cleric, who was in his twenties and had spent the last fifteen years in Najaf, could have been as ignorant as me.

CIVIL AFFAIRS

Anyone wishing to establish a republic today would find it easier to do so among mountaineers, where there is no culture, than among men who are accustomed to living in cities where culture is corrupt; in like manner, a sculptor can more easily carve a beautiful statue out of a rough piece of marble than he can from one poorly blocked out by someone else.
　　　　　　　—*Machiavelli*, Discourses, *Book I, Chapter 11*

OCTOBER 2003

Tens of thousands of civil servants like Hussein were at their desks; schools and clinics were functioning; half the population had piped water and sewerage; and there was electricity six hours a day. But services had not yet returned to pre-war levels. This was not only the Coalition's fault. After a decade of sanctions, systems were "tied together with bits of string"; civil servants broke equipment so they could steal money provided by the Americans to mend it; the systems were too big to monitor for corruption; and demand for electricity had increased as the borders opened to trade and everyone bought new televisions and air conditioners. Iraq produced only half the electricity that it required. It would take four years and billions to build generating stations to meet the shortfall. The only neighbor prepared to provide large amounts of electricity was Iran, and there were strong strategic reasons not to make Iraq dependent on Iran.

The pipelines and the powerlines were very difficult to defend, because they ran through large stretches of empty desert. Insurgents were blowing up oil pipelines. In Maysan, people pulled down electricity pylons with tractors: one pylon would usually bring down a dozen others as it fell. They then cut the copper wire, smelted it, and sold it in Iran. They made ten thousand dollars from eighty pylons, which cost us ten million dollars to repair. It is very difficult to restore basic services in someone else's country. Four years after the invasion of Kosovo and two years after the invasion of Afghanistan, the international community had still not provided adequate electricity in Pristina or Kabul.

But in Iraq this failure mattered more than in a place like Afghanistan, where the Taliban had provided very little. I had walked six hundred miles through the mountains of Afghanistan without staying in a single village with electricity or meeting a civil servant who received a salary. In Afghanistan or in Sierra Leone, where there had been decades of civil war and no functioning state, a Coalition could easily improve things. But Saddam's huge centralized bureaucracy had run almost every detail of society and the economy. Such a system was difficult to keep, replicate, or replace. Iraqis believed that the Coalition and Western technology could create immediate improvement in their lives. They couldn't.

Not everyone, however, had enjoyed a prosperous life under Saddam. Soon after my arrival, I accompanied the social affairs officer to a compound ten miles south of Amara, in an area of dried marsh. We stopped the vehicles at a low mud house that faced a courtyard thick with black flies. A man was leaning against a wooden pillar. One trouser-leg was still intact and he had a shoe. The rest of him, however, looked like a plaster statue left too long in the elements. The blood-caked clouts, loose round his wrists, revealed that he was missing two fingers on each hand. Three toes were gone and where his nose had been was a livid mottled section of flesh. A woman stood beside him and strained to give us the traditional cry of greeting— *wa wa wa wa*—ululating feebly up the scale. Her rheumy eyes had swelled to the size of old apples. The pupils, cataract-glazed, floated useless on the surface, and flies fed where the lashes had been. Charlie Morris advanced to embrace her and I very awkwardly held the man's wrist. I could think of nothing to say or do except turn away so the bodyguard team would not see me crying.

In my next six months in Amara, I never heard any Iraqi mention the existence of this place. The ten lepers said that they had once been in a hospital in Amara but through some change, which was blamed like everything on Saddam's son Uday, they had been expelled from the city and placed here. One old woman in the compound was not a leper. She had been their nurse. But when she tried to return home she was driven back with stones from her house.

I had not seen such conditions in Afghanistan. These humans could do almost nothing for themselves. Half were blind, all were missing digits and struggled to walk. Their families had disowned them. They were only alive because villagers occasionally dropped scraps of food on the edge of the road, three hundred meters from their compound.

Back at the office I asked Charlie Morris to prepare a project to build a new house for the lepers, with a generator and running water. Charlie had some suggestions of how to link the community to Iraqi medical and social services, and she offered to find clothes and medicine for them. Charlie's military boss, however, wanted to veto the project. The Coalition commander's mission was to support the ministries and do large-scale reconstruction projects. He said we were not here to help communities of ten, however sad their circumstances. I could see the officer's logic, but I used my position in the CPA to authorize and fund the project.

That evening, I stayed late at the office to drink some wine with the civil affairs team. Although I met them every morning and saw them throughout the day, I had a formal relationship with all except the agriculture specialist, an infantry captain, who ran with me in the evenings and called me "boss," "governor," and sometimes, I was told, "chicken legs."

Alcohol had been banned at the main base before I arrived. I was told that this was because one evening two soldiers had staged a box-ing match on the landing strip, preventing a helicopter from landing, and a military policeman had stuck a loaded weapon in his mouth while his officer collapsed in an alcoholic stupor on the ground in the act of trying to "talk him down." There were only two exceptions to the alcohol ban: the more special units, who drank beer while watch-ing pornography, which they had filmed themselves with their covert image-intensifying night-vision equipment after luring one of the camp's three women to their room; and our own unit, which was at exactly the opposite end of the spectrum of military operations.

I sat with George by the river and explained my plans to turn the waterfront building into a canteen. He nodded. We talked about fill-ing the pool with water so we could swim and he warned me of potential liability problems if swimmers injured themselves. I encour-aged him to go ahead regardless. Then I discussed restructuring our operations. I was concerned that we were not giving enough respon-sibility to the Iraqis and had ignored key clerics and politicians. He listened to me with an expression that was half a smile and half a grimace. "Rory, you're going to have to take it easy," he said. "You've been here a few days. Take your time."

I said nothing, and when we walked inside, I joined a group lis-tening to a visitor who wore jeans and a North Face jacket. He was six foot four and his chest was so broad that at first I thought he was wearing body armor under his T-shirt. He stood with his legs wide apart and a beer can in one fist and spoke in an accent that some-times sounded Yorkshire and sometimes like an upper-class drawl.

"Right, I'm going up to Majar now," he said, talking about a town twenty miles south, where six royal military policemen had been executed three months earlier. "I'll tab it myself. All I need is to strap on an M-4, a Glock, an M72A2, an L2, a twelve-bore, and a Minimi." Everyone nodded at this list of weapons though few of us had ever fired them. "I understand all that political shit but we need to get in there and flat-pack some people."

Some of the group laughed. The civil affairs team had more contact with Iraqis than anyone through their reconstruction work, but many of them missed being soldiers. Our agricultural adviser took every opportunity to put on his wrap-around Oakley shades and lead patrols into the streets. And when our compound was later attacked the team competed to climb onto the roof and man the heavy machine guns.

The visitor had been in Majar on the last operation designed to catch the killers of the Royal Military Policemen (RMPs). It had gone wrong. I asked him what had happened.

"You've seen *Black Hawk Down*? It was like going into the Katanga market. I felt I was going to be leaving town with only two rounds in my Glock, one for me and one for the last Arab that tried to get near me. It was summer, everyone was sleeping on the roofs—we were overlooked from every side—drove into a closed central square, surrounded on every side. And there's a geezer who's been working the case for months, points us toward a building. And one of the guys says, listen, this is the wrong building—it's the other one. But he's like, 'This is the right fucking building.' Fair enough, we'd only been briefed that morning and he'd been working it for months, so we go with him. We get in there, there's twenty inside. I'm pointing my weapon at them," he mimed it out, "illuminating them with the torch on the barrel; I'm thinking, this isn't right: the killer should be missing some teeth. That was it. Mission over. No hombre. We need to get back in there now and do the business."

"The time to go back was straight after," I interjected. "Then Majar would have understood what we were doing."

"That's right. Don't show any weakness. They're like, wha' hey? First they allow us to slot some RMPs, now it's anything goes. Arabs respect power—big, powerful men. I know they respect me because they know they are dealing with a big, powerful man."

"But it's a bit late now," I pressed the point.

"Bit late? The RMPs had wives, children."

"And three girlfriends apiece," someone added.

"Is that a crime now? Get in there," the big man countered.

"If we go in now, the province will go up in flames," I said.

"Do I care? We're not here for keeps. Americans would do it. They wouldn't get away with it from the Americans. What is our problem? Honestly, the problem is officers thinking about their own careers. That's why officers should not be allowed anywhere near this stuff—need some lateral thinking. And most of them couldn't hit a cow's arse with a banjo."

I mentioned that I had just been reading Bertram Thomas, who had been the political officer in Nasiriyah in the twenties. He had said something like, "Arabs respect three things in a government: power, the will to use that power, and a genuine concern for the welfare of the people."

"Spot on," said the big man. "For the first two anyway. I don't give a fucking monkey's about their welfare."

"I reckon you do," I said.

"I fucking don't. Try me."

PERSIA

Realizing that the subjects would have armed themselves in any case, it chose the honorable policy and decided that what ought to be done would be better done with its permission.

—Machiavelli, Discourses, *Book I, Chapter 38*

SUNDAY, OCTOBER 12, 2003

Paul Bremer, our chief administrator in Baghdad, had a seven-point plan for Iraq—seven steps to heaven. He had already appointed a twenty-five-member "Governing Council" (which included the Prince); it had in turn formed a constitutional preparation committee and selected ministers. Next a constitution would be written, a referendum held on that constitution, then a general election, and our CPA office would be dissolved. I had had little to do with any of this. I spent my first week in Maysan deciding how to mediate in a tribal war, deal with a flood, regulate religious flagellants, advise on the architecture of the souk, patch a split within a political party, set up a television station, arrange an election, and equip the police with guns. I operated at a level that had nothing to do with new constitutions. I intended to create a safer place with some economic growth and a government that responded to its citizens. I was mostly trapped in my office. And most of the time, I still knew almost nothing about the people who came to visit me.

One morning, the translator announced the arrival of three of the most powerful men in the province. He called them Abu Miriam,

Abu Ahmed, and Abu Maytham. But these were not their names—they were aliases, *noms de guerre.*

I asked the translator what he knew about these men. "None of us knows anything about them."

"But they are originally from Maysan."

"Perhaps. I don't know."

Abu Miriam entered first, as the elder. He was small and looked frail, with a grizzled white beard and tired eyes behind spectacles. Next was Abu Ahmed, a portly man with a broad smile. Even very poor men in Maysan generally took great care to polish their shoes and brush their hair, but his belt was untied, his beige shirt was hanging out of his trousers, his jacket was crumpled, and his shoes were scuffed. His combover had fallen forward, revealing a bald spot. He looked nearly fifty, although he was in his mid-thirties. Abu Maytham entered last, tall and broad-shouldered at forty.

Each man introduced himself as the leader of a different political party, although I knew they were all associated with the Iranian-linked Badr brigades.[1] I asked Abu Miriam how many members his party had, expecting to hear—as I did from everybody—"Oh, tens of thousands."

"One thousand one hundred and thirty-four," he said.

"How do you know so precisely?" I asked.

"Because I personally issued each man with a Kalashnikov," he replied.

I learned later that these three represented for the Prince of the Marshes all that was wrong in the province. He described them as Iranian secret agents whose objective was to colonize Iraq. It was true that, while these men had been born in Iraq, they had lived in Iran for nearly two decades and their families were still in Iran. They had been paid and supported by the Iranian government, and the senior

---

[1] Abu Miriam ran an organization called the Movement of the Party of God. Abu Ahmed was the representative of the Supreme Committee for the Islamic Revolution in Iraq. Abu Maytham said he was commander of the Badr Movement.

officers of their militias had been members of the Iranian revolutionary guard. They had fought on the Iranian side during the Iran-Iraq
war and their leadership had long been committed to creating a
single theocratic superstate, including Iraq and Iran under an Iranian Grand Ayatollah. They had crossed the border shortly after the
invasion and with the Prince's own (non-Iranian) militia seized most
of the district towns and established their own security apparatus, almost the only effective security presence in the province. Now their
followers had been incorporated into the police, by the hundreds. It
was their black-clothed followers who had glared and spat at me in
the souk. Hence the Prince's claim that "one-third of the police force
are agents of Iran."

If these groups still wanted, as the Prince of the Marshes claimed,
to turn Iraq into something resembling Iran, this was very troubling.
Iran had, of course, been through periods of mild liberalism: women
in the capital sometimes showed their hair under their headscarves
and cut their overcoats short, and the elite found ways for men to
dance with women and smuggle in alcohol. It was not a simple medieval theocracy. Iranians were highly educated; there were spaces for
dissent; some of their cinema was amazing.

But in the three months I had spent walking through the rural
provinces of Iran, I had seen little of this. The movies that won prizes
at Cannes were rarely shown in provincial towns, where instead the
fare tended to kung fu movies with Israeli villains and Iranian heroes.
In the provinces, women wore only black *abayas* and the Iranian state
was omnipresent, from plain-clothes and uniformed police, military,
security service, and intelligence service to the revolutionary guard.
Every village had its cell of Bassij militia, and in Hamadan I was
stopped by twelve-year-old boys in uniform, carrying guns.

We as the Coalition had particular reasons to fear the influx of
these Iranian-spawned groups. The Iranian government still described
America as the "Great Satan" and Britain as the "little Satan," and
funded terrorist groups in the Middle East. It was wealthy, aggressive,

and apparently embarking on a nuclear program. Washington wanted Iraq as a counter-balance to Iran—not to hand it to Iran. Inside Iran, newspapers were closed, intellectuals and dissidents assassinated. This was not the kind of society we wanted to create in Iraq. Nor, we thought, was it the kind of society Iraqis wanted.

The Prince of the Marshes claimed Iran was using political leaders like my visitors to foment instability in Iraq: they were behind the terrorist attacks and the demonstrations, a strategy to keep us occupied and to dissuade us from invading Iran next.

The elderly Abu Miriam began by demanding that I release one of his lieutenants, whom we had interned "unjustly." The man in question had been the leading light in the carjackings and kidnappings in the northern areas. He had been arrested by the British military and his supporters had attacked the unit as they drove off, killing a British soldier. The military were, therefore, very reluctant to release him. On the other hand, they had no firm evidence against him and it was only a matter of time before he was out. I promised to take up the matter with the military.

The Badr commander, Abu Maytham, said not enough had been done to de-Baathify the province. In the West, many commentators claimed that we had done too much de-Baathification—far more, they said, than in post-war Germany or Japan—and by doing so had sacked all competent staff and created unnecessary enemies. In Amara, however, few people had been sacked at the ministries. And I had already met many like the Badr commander who demanded more, not less, de-Baathification. "Many fedayeen and Baathists are infiltrating the province," said the Badr commander.

"Please give us their names," I said, "and we will pursue them."

"We have given you the names of God-fearing people, but you have not accepted them. You prefer corrupt traitors." I guessed he was referring to the Prince of the Marshes and the ministry directors.

"The more information you can provide, the better we can work against these people," I repeated.

"We hear you say that again and again," the Badr commander snapped, "but no Baathists have been removed. They are regrouping."

Abu Ahmed, the portly and scruffy commander of the Supreme Committee for the Islamic Revolution in Iraq (SCIRI)—which was in a sense the umbrella organization for all these groups—then began to speak in a shy voice. He said he had been active in the resistance against Saddam for thirteen years. Much of that time— he wouldn't say how much—he had spent in Iran, and he had re-entered Maysan at the head of the SCIRI militia shortly after the invasion. "But," he insisted, "there has been no bad behavior from our groups. Our leader, the martyr Seyyed Muhammad Baqr Al-Hakim, gave us permission to deal with the Coalition for the sake of Iraq. Our enemy is not you. It is Saddam and the Baathists."

I thanked him. I guessed he had prepared this speech on instructions from Baghdad—his party was said to allow little autonomy to local figures.

"We have come now to demand to keep security in this province," he continued. "We are not afraid. We do not care about the tribes and the criminals. We think only of our honor." His voice was soft, slightly at odds with his heroic language, and he scratched the hair on his neck as he spoke. "First we are Islamic sacrificers—second we are for our country. How much better it would be for you to work with educated people such as ourselves, in scientific cooperation. We want to make Amara a modern society and take it away from the influence of the tribes. It is not true that the heads of the tribes control the tribes. To give a role to the heads of the tribes is a mistake. Al-Sadr is a dangerous man who calls mobs into the streets. Although the existence of the Coalition is not legal, we will cooperate to keep the peace on the streets."

I warmed to this apparent candor. But I was struck by what his carefully prepared speech—which was spoken so fluently that it almost seemed memorized—suggested about his party's view of the Coalition. He assumed that I, like many middle-class Iraqis, had an instinctive mistrust for the tribes and the uneducated and unscientific masses, and an affection for Islamic sacrificers and confidence in their honor codes. He took it for granted that the occupation was illegal. And he could not see how little connection there was between his proposal to allow Islamist vigilantes to run security and the Coalition's vision of rule of law and democratic policing. But he was an intelligent and articulate man. I wondered if he was simply seeing something I was missing.

"And who is making trouble at the moment?" I asked.

"Everyone including Iran," he replied. "We want a national government for Iraq." This was a change for a party that had once aimed to include Iraq in a super state under the Iranian leader Khomeini.

"And what kind of government do you wish to establish?"

"*Wilayat-e-faqih,*" he replied smiling. The government of the jurists—or, in other words, an Islamic theocracy under a senior Ayatollah: the governmental system of Iran. No one in the Coalition wanted to establish an Iranian-style theocracy, and it was clear even in the few days I had been in the province that there was little enthusiasm for it from Iraqis. Was the man naïve, or somehow steps ahead of me?

The Prince was wrong. These men were not simply Iranian spies out to destroy the Coalition. They had been close to Iran. But they were also ambitious politicians who wanted power; they were Shia Muslims who wanted religion to play a large part in government and they were nationalists who wanted a secure and strong Iraq. And perhaps because of what they had suffered in a decade or more in the resistance, they were also dignified and direct. How much power should they have in the new provincial council? They had three thousand armed men behind them. But did they have votes?

Painted slogans had appeared on the walls, saying, WE REJECT YOUR OCCUPATION. The new politicians made public statements against us and appeared with their militias. There were many poor and jobless in Amara, and our visitors were campaigning for a better economy as the route to peace. One of the first to tell me this was seventy-year-old Sheikh Ismail of the Bahadil tribe, who began, "We will never forget Mr. Grimley."

"Mr. Grimley?" I said.

"Mr. Grimley, your British predecessor here in the 1940s. He irrigated the fields. He worked for the Iraqi people. He made prosperity. The Grimley canal. Ah, Mr. Grimley. These young men outside know nothing. They are bored they are lied to by their clerics. Dealing with them is very easy. If you just give them jobs they will be too busy to turn up and make trouble. No one here really supports these radicals. We are a quiet society, a rural, tribal society that looks up to elders. Simple jobs would be enough: a dollar a day, cleaning the streets and some help with the irrigation. Remember Mr. Grimley."

We were surrounded by half-forgotten history. I had met some people back home who still remembered British political officers who had served in Iraq between 1916 and 1958. St. John Philby was famous. Before he became political officer in Amara in 1917 and conceived his son, Kim, the British intelligence officer and KGB double agent, he had been a civil servant in the Punjab. The British representative in Basra remembered the old Etonian Dugald Stewart, consul in Amara, talking about driving his two-seater from Amara to Basra in 1952, for a black-tie dinner with the consul-general. But no one had ever mentioned Grimley.

And yet it was somehow Mr. Grimley who had imprinted himself on the mind of the old sheikh and left his name in the landscape. Grimley couldn't have actually paid for the canal—the British consular office by the 1940s was famously short of money. Nor could he really even have ordered it to be built—by that date Iraq had not been a British protectorate for twenty years. Perhaps he had used his position to champion the project with the Iraqi government in Baghdad. Sheikh Ismail remembered Grimley coming out weekly to inspect the progress, getting down into the ditch and showing people how to dig. The Sheikh left it to others to draw out the implications, which they did, taunting us in endless meetings: "What has the Coalition ever done for us? What will you be remembered for? Nothing."

It was not that we lacked money and power. We could get our hands on much more of both than Mr. Grimley ever had. Nothing was set in stone, and everything was newly invented, including our jobs. With enough confidence and theater it was possible to expand our roles, acquire millions, and do a great deal. But this involved manipulating people—not only Iraqis but also our own civilian and military colleagues.

Our position reminded people of colonialism. But we were not colonial officers. Colonial officers in British India served for forty years, spoke the local languages fluently, and risked their lives and health, administering justice and collecting revenue in tiny, isolated districts, protected only by a small local levy. They often ruled indirectly, "advising" local kings, tolerating the flaws in their administration and toppling them only if they seriously endangered the security of the state. They put a strong emphasis on local knowledge, courage, initiative and probity. But they were ruthless in controlling dissent and wary of political change.

By contrast, our governments, like the United Nations, kept us on short contracts and prevented us from going into dangerous or isolated areas. They gave us little time or incentive to develop serious local expertise, and they considered indirect rule through local elites unacceptable. They had no long-term commitment to ruling the country. Their aim was to transfer power to an elected Iraqi government. The British wanted to do it immediately. Bremer thought it might take a couple of years.

ICE CREAM

Never pretend to make a new world or unhinge the very constitution and institutions of knight errantry.
—*Cervantes,* The Advice of Don Quixote, *Book 2, Chapter 2*

The day before my meeting with the three Iranian-linked militia commanders, I drove with George Butler to the regional finance meeting in Basra, where we met with the other Coalition governorate teams. There were still only five British civilians contracted to work in the governorate offices outside Baghdad and Basra—besides Mark Etherington in Kut and John Bourne in Nasiriyah, Liane Saunders and Emma Sky were now acting governors in the Kurdish areas in the north. The rest of the eighteen governorates were to be run by Americans, most of whom were State Department Officers with backgrounds in the Middle East.

I sat opposite John Bourne, the veterinarian. I knew that he had left the British Foreign Office to join the agriculture ministry, and I had heard that he been educated at Eton, but there was no swank to him. He was a small, wiry man who was known to work sixteen-hour days, impatient of any idea of holiday or rest. No one knew as many tribal sheikhs, and few had such a nuanced understanding of the local social structures and political parties. He drove every day into remote areas and returned late. To be on his bodyguard team was to be frequently forced into the middle of gangster towns without a chance to perform reconnaissance and to be deprived of lunch and dinner. The bodyguard teams learned to carry military rations. John apparently rarely ate.

In Maysan, the British battle group was keen to administer the province, and the civil affairs team was happy to work closely alongside me. John however, received almost no support from his Italian military team, but he was serious in his beliefs about how government ought to function, and he flung all his considerable energy and courage into those beliefs. He did not like the evasions, manipulation, and compromises of much of Coalition office politics. He thought, with reason, that the head offices in Baghdad and London had little understanding of the local situation and that the contracting and financial rules were absurd.

I had practiced my speech on Major George Butler on the way down in the car. I was, therefore, able to give the Basra meeting a very structured presentation peppered with statistics. I painted a gloomy picture of the poverty in our province but was optimistic about our capacity: I told them that with our civil affairs team and the local NGOs as "force-multipliers" we could administer hundreds of projects. I requested a larger team, more security, and more money.

John Bourne followed with a lengthy and ironic disquisition on the complexities of Nasiriyah, the weaknesses of the Italians and the peculiarities of the agricultural system. After the meeting I visited all the senior officials in their offices, reemphasizing our requirements and capacity. My pre-packaged blarney was rewarded with a quarter of a million dollars in cash. John emerged with nothing.

As we walked back to our cars, John told me that he was waiting for a project officer to arrive before he began to apply for development funds. I offered to show him how I got round the rules. He declined, not approving of my indifference to procedure. He didn't have the authority to sign off on money and he intended to do it properly.

A month later, by which time we had gathered nearly two million dollars in Amara, he still had no money for his province.

Meanwhile I acquired, in part through good relations with the British military, far more money than I could spend.[2] The question was what to spend it on. Baghdad focused on electricity and oil. Billions had been spent studying, refurbishing, building, and yet the electricity supply remained poor and Iraqi oil production dropped.

Over the next six months in Maysan, our civil affairs team implemented 224 projects worth 6.5 million dollars—on building clinics, schools, and water networks and refurbishing government ministry offices—always with Iraqi contractors, and often in partnership with foreign NGOs. But these projects were often expensive and complex and involved inscrutable systems of contracts, invoices, and receipts.

With nearly four hundred schools to refurbish, I preferred to give villagers and the headmaster a very small amount of money and let them refit the doors and windows themselves. It meant that the money did not vanish into the pockets of wealthy contractors or the ministry directors. If money was skimmed off, at least it disappeared at the most local level. Later I discovered that a military predecessor had already successfully run a similar scheme.

Every new project brought more problems. Eight civil affairs officers, even with considerable help from the NGOs, could not fully monitor and manage two hundred reconstruction projects. There was an ever-present risk of inefficiency and corruption. I emphasized this to Andy Bearpark, the British director of operations, when he arrived from Baghdad in a large black armored Mercedes, followed by two jeeps filled with his South African security team. He was wearing a black suit and white opened neck shirt and was accompanied

---

[2]In May, I was encouraged to spend ten million dollars in a month with almost no restrictions. Auditing systems were primitive and the money arrived, vacuum packed in million dollar bricks. We received so much money that it was impossible to spend it responsibly. I ran out of projects in Nasiriyah which could be completed in the time frame and had to return one and a half million dollars.

by a thirty-year-old female policy adviser with large gold hoops in her ears and by a Bosnian who had been his bodyguard in Kosovo and got the best tables in mafia nightclubs in Belgrade. Andy had recommended me for this job and I owed my position to him.

"Rory," said Andy, "you are not here to run a development operation. Your staff is not going to grow, it is going to get smaller. Your resources are going to diminish. You better adjust to that. I know you want to do sustainable development. But that is not what you're here for."

"Well, what I am supposed to do with my money here?"

"You're going to only have enough to build an occasional clinic or school, and you can connect them as you like to your political programs and objectives. Your budget is meant to support your political work, not to provide the basis for a full-scale development operation. Focus on making us friends. We need them."

"And what will be my mission—what will you assess me on at the end of the year?" Andy coughed and stubbed out his Benson and Hedges in one of the corrugated peach tins that served as an ashtray. "If I can come back in a year's time and see that the province is reasonably quiet and has not descended into anarchy and you are able to serve me some decent ice cream, I will be satisfied."

BAKLAVA

In olden times, Marsh people were fervent believers in this "King of the Marsh," whom many claim to have seen—a gigantic negro, according to some; a great shining-faced, roaring shadow blotting out the stars, said others.

—*Gavin Young*, Return to the Marshes

A city could not call itself free when there was a citizen living there who was feared by magistrates.

—*Machiavelli*, Discourses, *Book I, Chapter 29*

WEDNESDAY, OCTOBER 15, 2003

If the province was to remain reasonably quiet, I believed I would have to build a close relationship with the Prince of the Marshes and since I had failed to make an impression in his house, I invited him to my office. He drove his small Japanese car right into the compound—no one dared to search him—parked beside an armored personnel carrier, returned the policeman's salute and strode down the path, lifting his fine gold-braided cloak out of the dust.

I felt nervous. I went to the kitchen and told Karim to make coffee. I gave the kitchen boy ten dollars from my wallet and told him to hurry to the souk and buy two kilos of baklava. Then I rushed into my office, cursing the fact that I had not used insecticide and there was now no time to spray and let it dissipate. I re-emerged with toothbrush and toothpaste, took some water from the kitchen because the bathroom water was too sewage ridden, and brushed my teeth; pulled on a tie and, returning to the office, swept my papers off the table into a cardboard box I hid under the desk; pulled some of my books out of my suitcase and arranged them on the shelf; put my laptop and satellite phone on my desk and then, thinking it would make me look more important if my desk were clear, removed them again before I went to the door to greet my guest.

"*A salaam aleikum,*" I said.

"*Waleikum a salaam.*"

"*Ahlan wa sahlan.*"

"*Shukran.*"

He swept past me into the meeting room, and everyone waiting for meetings stood to greet him. But he did not stop to shake hands or ask after people's health. He simply nodded and pushed through the archway and into the kitchen corridor without waiting for me.

At the door to my office, he said "*Ya Allah*" and entered. Behind him, I gestured toward a seat and he sat down. I smiled at him. He did not smile. He was immobile: his shoulders back, his hands quite still on his lap, his chin slightly cocked as if posing for a sculptor. Only his narrow eyes moved, glancing from me to the floor, over to the desk and back as I began the formal greetings. He thanked me briefly and then immediately asked, "What is your position here?" At this point Karim entered the room with the coffee.

The Prince refused to have any coffee. This would have been rude if I had been an Arab. I guessed it was rude even if I was not an Arab. I sent Karim to get some Coca-Cola from the fridge. The Prince took it and thanked me but did not open the can. We were joined by Ahmed, a Yemeni development officer who kindly agreed to translate. The Prince did not trust local interpreters.

"Please have a baklava," I said, gesturing toward the tray where the pastry oozed sugar onto the porcelain plate.

He inspected the plate. "No, thank you. This is bad for your health. This sweet food will lead to weight gain and then will clog the arteries and put pressure on your heart. Then you will die. I take care of my health. I do not eat sugary food. I exercise regularly. I try to avoid colds. Perhaps I can send some of my herbal remedies to you." I thanked him. I knew, however, that in certain circumstances he had taken ample risks with his health. It was said that five years earlier, when Saddam's security service had spotted him in a restaurant and tried to arrest him, he took a hand grenade out of his pocket and threatened to blow himself up, and the room along with him. The officers ran and he sat to finish his breakfast. Presumably a fat-free breakfast.

"What is your position here?" the Prince asked again. The General had already told him.

I wasn't sure how to reply. An acting governor shortly to be a deputy governor with little power who needed to be taken seriously.

I answered gravely, emphasizing the immense honor he had paid me by his visit. "I am a British diplomat," I said. "I have spent the last nine years in the Islamic world. Before I came here I was in Indonesia and Bosnia, then in Iran and Pakistan and Afghanistan. I am now the acting governor and the head of this office. I am the representative of Ambassador Bremer. I will be here for one year."

"What has happened to Major Edward? Are you working for him?"

"No. Major Edward will be working for me."

"So you work for Colonel Mark?"

"No. There is now a civilian government here and the military and Colonel Mark are here to support my office, which is the Coalition Provisional Authority." This was true at least in theory. One of the military's two formal missions was to support the CPA. But from my brief stint in the army I knew that the colonel was unlikely to consult me, let alone to take orders from a civilian.

The Prince of the Marshes was unimpressed. "And what of the American?" he asked. "I thought we were getting an American governor."

"I don't know. I think she is held up in New York."

"Yes, a very senior American woman, Molly Phee. I know all about her. She has very good contacts in the administration. The Coalition has done nothing for the people here, nothing. No construction, no jobs. The economy must be got going. People are poor and angry. Molly must come at once. She will get money for the province."

"Well, I intend to begin by getting money for the province. You will see now that I am here, that we will begin to get the development aid that you have been promised. I have very good contacts—"

"No, not you. We need an American. The British can do nothing for us." He had observed in Baghdad that the United States not only spent 90 percent of the money and took 90 percent of the casualties but also took 99 percent of the decisions.

"I think you'll find—"

"When is Molly coming?"

"In about a month. But I'm here and I will be here for a year, whereas—"

"She must come sooner. I will tell Ambassador Bremer to make her come sooner."

I nodded and we sat in silence for a while. I gestured toward his Coke can, which he opened and, to my relief, sipped.

"Abu Hatim," I said, "one of the tasks I have been given is to reform the provincial council to make it more representative and then to select an Iraqi governor. It seems to me that there are three powerful political groups in Maysan." I meant his group, the Islamist political parties, and the Sadrists. "The first is a group that is more secular and independent and is supported by the tribes and the educated people." He nodded approvingly at this description of his group, which was seen by others as a collection of criminal, illiterate tribal thugs. "The second is the group with some members who have links to Iran." I meant the three militia commanders who had visited us.

"All of which have links to Iran. They are run by the Iranian Secret Service," he interrupted.

"And the third is the group associated with Muqtada al-Sadr."

"Forget about them. They are unemployed illiterates who like to riot."

"I realize that some of these groups are better than others but I think we must try to give them all a voice and a position on the provincial council. We want them on the inside. We want them arguing in the council chamber, not on the street. Otherwise we will have civil war."

"No," he said firmly. "There will be no civil war. Shut down the other groups. They have no supporters and if they try to make any trouble we together will kill them."

I laughed. "I understand what you are saying. But they would say the same about your group—"

"Are you comparing me to them?" he shouted. "Do you know how much power I have in this province? Have you asked anyone in the streets who they support? What are these political parties? Do you know how many members they have? Three apiece. Forget the political parties. We will run it better without them."

"Abu Hatim, I completely sympathize," I replied, surprised by his vehemence. "But you know we are moving toward a democracy here and in the end we have to rely on political parties. We need to train them, give them a voice, bring them along, so they are ready for an election."

"Politicians?" he said. "I hate politicians, so do the people. And me? You talk about me as if I was a politician. I want to return to private life. I have no interest in power."

"I respect that and you. As does everyone. But I am afraid that these changes are going to have to happen. We have no choice, this is from Bremer."

"I will speak to Bremer."

"And from our governments in Washington and London."

I waited for him to reply but he didn't; I continued: "My second task is to choose a governor for Amara. We are the only province without a governor, which is why I, a foreigner, am acting as the governor."

"It would be better if you just stayed as the governor. The people would prefer it. They will not trust an Iraqi governor."

"What I was going to suggest is that the new provincial council should elect the governor."

"*La, la,*" he protested angrily, thrusting forward in the chair. "This cannot be. Absolutely not. The Iraqi governor will be appointed by the governing council in Baghdad. We have agreed that already in Baghdad with Bremer."

That was not the impression that I had been given in my briefings. But since we received very little information from Baghdad, it was difficult to disagree.

"What qualities do you think a governor should have?" I asked.

"He should be an educated, independent man," he replied without pausing, almost as though he were reciting, "with strong opinions, a good reputation, no political connections but experienced in the bureaucracy. Perhaps an engineer."

The only man in the province who seemed to meet the description was his brother Riyadh, who had chaired the ministry meeting. I said so.

The Prince snapped. "I did not mean to appoint my brother."

"Would you be against the appointment of your brother?"

"It would have nothing to do with me. It would be decided by the governing council." The Prince was the only representative from Maysan on the governing council, and he would have overwhelming influence on the decision. I was almost certain he would try to appoint his brother.

The conversation faded again and again I offered my guest the baklava, which again he refused. The translator had another, licking his fingers, and chuckled as Abu Hatim again told him that if he kept eating them he would have a heart attack.

I tried to ask him a few questions about his life. Most of the Shia resistance groups were tied to Iran. But he claimed that although he had spent a certain amount of time in Kuwait and Saudi Arabia and knew their intelligence services well and regularly met the Americans, he hated the Iranians and had never worked with them. I tried to ask him what exactly his group had done in the resistance. Some said that they had limited themselves to assassinations of local Baathist officials.

"We fought the old regime," he replied, and I could get no more out of him. I asked him about smuggling. He replied that it was going on in the marshes and indicated a broad area on the map but said he knew no more details. Then he said he needed to go. I thanked him and walked him outside. As we approached his car he pointed out that we were relatively safe from mortars if they were fired from the north but could easily be shot by a sniper on the west bank of the Tigris.

PAGODA

The people always desire two things: the first is to avenge themselves against those who were the cause of their being enslaved; the other is to regain their freedom . . . a small part of them desire to be free in order to command; but all the others, the countless majority, desire liberty in order to live in security.

—Machiavelli, Discourses, *Book I, Chapter 16*

"Amin masdar quwwat lel ferd we el mujtema," said Abu Mustafa in my first meeting with the supervisory committee of local leaders appointed by the British military. Security is the basis of the power of the individual and the community. Everyone smiled, recognizing the paraphrase of Saddam's favorite aphorism. Saddam had stolen it from a great Shia ayatollah, but what Saddam and the ayatollah had said was, "Democracy is the basis of power." Priorities had changed.

I had never believed that mankind, unless overawed by a strong government, would fall inevitably into violent chaos. Societies were orderly, I thought, because human cultures were orderly. Written laws and the police played only a minor role. But Maysan made me reconsider. A secure and functioning government was not emerging of its own accord, and Iraqis continued to insist that only a police state could restore security. The CPA in the Green Zone wanted to build the new state in a single frenzy. Instead of beginning with security and basic needs and attempting the more complex things later, we implemented simultaneously programs on human rights, the free market, feminism, federalism, and constitutional reform. We acted as though there could be no tensions between the different programs, no necessity to think about sequence or timing. But people in Maysan talked about almost none of these things. They talked about security.

"The chief of police is a fool," growled Sheikh Rahim. "We have been asking since June to run this province since you cannot do it." Then his voice rose to a higher pitch. "In the southern towns like Al Qala the district councils do nothing. The road from Basra is not safe, our relatives have been kidnapped, our power lines are looted. Iranian secret agents move freely through the province and we have become an auto route for drugs from Afghanistan and Iran. It was not like this under Saddam."

I found it difficult to disagree. Maysan had been relatively secure under Saddam. The peace had been kept by officers of the special units of the army, the Baath party, the special security service, and the intelligence service; with heavy armor and checkpoints every few yards; through secret surveillance; on the basis of arbitrary mass arrests, blackmail, torture, and execution. Some in the Coalition, apparently including members of the 320th Military Police Battalion, which had taken over in Abu Ghraib a week before, seemed to think Saddam's methods were still necessary. For them and for many Iraqis, like Sheikh Rahim, this was a hard-headed nation that could only be ruled brutally.

But most of the Coalition policy makers believed that Iraq could be both secure and democratic. There was, they argued, no necessary connection between order and brutality or truth and pain. They thought that secret police were unnecessary and dangerous; that torture was counterproductive; crowds could be controlled effectively but humanely; the old, cumbersome, violent, and unpopular security forces could be replaced by a small, well-trained, lightly armed, citizen-friendly police service.

Partly for this reason the Coalition disbanded the army, sacked all senior Baathists, and abolished the security and intelligence services. It refused to allow the police to carry heavy weapons or set up secret units. British police trainers talked of encouraging a sense of public service, and one discussed with me the possibility of psychometric tests for senior officers and gender awareness workshops for all.

But the police were weak and incompetent and the ordinary officer was little more than a fist and, if he possessed one, a gun. Most policemen men had no weapons, uniforms, vehicles or radios. Procedures were based on legalistic paperwork and illegal brutality, only officers were permitted to charge suspects, write reports or search, and the leaders of the old security apparatus were mostly our enemies. We had very little information on criminal gangs or insurgents. The police would not arrest members of political parties or Islamist militias for fear of reprisal; they could not target tribes for fear of blood feuds. No one was really afraid of the police, and the police were afraid of almost everyone. Many of the policemen did not work because they were injured, idle, or dead. But their salaries continued to be paid, and were collected by relatives or by widows, or by senior officers.

Clearly, we needed to reform the police. The British colonel in Maysan introduced a number of innovations. He appointed, for example, a man of uncertain provenance called Seyyed Faqr as the Islamic chaplain for the police; the police had never had a chaplain before, but he was convinced that this was a good idea "because every British regiment had a padre." He also conducted a long search for a police chief with "real leadership skills, courage, and charisma." He failed to find a candidate among the regular police officers and finally appointed Abu Rashid, a sheikh of the smuggling Nowaffel clan and commander of the militia that supported his kinsman, the Prince of the Marshes. Abu Rashid had been a guerrilla fighter for fifteen years and had never served in the police, but he had a reputation for courage.

Most of the Coalition forces were fixed in position, guarding specified areas of the province; there were few soldiers to spare for police training and they were not professional policemen. The British Police Association had decided that the danger in Iraq was so great that it could not be ordered to deploy policemen overseas, and the senior British police adviser had received only a dozen of the few thousand British police mentors he had been promised.

We needed security before we could create any kind of functioning government. I could help with development projects and political reforms, but all our policies depended on the rule of law.

I first talked to police chief Abu Rashid on October 17, in the company of the general and the colonel in the military camp. He entered in his new uniform, having just changed out of the dish-dash I had seen him wearing an hour earlier. The epaulets with his brigadier's stars stuck out a little beyond his shoulders, and he had clearly struggled to do up the buttons over his full stomach. He pulled a leather-backed writing pad from his case, put it neatly on the table and glanced down at his shirt-front. I could imagine that his full black beard and bearlike torso might make him an intimidating figure, but on this occasion he looked as though he'd found himself at a party in clothes he regretted.

He began speaking very quickly, "General, Colonel, Seyyed Rory. Mission. My mission is to keep security in the Province of Maysan. In support we have the tribal chiefs, religious leaders, political parties, and independent personalities. This is our province and we must take responsibility."

We all leaned forwards and nodded energetically.

"This is a hundred-and-twenty-day plan to change the police, with targets. We are currently paying approximately," he glanced down at his pad, "four thousand regular police, of which a quarter are in al-Amara; four hundred fifty traffic police; nineteen communications police; three hundred identification police; five hundred firemen;

four hundred from the guards directorate; and three hundred twenty highway police." He glanced at the pad again, "Budgets. We need to gain access to our operating budget and train accountants to manage it."

"Okay, we are aware of that and we have raised it with Baghdad," said the colonel.

"Structure: I will split up and integrate Emergency Brigades 1, 2, and 3 into different parts of the force."

We all stared at him. This was an important and risky decision. The emergency brigades were the heavily armed militia groups that had taken control of the province between the fall of Saddam and the arrival of the British military. Brigade 1 consisted of the followers of the Prince of the Marshes, mostly illiterate villagers from the Albu Muhammad tribe. They had fought with him against Saddam and were associated with much of the looting and smuggling in the province. Brigades 2 and 3—Badr and the Movement of the Party of God—were the militias whose commanders had called on me a few days earlier.

Together, these three groups consisted of thousands of men. They were the only groups to protect government buildings in the month of the liberation. But they were also involved in protection rackets and frequently threatened to fight one another or the police. With only a thousand men of our own in the entire province, we did not have the power to confront or disarm them. The British colonel had therefore decided to badge the emergency brigades as policemen. This meant that almost all the heavily armed militia were now employed in the official structures. Only one militia group remained outside: the explicitly anti-Coalition militia of Muqtada al-Sadr, which called itself "the Army of the Redeeming Imam," and continued to gather in the back streets of Amara and the southern city of Majar, recruiting young men who were capable of forming mobs, carrying out simple assassinations, fire-bombing buildings, and making explosives.

The official militias now dominated the checkpoints and the criminal investigation department. The Prince of the Marshes Brigade, which Abu Rashid had commanded, operated largely independently, from a former Baath party building it had illegally occupied, next to the Prince's residence. All these units were of questionable loyalty and discipline. To split them up and integrate them further into the police as the chief was proposing would be a difficult and unpopular task.

"Dealing with Baathists and bad policemen," continued Abu Rashid. He paused and consulted his pad. Many people in Amara, disgusted that we had chosen as chief of police a Marsh Arab guerrilla with no police experience or training, claimed that Abu Rashid was illiterate, but this did not appear to be true. "I will tell the policemen that they have to meet certain standards. They must come to work. They must patrol. They must capture criminals. And if they do not, I will discipline them. Also I will investigate which policemen are Baathists and remove them. Training: the Coalition has agreed to set up a training course in Jordan for the police and also in Basra."

We nodded.

"I will select people to go on the course. I have set a series of standards, forty in all, which will need to be met over the next one hundred and twenty days. At the end of that period I will see how we have measured up to the standards." He glanced at the Colonel.

It seemed a very curious speech. In my short experience in Maysan, people I had come across had a standard response to the security problems. Employ five times as many new policemen. Get heavier weapons. Impose curfews. Set up checkpoints on the roads. Establish secret services to gather intelligence. Be more brutal. Seal the borders. In short, recreate some of Saddam's police state. No one in the Iraqi bureaucracy, even in the finance ministry, was talking mission statements, targets, and one-hundred-and-twenty-day plans. This wasn't even really the language of the foreign civilians. The only people I knew who talked like this were the military.

At the time, although slightly confused, I was impressed. It is only now, recording it, that it dawns on me that Abu Rashid must have written that speech for the general with considerable help from the colonel, who had appointed him. It was the colonel's last week—the King's Own Scottish Borderers were going home, and the Light Infantry were replacing them, and this was the last time he would meet the General.

The General congratulated Abu Rashid on his vision and asked him whether he was comfortable in his new role. Then there was a pause. I wanted to try to reconcile the rhetoric with what I knew anecdotally about police actions in Maysan. Abu Rashid had imported hundreds of his tribal kinsmen from the Prince's militia into the police, some of whom were twelve-year-olds with very little education. I had heard that the previous day some of these boys had drawn weapons when Abu Rashid's mother had been told to wait in line in the hospital, beating up some of the hospital staff and threatening to shoot the doctors unless they treated her immediately.

"Excuse me, General, Colonel," I said, "may I ask a question? General Abu Rashid, I have heard that your militiamen have been attacking staff at the hospital. Is that true?"

Abu Rashid looked bewildered for a moment. "No, this is not true."

"What are the stories from the hospital, then?"

"The problem is that the hospital is employing members of Iranian Islamist militias as their security guards and discriminating in who they let in. Simply we were keeping them in order." He smiled.

"You understand that the police must be entirely impartial."

"Of course."

This was the first that I had heard of there being yet another militia group, this time connected to the hospital. Feeling that I was running out of steam in this inquiry, I tried a different tack. "Does everyone in the police have appropriate qualifications?"

"I am investigating that now."

He glanced at the colonel when I was talking, as though he were surprised that I was allowed to talk to him like this. The general, who sensed the mood, even if he did not understand the background, interrupted. "General, do you have what you need to do your job?"

"No," said Abu Rashid. "Sixty senior officers have pistols; about twenty-five percent of the other policemen have AK-47s; the rest are unarmed. They have only twelve vehicles—second-hand twin cabs—to serve nearly six thousand people. We have no budget for gasoline. More than half of us do not have uniforms. There is not enough ammunition and what there is . . ." He took two rounds of ammunition out of his pocket and handed them to me. One bullet was bent, the other calcified with green rust. "We have no communications equipment."

The colonel, who must have heard this a dozen times, interrupted. "As you know, we are getting those things for you. We have already bought you four vehicles and given you some Kalashnikovs. There is a new national communications system—the blue light system—about to be introduced in two to three weeks. There is no point buying your own comms if it is going to be immediately replaced from Baghdad."

"General," I said, shifting to support the colonel, "almost every man in this province has a weapon at home. And you operate in three shifts, so you would only be using a thousand weapons at a time. If you share weapons and license some people to use personal weapons you will have enough."

My comment was met with silence, and I felt that perhaps I had done enough speaking for one meeting.

"I have been told," continued Abu Rashid, "that we should be using the money from our ministry of interior budget to equip the police. But the treasurer is only releasing sums of a thousand dollars at a time. And he says that the things that are most urgently required are not authorized within the budget. The budget for all sections of the police is only eight hundred thousand dollars, and we would like two million dollars for our police force."

"What about smuggling?" asked the general, deliberately changing the subject.

"I am setting up a task force to look into it."

"Where does it take place?"

"Everywhere."

As far as I knew, most of the smuggling took place in Abu Rashid's home district and was run by his cousins in the Nowaffel clan. But what would be the point of implying that our new police chief was nepotistic, biased, violent, and semi-criminal? I didn't have any ideas on who else should do the job. And we needed to have the police chief feeling confident and supported if he was to perform.

"What is happening with the Sadr office and the Army of the Redeeming Imam here?" asked the general. We had received information suggesting that they were planning large demonstrations and strikes against the occupation.

"As you know, I am reaching out to all communities. I am impartial," said the chief, relaxed again and smiling broadly. "Everyone here knows me and likes me. I have done some favors for the Sadr Office. They have invited me to attend Friday prayers in their mosque. I could attend if you so wish next week and tell you what they are saying."

"Do, please," we said, and with that the meeting ended.

I had introduced a compulsory Friday holiday for the civil affairs team because I could see they were exhausted from working seven-day weeks, and I decided to use mine to visit the southern town of al-Qala, which was in the Prince's Albu Muhammad tribal area. I had spent my first two weeks almost entirely in my office or in camp, and I was eager to visit rural towns, which I heard were bastions of corruption, inefficiency, and political tension. Many of the problems seemed to be connected with the district councils. Al-Qala was by all accounts a typically lawless place with an inactive police force that I thought we needed to restore with a combination of development projects and political compromise. We had so far, according to our records repaired three schools and a clinic in the district and provided three hundred jobs.

Al-Qala consisted of a few blocks of cement houses on either side of the Tigris, surrounded by rich agricultural land. Much of the land had recently been marsh. Unlike many other communities, al-Qala had benefited from Saddami draining of the marshes and was strongly opposed to reflooding them. There was a pontoon bridge connecting the two halves of town, and a small open-air market on the right bank. There was, it transpired, not one district council in al-Qala but two—one on the west bank of the Tigris and one on the east, fifty yards across the river. They were not speaking to each other. The Iraqi translator who was with me explained that after the collapse of Saddam's forces and before the arrival of the Coalition, the Prince's militia had divided the seats on the council with the Iranian-backed groups. The British military had left this arrangement in place. Then the Sadrists, who felt excluded, had formed an alternative council that competed with the official one. The two councils were now in continual dispute. Some people thought there would be civil war.

I had already met Sheikh Raisan, the most powerful figure on the official council. His family, the Beit Feisal, a clan of the Albu Muhammed, had controlled the area for more than a century, and his great-great grandfather was the brother of the great-grandfather of the Prince of the Marshes. Other members of the official council were from Islamist parties and had been in exile in Iran and in the resistance against Saddam. They received salaries from the central government, when the treasurer got round to paying them, and oversaw municipal projects in the surrounding towns. People said they were selling government equipment and vehicles, taking bribes, and stealing from budgets. I called first on the official council and found only one man in the office, the deputy mayor.

"You have repaired no schools in this district," he began.

"We have repaired three," I said and named them.

"I meant," he said "no high school had been repaired. And there are no jobs."

"But we have just provided three hundred jobs for al-Qala."

"I meant no jobs for graduates. The Salvation Army has been dealing with the 'illegal' council across the river. That council is controlled by anti-Coalition Sadrists who are levying taxes on local ministries, issuing travel permits, intimidating anyone who breaks Islamic social codes, and stealing kerosene. This is only the calm before the storm. The government and the police have not been paid. It will take only the smallest thing to turn the tribes against the Iranians and the Sadrists and then you will have a civil war. You must give me a weapons license and grant us control over the local police force."

I did know why he needed a weapons license; I told him he should apply to the British military, not to me. Later I was told that he ran the local diesel smuggling ring.

I then crossed the river to inspect the alternative council. Whereas the official council offices had been empty, theirs, a school classroom, was filled with a hundred young men, who from their clothes seemed to be mostly poor. I introduced myself and then sat and listened. The discussion was dominated by religious rhetoric.

The many posters of Sadr II on the wall confirmed that these men were followers of the charismatic preacher who during the nineties had lectured on the evils of Western decadence, prophesied the return of the hidden Imam—the Shiah messiah—and talked of a new leader for the Muslim world, who had increasingly resembled himself. Samizdat videos of these sermons, like the one I had seen in the souk, were distributed everywhere. He had reached out to the poor with an extensive and well-funded charitable foundation. The most senior leader of the Iraqi Shia was still Ayatollah Sistani, a much more learned scholar. But Sistani was an Iranian and did not give public sermons—some said because he did not want people to hear him speak Arabic with a Persian accent. Young men sometimes mocked him in private, calling him "the silent leader" and gave their hearts to the unimpeachably Arab Sadr II. Tens of thousands of young men often from deprived backgrounds attended the mosques where Sadr's young disciples preached.

After they had finished the religious discussion, one of the young men asked if I could contact the Kut dam to let more water down the Tigris. Another told me to ask Turkey to release water from their dam. Others asked practical questions about the refurbishment of buildings. I promised on the spot to refurbish the al-Qala secondary school and to create another three hundred jobs in the town. After the meeting I was taken aside by a man who was the leader of the alternative council structure in Al Amara. He was dressed in a suit, spoke intelligent English and had a kindly face. The NGOs had praised him to me for the work he had done in distributing emergency rations and allocating jobs; others had told me that he was a dangerous revolutionary, connected to the Sadr office.

He wanted the official council to be replaced with his alternative council. The official council, he claimed, were tribal criminals who had stolen forty thousand dollars. Then he complained about the Prince of the Marshes.

"His kinsman the new police chief is a gangster, his Marsh Arab Albu Muhammed followers have looted the province and terrorized the people. No one supports the Prince, and I am astonished that the Coalition continues to deal with him. It is only a matter of time before the unemployed and frustrated Muslims take the law into their own hands."

The Sadrists were no friends of the Coalition, but they had many supporters in al-Qala, and I believed that if we did not begin to include them and give them representation they would take to violence. I promised to meet the man again to discuss the competing town councils. I was, in fact, tempted to merge the two, but I wanted to discuss this move with the supervisory committee in the capital before I announced it.

I finished in al-Qala by checking on some of the work being done on public buildings. In the center of town, the local hospital was being refurbished and reed huts were being constructed as emergency housing for refugees. I was surprised to see from the metal signs outside the buildings that many of these projects had been undertaken by international NGOs. Iraq was not Kosovo, with traffic jams of white Land Cruisers marked "Kuwaiti Relief Aid" or "Clowns Without Frontiers." This war was dangerous and unpopular, and few agencies came. During the time I was in Iraq, Tanzania was visited by a thousand donor missions, Maysan by a dozen.

The clinic in al-Qala was being refurbished by Gordon, a thirty-four-year-old New Yorker. His agency, Mercy Corps, was funded by the U.S. government, but refused to do joint projects with the Coalition: before he came to Iraq, he had organized large demonstrations in America against the war. His ambition was to leave Iraq and set up a beachfront cappuccino bar. I liked Gordon. I had been to his house in the evening for a lentil curry, which was shared with young Czechs from an NGO called People in Need, one of whom I had met before in a small village in Afghanistan. After dinner he had played the trumpet, Gordon played the trombone, a colleague played the guitar, and I and the others played the local drums, made from pottery and a stretched fish skin. These were increasingly difficult to obtain, since the Islamist parties had attacked most of the music shops, apparently considering music to be un-Islamic. Later the band came to play in our office but a drunk Marine punched the Czech guitarist and they did not return.

The reed huts for the refugees were being built by the Salvation Army. Many of its staff were priests at home. They received no salaries, and they did not participate in our brass band. One might have predicted disaster for a Christian missionary organization that called itself an army, operating in the Shia south. Yet the Salvation Army were probably the most successful and popular NGO in the province. Our local office funded many of their programs, from computer training to playgrounds. They had opened a dressmaking school, which was run by a very reserved young woman called Muna. Her father had died and she was the only breadwinner for five brothers and five sisters, all of whom had long black pigtails and wore purple and green smocks made by Muna. Even conservative fathers seemed happy to send their daughters to her classes. When Muna talked about her work, she lost her solemnity and smiled like her younger sisters, saying, "I am so grateful, more than words can say, that the Salvation Army has given me this chance, this hope, when before I had no hope."

The high school at the north end of town had, I found, no heating, no water, no electricity, and not a single pane of glass in its windows; and it was surrounded by an open ditch of sewage. Every classroom was missing its door and was occupied by a family of returnees from Iran, crouched round a kerosene stove. Two young men spoke to me for a few minutes in Farsi, seeming relieved to find someone who knew something about Iran.

"You can see the conditions in which we live. We have no work, we have no houses. We returned for this? We are thinking of going back to Iran."

On the way back to Amara, I saw a compound up a dirt track, off the main road, and decided to pay a visit to what appeared to be a typical farm. The farmer seemed happy to have a visitor to whom he could show his rusting machinery and his sheep searching for grass on the sandy soil. I asked him how things were. He said, "Look around you. I am rich. I have a tractor, seven sons, three hundred sheep, and all the land you can see is mine. There is nothing else I could want."

As I left, I asked him what I should be doing. "Don't trust the police chief," he replied. "He is a gangster. Don't trust anyone who lives south of al-Amara. They are all thieves and bandits."

"But you live south of al-Amara," I protested.

"Don't trust me either," he said. He presented me with a live guinea fowl in parting as a gift.

When I got back to Amara, I submitted a proposal for the Salvation Army to refurbish the high school, and the project was approved. With its own money, the Salvation Army built more emergency housing from traditional reed huts at the south end of town and resettled the refugees from the school into them. We were able to find work for the Farsi-speaking men. Six weeks later, the school was fully renovated and filled with teachers and children.

I did not ever see the farmer again, although I frequently tried to contact him. Perhaps he was not keen to spend time with an agent of the Coalition. The guinea fowl was christened "Larry" and released into our office garden, and Tommy Smith, our new agricultural officer, later established Larry was a female and brought her two companions. They roosted in the central courtyard, and they were so noisy that meetings had to pause while they shrieked.

Scowling militiamen with guns still appeared on the streets, and often when the British military tried to confiscate their weapons they produced police badges. The Iranians were said to be studying our buildings and arming political parties; the Sadrists were angry at being exluded from the government. Economic projects continued. I was able to mollify the ministries with the quarter of a million from Basra. A ten-million-dollar project was approved to install gas turbine generators at our small oil field and thus double the electricity supply for the province.

The civil affairs team suggested that we take the General to visit the girls' high school in Amara, which we had recently renovated. We arrived in a long convoy, an hour late, because the General had been detained by the Prince of the Marshes. The school was housed in a two-story concrete building with a courtyard. It had clearly been re-built since my friend Yahya Said's grandfather, a Baghdadi Jew, had been the headmaster in the Ottoman period. Yahya's father, one of the most famous Communist leaders in 1950s Iraq, had been born in the school.

The current head teacher was a woman in black Islamic robes and a tight veil. She said she had held some students after class to greet us, but when we were late she had sent them home. When the General reached out to shake her hand she did not take it.

"I have said before," she said scowling, "that you should not come to this school. This is a women's school. It is not suitable for men. I have only agreed to this because you gave the money for the repairs." The General looked politely at the walls and said nothing. We followed her into a long, empty room. "This is what should be the chemistry lab. We have no equipment. You have not given us equipment and textbooks." She told her assistant to take us onto the roof.

Most of the money, explained J.D., the officer in charge of our gate security, had been spent on reinstalling stolen roof tiles. The work has been assessed by our own team of Iraqi engineers, who were trained by U.S. military engineers. We had invited tenders, re-viewed them with the Iraqi director of education, selected the lowest quote and supervised the work. "And as you can see," said J.D., "it's pretty good. A good feeling, if I might say so, sir, to get the girls back to school."

As we reached the ground floor again, we were surprised to find the Prince of the Marshes questioning the headmistress. He turned to the general's interpreter and said, "Tell him this is a disgrace. A com-plete disgrace. Forty-five thousand dollars for this!" He ran a finger-nail down the wall. "The paint is mixed with water. Nothing has been finished. This is five thousand dollars of work."

"But, with respect, you haven't seen the roof," I said.

"The roof? What? It is a golden roof? A Buddhist pagoda? This is a disgrace. You always do this, you never consult me, you have no idea what you are doing, you award the tenders to all the wrong people. If you had come to me I could have done it all for five thousand dollars." He raised his voice and the headmistress nodded approvingly. "Now I need to find the contractor who did this work—tell me his name, and I will rip his tongue out."

THE SUPERVISORY COMMITTEE

But in this degenerate age, fraud and a legion of ills infecting the world, no virtue can be safe, no honor can be secure; while wanton desires diffused into the hearts of men, corrupt the strictest watches, and the closest retreats; which though intricate and unknown as the labyrinth of Crete are no security for chastity.
— *Cervantes,* Lament of Don Quixote, *Book 2, Chapter 3*

SUNDAY, OCTOBER 19, 2003

Maysan needed strong Iraqi leaders. The vacuum left by Saddam in Maysan had been filled with the supervisory committee, whose members had been appointed partly by the Prince and partly by the Coalition. I needed to form a new provincial council and I was not allowed to hold an election. Whom should I appoint? The old Baathist ministers and policemen had at least been educated career civil servants or graduates of the police academy. The current leaders had only one qualification—their time in the resistance, where operations were so secret it was difficult to know precisely what they had done. The Prince's semiliterate Marsh Arabs had confirmed their reputation as thieves by thoroughly looting Amara. The other militias were beginning to enforce very restrictive Islamic social codes. All the waterfront cafés and the alcohol shops were closed, minority religious groups were fleeing the province, women were now afraid to appear unveiled, Internet cafés had been bombed. Mafia gangs

connected with diesel smuggling, kidnapping, and carjacking were
flourishing. Only the three militia commanders who had visited me
claimed to be leaders of political parties. The rest of the supervisory
committee leadership had as yet no clear affiliations.

The existing committee included some rural figures who seemed
to sympathize with the Prince, some middle-aged men who liked to
talk about Islam, and some representatives of marginalized communities: a woman, a Sunni, a Christian, and a Sabian follower of John
the Baptist. The latter group almost never spoke. The others were
unruly and querulous. They complained that the Coalition had given
them no responsibility, so they took no responsibility. They were despised by many. At the same time, it was clear that at least one powerful faction had been excluded from the committee, the "alternative
councils."

Since the Sadrist-led meeting I had attended in al-Qala, the alternative councils remained mysterious. Although they had clear Sadrist
sympathies, they claimed not to be Sadrists, and Islamist though they
were, they were opposed to Iran. Unlike the other groups, they were
supported by the urban poor. They had a violent militia, but they
had been effective in distributing kerosene and emergency goods.

Educated Iraqis, who saw themselves as modern nationalists,
hated the alternative councils as much as they hated the groups on
the official committee and accused them both of "backward tribal
feudalism and religious superstition." Nonetheless the Islamist alternative councils were too powerful and popular to be excluded. Such
broader participation, however, would also dilute the power of the
Prince.

The Prince was perhaps the most famous resistance leader in
Iraq; he was not radical either politically or religiously, but he would
be a dangerous enemy; he had taken substantial risks to support us in
the past. Many criticisms of the Prince were unjust. The snobbish
urban elite said he had not completed his high school education, had
failed to become an officer in the military and was only "a jumped-

up corporal turned dictator." He had, it was true, probably participated in the looting of the province, profited from the sale of stolen ministry vehicles to the Kurdish areas, stuffed the police and the administration with his tribal relatives, and assaulted his political enemies, but these things were also true of his chief opponents and allies. Some Iraqis claimed he was in league with the Iranians and that everyone in the province hated him; there was no reliable information on public opinion in rural areas. It was more likely that he hated Iran. His rivals were almost all Islamists who, if given power, could divide the province and oppose the Coalition. For all these reasons, the colonel, who knew the province well, had relied strongly on the Prince.

But we had arrived promising democracy, not a warlord. We could not continue to rule solely through the Prince. I hoped to include in the new council, in addition to the Islamist alternative councils, some more moderate educated figures. And I intended to give the new council clear autonomy, responsibility, and its own budget, so that it could run the province as soon as possible. Morality, necessity, and something approaching political theory were all involved in my decision. I hoped that subconsciously I had not been overinfluenced by the Prince's ignoring me, rejecting my proposals, and insulting our projects.

In the end, I wrote to Baghdad promoting my new plan for the council. I did not say that the councils were dominated by unpopular mafia gangsters. This was partly because the reality was so far from what Baghdad believed about the province that I would be accused of exaggerating; partly because the military would read my account as a criticism of what they had done before my arrival; and partly because I might be blamed for the mess. Instead I wrote a draft in bureaucratic prose, talking about a "more inclusive approach." No reply came from Baghdad. I was not surprised. There was a lot going on outside our small province.

My first opportunity to explain my new policy was a meeting with the supervisory committee. At the far end sat the burly mayor of Maimuna and the aged sheikh Ismail. These were the Prince's people, but they were in a minority. The Prince's brother Riyadh had quarrelled with the committee and resigned; they said he had been trying to act as the governor, and they were not sad to see him go. Beside them was a charming former national basketball champion with mildly Islamist sympathies who was a close friend of our office at least until he began plotting to take over the local Olympic committee. At the other end sat Abu Mustafa, a forty-year-old cleric who often stopped by my office, seemingly to entertain himself and dispense a brand of wisdom; and the militias who had been in Iran.

The council members' first complaint was that they had not yet been paid their salaries. They were very angry. I was angry on their behalf. Our primary objective was supposed to be getting the Iraqi government on its feet and yet Baghdad had not managed even the tiny sum required to pay the salaries of the provincial council.

Then Sheikh Rahim spoke. He had been tortured for ten years by Saddam. I liked him: he was unafraid of me and often rude to me, but he was equally rude to the other factions in the province. "You must let us form secret police units. That will be the only way to keep order in the province."

"I'm afraid I cannot allow that to happen. You are not policemen. This is not a democratic suggestion."

"You give us no responsibility. You never listen to our advice," he said. "The people come to us demanding things and we cannot deliver. There isn't even a governor in this province. You are a dictator."

I explained that I would increase the council, give them clear legal powers and funding, and allow them to elect a governor.

"When? We have heard similar promises before."

I looked round the table. "There will be a new provincial council in six weeks," I replied, inventing a date. "And once it is formed it will elect a governor."

"And will we all keep our positions?" persisted Sheikh Rahim.

"No. I cannot guarantee that. Some people may have to step down. But I intend everyone in the province to be represented on the new council. This body, the sheikhs—"

"Why the sheikhs?" asked an Islamist politician. "We are modern people. We reject the tribes."

From down the table a sheikh bellowed, "We in the tribes have equal rights with others. We took part in the 1920 revolution against the British and the 1991 uprising against Saddam. We too have our martyrs."

"I will also," I continued, "include the political parties, the religious groups, the mayors of the towns, educated and experienced people, the alternative councils—"

"The British policy of divide and rule," drawled the cleric, and then in a sharper tone added, "The alternative councils are worthless Sadrist criminals. You should not include them."

"They have support," I replied.

"Only among the ignorant," said the cleric.

"You insult them and they insult you. But I would rather have them inside the tent than outside."

"They are Sadrists, your enemies even more than ours," he replied.

"If they are our enemies then we must hold them doubly close," I said. "If they are not included you will take all the blame for all the difficult business of government, they will accuse you of corruption and incompetence and their support will grow."

There was a sour silence. Excluding the Sadrists was the one point of agreement between the Prince and the Iranian group. And Baghdad hated them too. In fact, no one was going to thank me for bringing the Sadrists into the council, including the Sadrists, who rather enjoyed criticizing from the outside.

"I have a request for you to do some more mine-clearing," growled Sheikh Rahim. I agreed to look at it but I reminded him that the NGO charged nearly a half million dollars a month. We could re-furbish twenty schools for the cost of clearing a few acres of mines.

"How about the corruption in your contracts?" continued Sheikh Rahim. "You are awarding all the tenders for the reconstruction to corrupt men and Baathists, and you do not listen to us when we tell you so."

"Three members of this council have sat in on our tender panels. You yourself have sat on panels, sheikh. I am going to formalize this. Henceforth, tender panels for our contracts will consist of one member of the local council, one member of the provincial council, and the director of the relevant ministry. My civil affairs team will only be observers, with power of veto."

"These are promises, Seyyed Rory. But the question is, will you be able to deliver? Perhaps we will believe you more when you have paid our salaries."

I took from my pocket ten thousand dollars in cash and handed it to their accountant. There was a silence and something resembling surprise. I had proved I could deliver. Only I knew that I had only borrowed the money from another account and was gambling that Baghdad would finally deliver the payroll and allow me to get the money back. The meeting finished without any strong protest against the reorganization of the council.

HIGH COMMAND

A prudent founder of a republic . . . should try to have the authority all for himself . . . nor will a wise mind ever reproach him for some extraordinary action performed in order to found a kingdom or a republic.
　　　　　　　　　　　　　　—*Machiavelli,* Discourses, *Book I, Chapter 9*

THE GREEN ZONE

When, a few weeks after my arrival in Maysan, I flew up to Baghdad to attend a conference with Bremer, I found an operation on a scale inconceivable in my small, shabby office in Maysan. I went for dinner at a hotel where I had swum on my first visit to Iraq. There I met Marla, a Californian whom I knew from Kabul and who had stayed in my room in Baghdad; my good friend Matthew MacAllester, who had been imprisoned in Abu Ghraib by Saddam; and Georges Malbrunot, a French correspondent for *Figaro*. Georges was gloomy. He said a civil war was coming. "I recognize the feeling: it is like Beirut in 1984."

I drove back past the old UN headquarters in the Canal Hotel. I had been there too on my earlier visit. A friend who knew I was looking for a job had suggested that I come to a meeting with the UN special representative, Sergio De Mello. The UN dominated most post-conflict situations, but in Iraq they were marginalized, their office was small, and they were able to do little. I had wandered past the security point without anyone attempting to search me or ask my business. The Iraqis coming in and out of the compound were good-humored. I had said to my friend that things seemed pretty relaxed.

She had replied that the special representative was proud that Iraqis could approach the UN building—unlike in the Green Zone, whose barriers were a half mile from the main offices.

My friend went into a small office and soon came out, apologizing; it might not be possible for me to join the meeting after all. I saw De Mello passing. I had met him in Indonesia, but he did not catch my eye or recognize me and I went to the canteen, where I sat from ten until two in the afternoon, talking to local NGO staff who came in to eat and use the Internet. I particularly liked a Tunisian security adviser who had served in the Balkans and was worried about terrorists targeting the UN.

I left at two, intending to return later in the afternoon to use the Internet. But when I came back at 4:30 a thick column of smoke was rising from either end of the building, families were screaming and pushing at a cordon of U.S. soldiers, and the woman who had served me my salad in the cafeteria was running toward us. A suicide bomber had driven his truck up beneath De Mello's office window. The explosion had killed twenty-five UN officers and some of the NGO staff who had been working on orphans. I never found out whether my Tunisian lunch companion was killed. De Mello was trapped in the rubble and died that afternoon. Most of the UN staff was evacuated, and the UN never returned in strength to Iraq.

Now, two months later, I could not get close to the building. There were roadblocks on every street. I guessed, however, that like the British embassy and a number of other sites in the city it had been abandoned and that the staff had withdrawn inside the Green Zone.

I was dropped back beside the Green Zone, in an empty parking lot. Concrete boulders were strewn across the road to stop suicide bombers getting a clear run, and behind me, on the highway, street stalls were lit with fairy lights. An Iraqi shouted, "Careful, my friend. Do exactly what these soldiers are saying."

I passed a sign saying "Military Area: Lethal Force Authorized" and, entering a tunnel of concertina wire, could see almost nothing

but searchlights. After a minute, I reached thick pillars of sandbags and there was a shout in a Southern accent from behind the
searchlight:

"Raise your hands . . . away from your body."

I did so very carefully, concerned that the book in my hand might
resemble a bomb. "Good evening," I shouted in my most English
voice.

"Keep walking."

Twenty yards on, I saw a silhouette in helmet and heavy body
armor, pointing a machine gun at my chest. A man stepped out from
a booth draped with camouflage netting.

"Face the wall. Hand me the object. I am now going to search
you." He spoke with a Spanish accent and searched me very carefully.

"Okay, wait here."

I was motioned to a wooden bench. For the next five minutes I
listened to the roar of the diesel generators in this desert of check-
posts and armor. The sand was lit orange by the halogen spots and
tiger-striped by the thin shadows of the razor wire and the squat
forms of sandbags and armored vehicles. The night sky was invisible.
We could hear and see nothing from either the city behind us or the
Green Zone ahead. Although it was eight at night, it must have been
38 degrees centigrade and I was grateful that I was not wearing a helmet and body armor.

"Where are you from?" I asked, as I usually do.

"Me? Puerto Rico," replied the sergeant. I had met many Puerto
Ricans serving in the U.S. army in Iraq, many of whom had scarcely
visited the continental U.S.

"You enjoying your job?"

"It fucking sucks," said the other man grandly. He turned out to
be a nineteen-year-old from Florida. "Eight months. Twelve hours on
manning the gate. I haven't been out of this place since I can't remember. I want out of the Guard. But did you see today? They're ex-
tending. Obligatory. No deferral."

"It's an important job," I suggested, "guarding the gate."

These men seemed destined to spend their entire twelve month tour on guard duty, perhaps never firing a weapon in anger. They probably knew little about the Coalition Provisional Authority, whose headquarters they were defending, and their days must have seemed long, hot, and repetitive. I asked why they thought they were there.

"To take their oil, right?" said the Puerto Rican, laughing. And I smiled. Later I heard a British soldier say the same, and I wondered whether some soldiers didn't half-wish that the conspiracy theorists had been right and that their country was at least getting free oil out of the invasion.

"Far as I'm concerned, we've got rid of Saddam. Finish. Time for home," said the Floridian. "Here comes Ali." He peered down the sights and bellowed "Raise your hands. Away from your body."

A big Iraqi in a baseball cap and T-shirt held up a translator's ID card.

"Hey guys," he said in an improbably convincing American accent as the sergeant patted him down. "How's it hanging?"

The sergeant grunted.

"You had a good night?"

The sergeant grunted again.

"Stinks out there," said the Iraqi. No one replied.

When they had finished checking him they waved him on.

I walked on down a further corridor of concertina wire to another check-post, where I found the Iraqi and sat next to him.

"These guys," the Iraqi whispered to me. "You see how they treat us? Like dogs. Do you look like a terrorist? Or me? I am a translator here. With Marine Corps. I go on raiding every night. I have to hiding my face." Translating was a dangerous job. Translators lived outside the compound without any protection, and their neighbors soon discovered what they did for a living. Many had been killed. "Saddam's police beat people. But to educated men, foreigners, they knew politeness. Iraqis are very proud people. In our culture it is very bad to be searching like this. Why are Americans so aggressive to everybody?"

I muttered something about America being an egalitarian society.

"I know that," the translator said, raising his voice so the sentries could hear. "We know these are just young kids. They are frightened and hot and don't know anything. But they should learn something. Why don't they learn a little? Just a few phrases. Yesterday, I was on the highway at a checkpoint and they stop a car and they are shouting at the driver, 'Stay in your car' in English. He cannot understand what they are saying—he was not educated man—he is opening the door. And I am running to him and saying in Arabic, 'Don't get out.' But I cannot in time and they shoot him. Dead."

I looked at him.

"You don't believe me. Listen, I saw this with my eyes. This is why they are losing Iraq."

I walked down more razor-wire corridors, through three more checkpoints. There were white lines on the road, and street signs, and I realized that I was still on the four-lane highway on which I had just seen the stalls and fairy lights, but suddenly the highway stood in the wasteland of the Green Zone without a person, car, or stall in sight. I continued past a fountain and, walking through the tall glass doors, entered the marble and chandelier lobby of the al-Rashid Hotel, where I was staying.

The lobby was filled with men, mostly in jeans and desert combat boots. A group wore T-shirts that said "A Can of Whup-Ass" or "Who's Your Baghdaddy?" The hotel and its staff had been requisitioned, and these men were Coalition personnel who had been billeted two to a room. Some were shopping in the boutiques for Saddam watches and mosque-shaped alarm-clocks that woke you with the call to prayer. Others examined the oil paintings of windswept horses, forever galloping from a desert sunset, perhaps in terror at the chemical intensity of its puce and vermillion rays.

Up an escalator beside the ballroom and through a double door, loud hip-hop morphed suddenly into the Gypsy Kings. At a bar on the left, young men were drinking beer and a small middle-aged woman was trying to read a book. A Colombian man who had been introduced to me as the acting planning minister held a young, taller English girl tight into his body, his little legs driving her back, step by step, toward the DJ. Putting his right hand behind his back, he took her left, twisted her round twice, caught her again, and then, pressing her tight again, began whispering something into her long brown hair.

Later, I danced to the Stones with a woman in a tube-top and mini-skirt. She was Bosnian, had worked with the U.S. military in Sarajevo, and was now working doing the laundry for the officials in the Green Zone. But I must have bored her with my bad Bosnian, because she turned her back on me and went to join a group of women who from their build looked as though they were in the army. The DJ cut from *the time is right for fighting in the street, for a palace revolution* to R & B. Each change brought a different group onto the dance floor.

It was now one in the morning. Outside the fence the restaurants had been shut for four hours; families were in their homes. Baghdad was silent, from the ruined Ottoman Place on the Tigris to the date palm plantations on the city's edge. Most Iraqis were not particularly pious, and senior civil servants might do some surprising things in private places, but Iraqis did not spend the small hours dirty dancing in public with strangers.

The music cut to salsa and then Justin Timberlake. To the waiters leaning against the wall, arms folded against the air-conditioning, it must have seemed as though they had been transported to an alien bar in another galaxy. They stared at the British ex-Gurkha officer in an Austin Powers purple satin shirt with four-inch collar tips, and the shoulder roll of European women, doing French rock whatever the music, and two men wrapped round each other. On the edge of the floor experts on monetary policy, gender counsellors, engineers, colonels with bare midriffs thrust their hips out at the drunken audience from under the spinning disco ball. I wondered whether the waiters thought this enactment of every Islamist image of Western decadence was how we behaved every night. I enjoyed it very much. I danced with people from very different places, who would never have been in the same club if they had not been in Iraq: truck drivers and soldiers, spin doctors, and economists. I met a fifty-year-old man with a ponytail who belonged to a Hells Angels chapter in Alabama and who had come to work on water projects. This was his very first time outside the United States.

A friend and I went down to the coffee shop for some tea, stale bread, and hummus. One table down from us was Bernie Kerik, the ex-New York police commissioner, now the Iraqi interior minister, sitting alone. My friend told me that he was often with a personal PR team who organized the press photos of him in shades, gun in hand, bringing zero tolerance to Baghdad. At the other end of the coffee shop, I was introduced to another man who also believed himself to be the interior minister. And earlier I had met two men, each of whom thought he was the media commissioner. There seemed to be too many chiefs in the palace, multiple people who had been summoned to the White House and told that they had been personally selected to run a huge part of Iraq, only to arrive and find that someone else had been told exactly the same thing. Then there were the non-Americans, who had been appointed by their own politicians to do the very same jobs. Much of the energy of the CPA went into trying to establish office space, size of personal protection detail, access to cars and helicopters, reporting lines and access to Bremer. This may partly have explained why Bernie Kerik had not yet managed to provide the minimum of weapons, radios, vehicles, and uniforms to the Iraqi police.

As I walked out of the building, a man in jeans with a pistol on his right hip and a Kalashnikov on his shoulder asked for my pass. I

recognized him as an American ex-Marine working for a private security firm. I knew some of his colleagues from Afghanistan, and I
had had a drink with him two nights earlier. He was well-liked, and
I had found him funny and relaxed and ironic about Iraq.

"Hi, Dave," I said. "I'm afraid I don't have one. I am being escorted by Catherine. I'm Rory. We had a drink together two nights
ago. You remember . . ."

"No. I do not remember."

He grabbed me by the collar, spun me round, and pushed me
hard toward the wall. Some people I knew walked past and looked
away. Then Catherine appeared.

"Dave, he's with me," she said, lifting her pass.

Dave ignored her, and when he finished searching me he pushed
his face close to mine and shouted, "If I find you more than five yards
from your escort again, I am gonna stick my boot up your ass and
you are flying out of this compound. Okay, chief?" He left without
waiting for an answer.

I had breakfast the next morning in a canteen that had been set
up in the old ballroom of the Republican Palace. The central core of
the palace had been built by a British engineering company for the
king. The wings had been built by Saddam, and he had mounted
four giant statues of his own head in a helmet on the corners. Noah
Feldman, the CPA constitutional adviser, called the statues "pseudo-
Andalusian dictator rococo," and the helmets "a combination of
Prussian Pickelhaube and an Arab kaffiyeh." Mustache size matters
in the old Ottoman world. One of the greatest Ottoman sultans had
mustaches so long they had to be tied behind his neck when he
fought, and in the tragic last scene of the Montenegrin national epic,
a companion says to the dying hero, "Let me lift up your mustaches
so that I can see the wound in your chest." The neat mustaches on
these statues of Saddam were the size of surf-boards.

———

The high-domed ceiling of the marble entrance rotunda had been painted over to cover another painting of Saddam. In a side alcove marked "Distinguished Visitors Waiting Room" were elaborate gilded sofas and a table inlaid in green malachite. The throne room, I noticed, had become a chapel, and some U.S. colonels appeared to be holding a Bible study group.

The main ballroom canteen was run by a subsidiary of Halliburton. On the door a sign read, "Strictly no weapons: i.e., M-16s, Kalashnikovs or sawn-offs," and on the next line, "Handguns permitted." It was staffed by Muslims from Pakistan, Hindus from northern India, and some Nepali Buddhists who were paid a hundred dollars a month, apparently because local Iraqis were considered a security risk. I was accustomed all over the world as a civilian in post-conflict zones to eating food made from local ingredients. The BBC in Kabul might serve fried chicken and salad, but they bought in the market. Here everything had been imported, much of it directly, twelve thousand miles from the United States. Meals were dominated by burgers and ice cream; breakfast included hickory-smoked streaky bacon, pancakes and maple syrup, peanut butter, and half-and-half. I was able to use my little Urdu and Nepali to sneak a *paratha* and some sweet tea with the staff a little later. I sat on a table with a young man from the British treasury. He was polite but he did not seem to have heard of my province, was over-worked, and left quickly.

On the upper walls outside the dining areas were proverbs in Arabic, worked in marble. One ran:

Ask not what your country can do for you but what you can do for your country.
—Saddam Hussein

The conference was held at a giant, hollow, round table with microphones all around. All the governorate coordinators and two- and three-star generals in the country had been summoned. John and

Mark had driven from Nasiriyah and Kut, and the coordinators and generals from the Kurdish regions had come in helicopters. The ministers and senior advisers, many of whom rarely left the palace, had simply walked down one floor from their offices. There, in U.S. Marine Corps desert camouflage, Polish gray, tailored women's suits, or black and white *keffiyahs*, were gathered a hundred or so of the most senior people in the administration in Iraq.

Bremer sat at the end of the table, in his suit and combat boots, with a lined face and a full and carefully combed head of hair. He spoke very softly and frowned a lot and did not seem to enjoy giving his introduction.

Andy Bearpark, who was on Bremer's right in his undertaker's suit, spoke next. "I know that a lot is going wrong. Jerry and I are aware of that." It was typical of Andy to refer to Bremer by his nickname. Everyone else called him "Ambassador Bremer." "Now it's time for the plan. Don't expect perfection."

A major from the "strategic planning unit" showed us a slide of black dotted vertical lines, eight yellow horizontal arrows, punctured by red and white equilateral triangles and rimmed by aubergine, sky-blue, and burgundy horizontal bands. This geometrical design was covered with text. He began to speak about some of the priorities for the three main cities.

After a minute, General Odierno, the six-foot-four, two-hundred-pound bald commander of the Fourth Infantry Division, brought his two huge hands down on the table and said in a high-pitched, passable imitation of the speaker, "Baghdad, Basra, Mosul. Baghdad, Basra, Mosul." And then, returning to his normal voice, he continued, "All you ever talk about is Baghdad, Basra, Mosul. Do you know what it is like there on the ground in Tikrit or Fallujah, for the guys, operating . . . I gotta tell you, it's frustrating—it's hard. It's frankly hard." His voice cracked and he stopped abruptly.

The major, who was not used to talking to a two-star general, returned somewhat nervously to his slide. He pointed to a series of yellow arrows, which were labelled:

> Governance
> Economy
> Essential Services
> Ministry of Justice
> Security Affairs
> Ministry of Interior
> Strat Comms: Strategic Communications
> CJTF-7: The Coalition Military Command

Each arrow was cut by dotted lines representing various dates between then and December 2005, more than two years off. The sky-blue lines had labels like "OIF 2 rotation" and "accelerated army recruiting." The aubergine lines, more purple at one end and more blue at the other, were labeled "job creation" and "transition to Iraqi control." The triangles represented key indicators.

It appeared from all of this that we were being told that within the next seven months we should, among many other things, elect a transitional assembly, privatize state-owned enterprises, install electronic trading on the Baghdad stock exchange, reform the university curriculum, generate six thousand megawatts of electrical power, vet all the judges, and have thirty-two thousand Iraqi soldiers selected and trained in the new civil defense corps and ensure that 90 percent of Iraqis received terrestrial television broadcasts. Each arrow had its own more detailed plan, we were told, as did each triangle. A full interactive hundred-page document breaking this down was available and was being continually updated on the CPA intranet. And it had been already briefed to the "highest levels in Washington."

Sir Jeremy Greenstock, the senior British representative, said, "We will not be presenting this plan to a static audience." He meant that Iraqi public opinion would change.

There was a silence and then a general said, "I'm sorry. Did I misunderstand you? Did you just say that you have briefed this plan to the highest levels in Washington without consulting any one of us round this table?"

Bremer cut in. "General, there has been an extensive consultation process—parts of this plan have been shown to people all over Iraq—all the relevant departments have been canvassed."

"Well, I sure as hell know that I haven't seen it," said the general. "Has anyone else seen it in this room? Any of my military colleagues?" Heads shook. "Any of the governors?" We civilians shook our heads. "You don't think you could have shown it to some of us?"

"We are showing it to you now."

The major now tried to speak about some of the theoretical aspects of de-Baathification and property claims.

"Theoretical?" said General Petraeus, the commander of the north and, with Odierno, one of the most respected generals in the room. "People are shooting each other over these issues."

The general next to him drawled, "Every day we are being told to do less and less, with less and less resources. I hear everyone talking about policy direction, but in practice we are being made to step aside."

During the coffee break, I approached a man from the governance team. He was a twenty-three-year-old political appointee from Washington. He was looking harassed. The team were reputed to work twenty-hour days, and to be perpetually worrying about criticism from Washington and the reactions of the new Iraqi governing council. They theoretically oversaw our work in the provinces.

I asked him what he was doing. "Coming up with ideas to change the governance structures," he replied. Under Saddam, all money, appointments, and power came from Baghdad. Almost nothing happened at the local level. Washington wanted to introduce a "devolved, federal" structure to give more power to the provinces. They wanted local ministries to prepare and submit their own budgets and propose projects rather than waiting for central instructions, and they wanted provincial councils to be able to sack and appoint ministry directors. This was a substantial change and it was going to take a long time to work out, agree, and promulgate these new arrangements.

I nodded and said that the Maysan provincial council desperately wanted to know what its current powers were. Council members were getting increasingly angry, and we could not transfer power to them if they had no legal authority.

He said that this would not be possible until an interim constitution had been worked out and approved by the governing council.

"But that could take till next spring," I said. I repeated that it was better to give the provincial councils clear powers now and change them later rather than leave everyone in limbo while we waited for a more perfect solution. I suggested we should stick closely to the existing 1968 law with its emphasis on central control. I did not think the local ministries were ready yet to prepare and submit their own budgets. I did not think that the provincial councils had the experience or capacity to appoint, monitor, and sack ministry directors. If we wanted to develop the capacity of the provincial councils, we should do so by giving them their own budget and leaving the old administrative arrangements in place.

He shrugged, said he had listened to my opinion and would be listening to many other opinions, and excused himself.

"When are we going to get salary payments for our provincial councils?" a coalition governor from another Shia province asked as the meeting began again. "We are supposed to be supporting Iraqi government. These guys are working unpaid. The salaries proposed are a joke. We need bigger salaries for the councils, and we need them now."

Bremer looked down the table, and with a decisive gesture and a tone that seemed to come from his past at the Harvard Business School, said, "Make that happen."

An official replied, "Yes, sir."

The American governor from Najaf cut in. "I cannot travel and I have a staff of eight to cover a province of more than a million. We are lucky to even feed ourselves. There is no way we can achieve one tenth of those things. And my office has no access to the CPA intranet, so how are we supposed to see the plans?"

"Neither do we," came a chorus from around the room.

"Well, Tom," said Bremer, "we're working hard to get you those things but in the meantime you're just going to have to do the best with what you've got and I know everyone here will work very hard to ensure you get all the support we can give you."

A general said, "This is not just a security problem. At heart this is an economic problem. Hundreds of thousands of young men do not have jobs and that is why they are joining the insurgency. We have an economic problem with a security dimension."

At last Bremer raised his voice. "Get real," he snapped. "We do not have an economic problem with a security dimension. We have a security problem and it is your job to solve it."

He concluded by reminding us that our objective was to create "a democratic Iraq where a government, elected on the basis of the constitution, respected human rights."

Back in Amara, I decided that I preferred Andy's mission: quiet and ice cream. But whoever's plan I followed—and there was one from the military and one from the aid agencies and one from the southern regional headquarters as well—my bosses were hundreds of miles away, and I was improvising with very limited resources. My mother kept sending me links to articles by journalists, politicians, academics, international bureaucrats, and all other amateur pundits who thought they knew about Iraq. They all agreed that those of us on the ground had not planned adequately and did not have the first clue about what we were doing. That was, however, almost their only point of agreement. Some said that if we read history we would be much firmer and stop appeasing (the 1938 school); others that we should withdraw from a hopeless situation (the Vietnam school). They told us that we had purged too many members of the old regime or left too many in place; that we made too much use of the tribes or not enough; that our reforms were too swift or too slow; that we were too brutal or too soft; that we would never have security without economic growth or economic growth without security; that Iraqis needed much more foreign support; that they needed to be allowed to run themselves.

Of course all this was true—we needed to do more and we needed to do less—and we knew it. Iraq needed decent security, education, and health; the rule of law; a good economy; less corruption; the protection of human rights; robust civil society structures; and a democratic government. We came from societies where many of those things existed. But none of these platitudes, nor the "lessons learned" from post-war Germany and Japan, the Balkans and Afghanistan, and the history of the Middle East, told us much about how to achieve these things in modern Iraq. Still less did they tell us how much corruption and violence and incompetence we should tolerate before intervening. When to appease and when kill? In what circumstances were our governments prepared to kill Iraqis and in what circumstances were they prepared to have their own soldiers killed?

When the British took over Iraq after the First World War, it was a simple rural society. Nationalism and Islamist politics were only beginning to gain momentum. British officers were Arabists with decades of experience in colonial administration and a long-term commitment to the region. They had strong institutions, and they had the freedom to be as Machiavellian as they liked. And yet, because the Iraqis didn't want them and the British public didn't support them, they concluded, after a decade, that the best they could do was establish basic security and a functioning government and get out as soon as possible. Better plans, better people, more troops might have given us a small advantage in 2003, but direct foreign rule, I guessed, was never going to turn Iraq into a liberal democracy.

And somewhere within these anxieties was guilt. We had promised democracy and believed, as Bremer said, that it was the only legitimate basis of government, but we did not think Iraq was yet ready for elections. We felt we needed to stay but felt ashamed of occupation. We were controlling the lives of people who had not invited us in and who had not voted for us. We wanted to justify the invasion by doing some good; but we knew little about the people who surrounded us, or their culture. Every day we gambled on insufficient information, trusted and suspected, persuaded reluctant bureaucrats, threatened, rewarded, and charmed. I needed to keep taking risks and taking sides, and people were going to be killed almost whatever we chose to do.

PART TWO

DEATH OF A HERO

To deal effectively with his enemies, to gain allies, to conquer (whether by force or cunning), to inspire both devotion and respectful fear in the people, to be obeyed and respectfully feared by the troops, to neutralize or destroy those who can or must be expected to injure you, to replace old institutions with new ones, to be both severe and kind, both magnanimous and open-handed, to disband disloyal troops and form a new army, to maintain alliances with . . . other rulers in such a way that they will either be glad to benefit you or slow to injure you.

—Machiavelli, The Prince, *Chapter 7*

FRIDAY PRAYERS

He was regarded by many as ambitious, a man who would transgress lawful government because of his audacity and hot temper; and since there was no means within the republic's existing institutions of resisting him without establishing a rival party, it came about that he set out to enlist partisans, not fearing anything but illegal methods; on the other hand since those who opposed him had no legal way to suppress him, they turned to illegal methods and eventually resorted to arms.

—*Machiavelli*, Discourses, *Book I, Chapter 7*

FRIDAY, OCTOBER 24, 2003

On Friday, October 24, 2003, a photograph was taken of Private First Class Lynndie R. England holding a leash tied to the neck of a naked prisoner. On the same day, police chief Abu Rashid strode up the steps of the main mosque, greeting people as he passed. In the forecourt, he took off his socks and shoes and handed them to the shoe-keeper. He walked to the basins, feeling the warm tiles under his bare feet, rolled up his sleeves and trouser legs and carefully washed his feet and his broad, muscular forearms, ran his fingers around the rims of his ears to rinse them, and then stepped onto the carpet in the hall to join the other men for the midday prayers.

When Abu Rashid first left for Iran in the 1980s, few Shia went to Friday prayers; they were seen as something associated with the Sunni and the government. But in the early 1990s, Sadr II had begun promoting the prayers, in which he and his young followers preached highly emotive sermons against unveiled women; invoked the glorious martyrs and argued for a more religious government.

Saddam, who had initially supported Sadr II because of his nationalism and anti-Iranian stance, was pleased when Sadr II called the leader of the Iranian-based Shia parties a traitor and a spy. But by 1998, Sadr II's criticism of corruption, secularism, and decadence seemed increasingly dangerous. Although Saddam claimed to be a descendant of the prophet (and, therefore, a distant cousin of Sadr II) and had begun to give money to Shia mosques and to pray in public, he was at heart a Sunni leader of a modern secular party. He felt the Shia clerics had betrayed him when they joined the rebellion in 1991 and, while sipping his favorite Portuguese rosé, he probably felt, like many privileged Baghdadis, a slight horror at this white-bearded, turbaned radical. He banned the distribution of Sadr's Friday sermons, and in 1999, he killed Sadr II and two of his sons.

This murder propelled what was already a growing movement into the most powerful popular religious sect in Iraq. Sadr II's legacy was continued by his chief of staff, a learned, middle-aged engineer turned theologian, and by his young son, Muqtada.

On the Friday Abu Rashid entered the main mosque, the sermon was to be given by the twenty-nine-year-old Sadrist leader Seyyed Hassan, a friend of Muqtada. He was expected, as often, to preach against the Coalition. Hundreds of men were in the congregation, most of them having spent the morning at home with their families, as the Muslim weekend begins on Thursday evening. Perhaps the knowledge that the Ramadan fast would begin the following week have given an added pleasure to a late breakfast. Some had brought their sons. Abu Rashid, however, was alone. Seyyed Hassan noticed him, caught his eye, and smiled, delighted, he told me later, that the police chief had attended. After the service, Abu Rashid went to the door of the mosque, put on his shoes, and began walking down the steps.

A short while later, someone ran into our office shouting, *"Mudir-as-shurta . . . jamia . . . shabab . . . sadriin . . . Quwat-al-ihtilaf . . . silah . . . kut-el-e."* Police chief . . . mosque . . . youth . . . Sadrists . . . Coalition forces . . . weapons . . . killed. Knowing more vocabulary than grammar, I could not initially understand who was doing the killing and who had been killed, but the translator soon filled in the blanks. As the police chief reached the bottom step of the mosque, there were two shots. Abu Rashid fell backwards. Blood spread across his chest. There was a scuffle, then two more shots, and someone ran.

Our police chief had been killed; the assassin escaped.

An hour later, some of Abu Rashid's hundred cousins in the police force stormed the mosque. They kidnapped Seyyed Hassan and another young cleric and took them to the Nowaffel tribal area in the marshes. They locked them in a hut and beat them and threatened to murder them unless they revealed who had killed Abu Rashid. The office of Sadr II, desperate for the return of their leader, called the congregation into the streets and marched on the police headquarters; the Sadrist militia, the Army of the Redeeming Imam, joined them, carrying Kalashnikovs, rocket-propelled grenades, and cutlasses. The Prince of the Marshes' militia defended the roof of the police headquarters with heavy weaponry. And at this point, according to some witnesses, a mysterious SUV with darkened windows drove onto the bridge over the Tigris, stopped, opened fire at both sides, and drove off.

At the time, we knew little of this. All we saw were crowds gathering in the streets and then, at dusk, the flares of rocket-propelled grenades flying over the Tigris. The ragged bursts of gunfire and the muffled explosion of grenades continued for a couple of hours. One witness claimed that the Prince was the first to open fire. Others blamed the occupants of the mysterious car, who they said variously were "Baathist provocateurs" or *"Ittila'at, al-Haras al-Thawri"*—Iranian intelligence, revolutionary guard.

The colonel and his battle group—the King's Own Scottish Borderers—had come to the end of their tour in Iraq and were in the midst of handing over to their successors, the the Light Infantry Battle Group. This meant that the outgoing Colonel was able to order an impressive number of heavily armored British vehicles to drive between the two warring groups; the firing stopped and the Iraqis rushed to clear away the dead and wounded. Some children had been injured by the RPGs. The next morning someone claimed that only two people had been killed, but a British cavalry officer said that he had driven over at least two dead bodies in his tank alone.

At ten the next morning, Seyyed Hassan was released by the Nowaffel, and the old colonel and I, accompanied now by the British police adviser, went to see the Prince of the Marshes.

It was a bright, cool day and I was enjoying sitting in the open back of one of the outgoing colonel's Land Rovers as we came up the main road into town. Theoretically, as a civilian, I should not have been in the unarmored vehicles, although the sharp edge of my body armor was digging into the small of my back and I was surrounded by armed soldiers. We were followed by a large convoy of troops because there had been rumors of further riots.

Over the radio I could hear the acronyms the military use to mask both farce and tragedy: VOR, a breakdown (vehicle off the road); RTA, a car crash (road traffic accident). Glancing at the map beside me, I saw that the military had imposed upon the landscape its own divisions and nomenclature. Whereas in a civilian taxi I had traveled from Route 1 to Route 6, and with my bodyguard team from Red 11 to Green 4, with the military I traveled from "Tampa" to "Quebec" (the U.S. military and the British military divided the naming of roads between them)—each time the same route.

A private on the roof-mounted gun behind me wore a dark green flak jacket—there was a shortage of desert camouflage. He had one sleeve rolled up, revealing a geometric tattoo on a sunburned forearm and, unaware of or unbothered by the previous night's events, he was giving the thumbs-up to anyone he could see. But there were no vehicles on the road, and the few Iraqis we saw did not meet our eyes. Two young men were crouching behind a wall, perhaps afraid of reprisals.

The colonel had implied that he had already appointed another member of the Prince's militia—"Colonel" Nadhem—as the new police chief. I did not want another controversial militia man who could be shot in days, nor a chief who was under the Prince's control. The assassination was an opportunity to find a figure who commanded more general respect. I wanted the provincial council to play a role in selecting him. But when I had tried to raise the topic with the colonel, he told me he was too busy, and when I confronted him, he denied that he had appointed anyone. I had therefore contacted Basra and told them that the current deputy police chief, Brigadier General Sabih, would serve as acting interim police chief while we looked for a successor.

We clattered under the bridge and along the river-side avenue, still meeting virtually no traffic. I noticed a black tent being constructed on the bank. Then we turned into the Prince's compound. But the Prince was not at the gate to meet us when we arrived; we found him in his office. He stood, shook hands quickly, and sat down.

"We are so sorry, Abu Hatim, to hear what happened," said the old colonel.

"Thank you, Colonel."

"He was killed because he was doing a good job," I added.

The Prince nodded. "You do not throw a stone at a palm that does not bear dates."

"A terrible day."

Pause.

"Can you tell us what happened?" I asked.

"I have already told the colonel. First the Sadr office killed Abu Rashid, and then they fired at me," he said, "and at my family. The Sadr office—the Army of the Redeeming Imam. With RPGs. Last night. Did you see that?" He looked round the room. "Now is your chance, Colonel. You must attack this cave of snakes. They are illegally occupying that building across from me. March on them now, seize their weapons, drive them out of the building, for they are murderers; murderers of Abu Rashid; Abu Rashid the martyr. They tore out the eyes from the corpses last night." This was the second time I had heard him claim to have seen bodies with their eyes plucked out—it seemed to be his shorthand for war crimes.

Wary that the Prince was using the situation to eliminate his rivals, and that if we complied we risked escalating the situation beyond what we could control, I said, "Abu Hatim, we have the utmost respect for you. We know what a good friend you have been to the Coalition. But the Sadr office was provoked. Someone kidnapped their leader. They were not the first to open fire."

"Are you putting me on a level with the Sadr office?" said the Prince. "My men fired in self-defense. The Sadr militia were attacking the police. Colonel," he said, dismissing me again, "will you attack the Sadr office this afternoon? If you don't, I will."

"Abu Hatim," I broke in again, "you will not attack the Sadr office. You have no legal authority to take armed men into the streets, and anyone who does will be fired on by British troops."

The Prince looked at the wall and waited for the colonel to say something. The colonel said nothing. The Prince's long brown fingers played with the gold hem of his robe and then, as though he had decided to ignore my rudeness, he turned to the colonel again. "Have you seen Abu Rashid's body?"

"Not yet."

"He was killed by two high-velocity shells—you can tell by the exit wounds. They were fired from a room above the square. The assassin came down the stairs and was seen by one of my men, who shot him. But he managed to run away, bleeding into his white shirt, and then we lost him. Has Colonel Nadhem taken office yet as the new police chief?"

"Well, Abu Hatim," said the colonel, "we are going to have to discuss this a little more."

"There is nothing to discuss. It was an excellent decision." He stood up, walked to the door, shouted at someone in the corridor to hurry up, and walked out himself. He came back a minute later followed by a man carrying a tray of Cokes and Fantas. He gestured to us all to take one and smiled at me.

"Abu Hatim," continued the colonel, "Nadhem was only an interim appointment."

"There are no interim appointments in Iraq, Colonel," said the Prince. "Once a police chief always a police chief. There cannot be a vacuum. Nadhem is the only man."

"Abu Hatim," I interrupted, "Deputy Police Chief Sabih will step in for the moment."

"Sabih? Brigadier General Sabih?" The Prince snapped his head round to look at the translator as though he had misheard.

"Sabih," I repeated.

"Sabih," he spat, "is an incompetent Baathist."

"Sabih is the deputy. This is the legal procedure. We will then form a public safety committee from the provincial council to choose the new police chief—"

"You call a group of Iranian spies a committee?"

"—supplemented by independent members of the public."

"And in the meantime, Sabih," he said with disgust.

"Assisted by Nadhem," I offered.

The Prince was quiet for a moment and then, again ignoring me, he looked round the room and said quietly and slowly, "It is up to you if you don't want to listen to me—if you want to destroy this province, if you don't care what happens, if you won't trust a patriot. I have told you that this is your chance to destroy the Sadr office, that no one supports them."

"You said they brought thousands into the streets last night," I

said. I noticed that all the foreigners in the room was looking uncom-
fortable. They did not like my arguing with the Prince but I guessed
they were equally wary of taking his advice.

"Hired crowds. You have one other choice, which is to arrest the
Sadr preacher Seyyed Hassan."

"But he was still being held by his kidnappers when the battle
happened, so he cannot be directly responsible," I persisted.

"He is your enemy," repeated the Prince slowly. "He preaches
revolution against the Coalition. Intern him, send him to the military
prison in Basra."

"I am very keen to take your advice, Haji. My respect for you is
immense. But can you point to something he had said, some weapons
he possessed, an act of insurrection?"

"He is a bad man," replied the Prince of the Marshes.

"But what has he done?"

"He is bad. Everyone knows this. I give you my guarantee of that.
If he had not been a bad man, I would not have told you to intern
him. We have no respect for this man or his authority. Our loyalty
now is to Bremer. Now, Colonel, come with me to see the murder site
and the body of the martyr."

On my way back to camp, I passed the old British war cemetery,
which had been converted to a rice paddy. A few headstones lay by
the fence, and there was a white cross in the center of the field, a long
wall, and a dilapidated Mughal dome that must have marked "the
graves of the Hindus and Muhammadans." On a dark granite wall
was carved:

**1914–1920. The officers and men of the Forces of the
British Empire whose names are here recorded are
buried or commemorated in this cemetery which
contains also the graves of 925 of their comrades
whose names are not known.**

The wall continued for fifty yards on each side, with scores of cap-badges and thousands of names. My regiment, the Black Watch, had lost more than anyone—there were three hundred names, half a battalion, including a Black Watch brigadier. Beside them were the names of men from regiments since vanished from the British Army: the Durham Light Infantry, the Bicycle Corps, Sikhs, Punjabis, Baluch, most of whom had died trying to rescue the British General Townshend from the siege of Kut in 1916. No one I'd spoken to in Amara had referred to this period in their history, when Amara had contained a large British garrison and military hospital, although it was well within the lifetime of many of their fathers.

While I waited for the security committee at the camp, I wrote an e-mail to the Commonwealth War Graves Commission, asking for a salary for the caretaker of the cemetery, who I knew had been working for a decade without pay. Then I walked up and down, squinting at the midday sun, kicking small clouds of pale dust into the air with every step, wondering what, if anything, we could do. The death of Abu Rashid did not feel particularly real to me. He had seemed so strong and robust in our meeting the week before. Had I half-expected such an end to a dangerous life, or was I still not engaging fully? Perhaps the nature of my interaction with Iraqis—formal meetings, with carefully chosen words and mutual suspicion, followed by analysis and written reports—prevented my feeling full sympathy for them. I guessed the Iraqis would feel much the same were I to be killed.

I entered the conference room with the police adviser, a deputy chief constable from the Northern Ireland police service, the out-going colonel and his successor, a broad-shouldered English infantry officer, who looked tired. Some of the provincial leaders sat facing us in white plastic bucket chairs. The blackout curtains had been lifted, revealing fragments of sand-smeared glass patched with cardboard. No one had yet painted over the many small holes in the walls.

The cleric Abu Mustafa caught my eye and lifted his hand in greeting. *"Allah bakheir."*

"Allah bakheir," I replied. Then the burly mayor from Maimuna, a provincial town, lifted his hand and greeted me as well. He was representing the Prince and his brother. Brigadier General Sabih, my candidate for police chief, had his long legs stretched before him as though to afford a maximum glimpse of his black silk stockings. He had been a policeman under the old regime for thirty years.

The deputy chief constable began in his gentle Irish voice, "The first thing I wish to express is my deep sympathy with you all for the death of Brigadier General Abu Rashid. He was a patriot and a hero and a great leader of the police." Everyone nodded. They had said it themselves, even the many among them who had asked me to sack Abu Rashid and those who may have wanted him dead. "I know what it feels like. During my time in the force, we have lost over four hundred officers in northern Ireland, many of them friends of mine. We must show now by our resolve that we will not be cowed or intimidated and that we will continue his legacy."

When he finished, one of the leaders of the Iranian faction said, "The police are relics of the Baath. Criminals are not afraid of them. If you had followed my advice of adopting the Iranian model in which civilian militias gather information from the public, none of this would have happened."

"We need to set up three independent secret police organizations," added Sheikh Rahim. Neither expressed any views on who had killed Abu Rashid or why.

The outgoing British colonel said that the royal military police would be setting up a full investigation into the death. The Badr commander muttered that the police and the Coalition were doing nothing and then lapsed into silence again. He seemed distracted. I assumed it was because of the fighting, but later I learned that his fifteen-year-old son had just killed himself at home, playing with a pistol.

"And you, Colonel Nadhem?" I said. "Can you explain what has been going on in the police?"

Colonel Nadhem looked at me and laughed. Then he looked round the room and laughed again. It was a rich, natural laugh. He was a man of about forty, fit and slim. He had been sitting forward in his chair, staring at the ground as though the sand patterns on the floor were more engrossing than our conversation.

"Well?" I said.

"Let's be honest," he said, standing up. "All that matters is catching the man that killed Abu Rashid." He shifted his feet as he spoke and glanced again at the floor. "There are ninety-five policeman in my force related to Abu Rashid, and they are in shock. Let's not waste our time talking about 'special investigations' and the 'rule of law.' We all know that the best way to do it is through the tribal channels, and if people play fast—putting on police uniforms and taking them off, giving a few people a rough time—well, that's just how it goes. I don't know where you think we are living . . ."

"You should behave a bit better than this," said the newly arrived Colonel from the Light Infantry Battle Group, speaking gently. "That is not how we do things. I know this will be a long journey but—"

"You are a policeman, Nadhem," I interrupted. "This is entirely inappropriate—your duty is to the law."

"My first duty and all our duties ought to be to Abu Rashid. We should get round the law. Now I can talk you through the steps we have taken." Nadhem opened his notebook.

An older Iraqi man got heavily to his feet. "That is unacceptable, Nadhem. I was a policeman myself before I was a judge, a graduate from police academy, and what we have seen over the last two days is a disgrace—policemen without uniforms or search warrants, assassination, kidnapping, civil war. We must work within the law. It is our responsibility—all of ours—to uphold the law, not to flout it."

The Badr commander, Abu Maytham, snapped, "You, Nadhem,

when you use tribal methods, you forget that the men you attack also have tribes and the cycle will only continue."

Nadhem, who until two months before had been a guerrilla in the marshes, was not going to be drawn into this. He looked around, laughed again, and then sat down.

The Irish deputy chief constable said, "Nadhem, when you put on the police uniform you take on a difficult and brave responsibility—you cannot take it on and off at will as I hear these people did who kidnapped the priest—you cannot betray that uniform and what it represents."

Nadhem nodded, unconvinced.

The next speakers were from the Iranian-linked militias. They emphasized that the real fault was with the Sadr office. They must be closed down. The Sadr office was not represented at the meeting and no one defended them.

Then Brigadier General Sabih made a speech about how he was determined to be brave, to face the criminals and never to act outside the law.

At three o'clock various members of the Iranian-backed militia began signaling to me from the back row—holding their hands palms upright and then stroking them down their faces in the gesture of prayer.

I interrupted the meeting. "I believe it is time for afternoon prayers. Thank you all."

I was left standing with the outgoing Colonel, his successor, and some of his senior officers. I explained to the new Colonel that the Sadr office hated the Prince partly because they had been excluded from power. I added that I was considering ways of including them in the new provincial council.

The outgoing Colonel turned to me. He was usually a controlled man but suddenly he seemed very angry. "This is your fault," he said, his clipped Scottish voice rising. "You and your CPA have been playing with fire. You have encouraged these people in the Sadr office by talking to them. You are as bad as the people who put Irish terrorists like Gerry Adams and McGuinness into the parliament in northern Ireland."

I shouted back, but before I had finished he was out of the door, leaving me unable to reply that we'd had no option in northern Ireland and we had no option here. And by the next day, he and his regiment had returned to Britain.

The following morning the supervisory committee of "local leaders" was very angry. The security problem in the province was our fault, the chairman said, for failing to give them any power. The burly mayor of Maimuna talked about marching against the Sadr office. Almost half the committee threatened to resign. I reminded them of all I had done in the previous month to get things moving: the new secretariat, the renovation of their building, the new development projects, the efforts with Baghdad to clarify their powers and secure their salaries. I reminded them that I was now going to reform them into a provincial council and give them the power to elect a governor. Then I asked, "Whom would you like to be the temporary police chief?"

The discussion tended toward the silk-stockinged Brigadier General Sabih. When I was sufficiently confident that the mood was in his favor, I called for a vote and everyone voted for him including, to my surprise, the Prince's supporters.

"Fine," I said. "In accordance with your wishes, Brigadier General Sabih will be the temporary police chief."

"We still have no power," rasped Sheikh Rahim.

"What are you talking about?" I said disingenuously. "You just chose the police chief for the province. What more power do you want?"

One of the clerics said, "This is an important start. But only a start. But thank you, Seyyed Rory, for giving us this opportunity."

As I left the provincial council I received a message asking me to go immediately to the battle group headquarters. The Prince had changed his mind and had decided that a man called Seyyed Talib should be the police chief, and Seyyed Talib was in the new colonel's office right now.

Seyyed Talib was barely five foot four, and his turban hung drunkenly on his head. He was accompanied by the tall, confident Colonel Nadhem, the police chaplain Seyyed Faqr, and one of the brothers of the dead Abu Rashid.

I asked him what police experience he had.

He looked confused. One of the others stepped in and said that Seyyed Talib was new to policing.

The new colonel asked him what thoughts he had on security.

Again he looked confused and did not speak. Abu Rashid's brother muttered something about checkpoints.

It emerged that Seyyed Talib was from a respected religious family connected to Abu Rashid's Nowaffel tribe. He was a prominent figure in Al Uzeyr, the biggest town in southern Maysan, famed equally for being one of the tombs of the prophet Ezra and for its dominant role in the Iranian smuggling trade. Although he seemed to the colonel and me a slightly pathetic figure and a ludicrous choice for a police chief, he was in fact well-respected within his immediate area for his arbitration in tribal feuds. But we could not appoint him without alienating all the supervisory committee. The new colonel told him politely that the temporary chief was Sabih. Seyyed Talib would have a good opportunity to apply to be the police chief when we held a public selection process. He did not seem troubled by this news and when the time came he did not apply.

I went next to the stadium, where four hundred policemen were waiting for me. The wind was strong and I had to shout to make myself heard. I told them that Abu Rashid was a martyr but there was no expression in their faces. I spotted Seyyed Faqr, the regimental chaplain, in the front row. He was in clerical dress but everyone else was in uniform, making it impossible to tell who was from the Prince of the Marshes' faction, who was from an Iranian brigade, and who was part of the old Baathist police. One policeman interrupted me to ask whether I would consider his engineering design for a new road bridge. Surprisingly, few made long speeches praising Abu Rashid. They seemed to take it calmly when I announced that Brigadier General Sabih was the interim police chief appointed by the provincial council.

AND WOULD NOT STAY FOR AN ANSWER

False accusations have no need either of witnesses or of any other partic-
ular corroboration to prove them, so that anyone can be slandered by any-
one else.

—*Machiavelli*, Discourses, *Book I, Chapter 8*

MONDAY, OCTOBER 27, 2003

I sent some of my own money to buy an ox for the funeral of Abu
Rashid (such things could not be claimed as official expenses) and,
as it was the third day of mourning, went to pay my respects. The
family was gathered in the black tents that I had seen being constructed on the riverbank by the Prince's house two days before. At
the entrance was a sign recording my gift as an "expression of the
appreciation and the sorrow of the CPA." The goat-hair tent formed
a long tunnel and perhaps three hundred men were seated on plastic chairs along both sides.

Silent and rigid as a statues, in flowing robes of wool fine as silk,
sat the sheikhs. In their center was Muhammad Abbas Muhammad Al
Araybi, paramount chief of the Albu Muhammad, the confederation
that included the police chief's tribe. His grandfather, Muhammad Al
Araybi, had been an immensely wealthy feudal lord, famous throughout Iraq, who had fought against and then alongside the British in the
First World War. People claimed that just before the 2003 invasion,
Muhammad Abbas had appeared on television signing in blood that he
would give his life in defense of Saddam and calling on his tribe to op-

pose the invasion. He was now one of our prominent allies. He stood, kissed me, and motioned me to sit beside him. Around him were some lesser sheikhs, including the police chief's brothers. I embraced Abu Rashid's father and repeated my sorrow, admiration, and condolences. Then I sat for a few minutes in silence among the men. Occasionally I caught the eye of one of the family and bowed. Everyone's eyes seemed dulled with grief. Many seemed to have been crying.

Back at the office the three leaders of the Iranian-linked militias were waiting for me. They announced that the Prince of the Marshes has just kidnapped three people and wrote the names of the hostages on a sheet of paper.

"Why were they kidnapped?"

"We have no idea."

After they left, a translator knocked at the door. "Sheikh Kadhem Mushettat is here to see you."

"Who is he?" After a month I could recite the names of a hundred local leaders and forty different tribes and parties. I was, therefore, frustrated to find another sheikh whom I did not know. "From which tribe?"

"I don't know. A big sheikh—maybe from the Albu Muhammad."

"Show him in."

Kadhem Mushettat was a large, middle-aged man, wearing robes, whose rapid and confident entrance implied that he considered himself important. He began by telling me that I was myself a tribal sheikh, famous for my knowledge of Iraqi tribes. This prevented my asking what tribe he was from. He complained that no one in his tribe had a job, and that his construction company had received no contracts. He gave me a binder that explained in erratic English that his company was able to undertake any work, from brick-laying to "ariospace" industry. Then he got down to business. "But all this is for the future. The problem today is that three people from my tribe have been kidnapped. You must get them released now or there will be civil war."

"Are these their names?" I read off the piece of paper I had been given five minutes before.

"Indeed, Seyyed Rory, as it is said, you know every leaf that drops."

"But why were they kidnapped?" I asked.

"They were innocent."

"Na'am," I replied—yes. "But what are they accused of doing?"

"The Prince believes Dr. Amin killed the police chief."

"So he has kidnapped Dr. Amin?" I had never heard of Dr. Amin.

"He kidnapped the brother and nephews of Dr. Amin."

"And did Dr. Amin kill the police chief?"

"No. He was in Baghdad when it happened."

"And is Dr. Amin connected to any political party?"

"No, no, he is completely independent."

"But," I guessed on the basis of my previous visitors, "Dr. Amin has spent most of the last ten years in Iran?"

"Because he was in the jihad against Saddam. If this is not resolved immediately," said the sheikh, "I will be unable to control my tribe. They will be forced to go into the streets and attack the Albu Muhammad—and the Serai are the second-largest tribe in Al Amara." The translator was wrong: the sheikh was not from the Albu Muhammad; he was from the Serai. It would be near suicidal for his tribe to try to attack the Albu Muhammad, the tribe of the Prince and Abu Rashid. The Serai may have been big in the city itself, but they were only medium-sized in Maysan province, and the Albu Mohammed dwarfed them perhaps by a factor of ten.[3] But they might

---

[3] I was reminded, however, of a story recorded in the 1920s. A stranger asked a Marsh Arab for a lift but explained that he wanted to go through territory controlled by the Suwaad tribe, who were his enemies. The Marsh Arab agreed because his tribe had a special agreement with the Suwaad, who would not attack a stranger if he was under the Marsh Arab's protection. A few miles into their journey they were challenged by men of the Suwaad who demanded that the Marsh Arab hand over his passenger. When he refused, invoking the laws of protection, they flung their spears at the passenger and killed him. The Marsh Arab returned sorrowfully to his own tribe because they were now obliged to attack the Suwaad. The Suwaad outnumbered them greatly. During the attack the Marsh Arab lost all his sons and many friends while the Suwaad lost almost no one. Thus the penalty of giving a lift to a stranger. Something of this remained.

still attack. In the 1920s a tribe had almost wiped themselves out attacking a larger neighbor. Tribal fights were still very common—it was not rare for two or three men to be killed in a week in tribal disagreements. And in this case, it was clear that the Serai would be aided by the Iranian-linked Islamist parties and their militias which had now been incorporated into the police force. It was only the third day after Abu Rashid's death and it seemed the fighting was about to start again.

I told the Sheikh that I would act immediately and sent a translator to the office of the Prince of the Marshes, asking politely if he knew anything about the whereabouts of these men. While I waited for his denial, various Iraqis came in with explanations for the assassination. The phrases they used were almost identical. Each began by assuring me, *"Shakhsian ana ma ahtam bi sultan."* (Personally, I am not interested in power.) *"Mali 'alakqa bi ay hizab. Ana mustaqil,"* they continued. (They were not connected to any party, they were independent.) This was usually a lie, but I would nod politely. Then they would say that Abu Rashid provided leadership that was brave and strong. But he had enemies and I should understand the risk they were taking in discovering and telling me the truth.

From that point on, however, their stories diverged. The first claimed that Abu Rashid had been killed by a rival criminal gang because he controlled the cross-border cannabis trade. The second assured me that the criminal bosses swore that no one would have challenged the police chief's cannabis monopoly; he had been killed by his relatives, who were eager to inherit the three hundred thousand dollars he had managed to amass during his short tenure. The third blamed the Syrians.

The final visitor told a story that was surprisingly detailed. He said that Abu Rashid, after deserting from the army, had fled to Iran and worked with Iranian intelligence on undercover operations inside Iraq. He had, however, been captured by the regime and while in prison had cooperated with his Baathist interrogators. This was proved by documents seized after the war, which also showed that he had continued to meet them after his release, while serving in the Prince's militia. When he became police chief he tried to disband the Iranian-linked militia in the province and attacked Iranians' covert cells. The Iranians had, therefore, killed him because he was a Baathist traitor and because he was a threat to their operations. The Iranian involvement was proved by the efficiency of the attack and the escape of the assassin.

But with this story, as with the others, there was a point where information suddenly ran out. When I pushed for more details, my informants would simply reply, *"enta—ti arif kul-shi"* (you know every-thing) and *"madri—la arif"* (I don't know), make their excuses, and leave.

The Iranian-linked leaders returned shortly thereafter. They claimed that the Prince had ordered the killing of Abu Rashid in order to discredit Dr. Amin and the Iranians. But they insisted that Dr. Amin had no connections to them or to Iran. They conceded that Dr. Amin was an old enemy of the Prince.

I was sitting alone in my office, still trying to work out what to do, when a translator told me that that Seyyed Hassan, the kidnapped Sadrist preacher, was here to see me. I asked the translator to bring him in while I went to the kitchen for a cup of coffee. In the kitchen were two military officers whom I had never met before, studying blueprints with an Iraqi man who was rumored to be one of the most corrupt contractors in the province. As soon as he saw me he sprang to his feet and asked if he could have a minute of my time. I replied that I had a guest in my office.

"Please, Seyyed Rory, one minute?"

I shrugged helplessly. I had made no progress in resolving either kidnapping or preventing what was beginning to seem like an almost inevitable collapse into civil war. I didn't suppose meeting the con-tractor would do any harm.

"Seyyed Rory, I need a job for my nephew—he is very qualified, he speaks very good English."

"I see. I will see what I can do."

"When can he see you?"

"I don't know . . . Thursday afternoon perhaps."

"What time?"

"Three o'clock."

"Thank you, Seyyed Rory."

On the way down the corridor I was intercepted by four different groups: Charlie Morris wanted to discuss a report of flooding in the southern province; the legal specialist wanted to check where he could put the four hundred thousand dollars he had just been given to build a prison; the bodyguard team wanted to know if they could do some weapons training; and a decision was needed on whether to build a sniper screen along the edge of the river. I said I thought it would be a pity to lose the river view and told everyone else to do whatever they liked.

On a wall in the civil affairs room, a translator had written "In the memory of Abu Rashid: like a tree he was cut down." Whether consciously or not, the translator was echoing a Sumerian death hymn found on a clay tablet on the edge of the Marshes, recording the death of King Shulgi four thousand years earlier:

As if he were a boxwood tree, they put axes against him in his joyous dwelling place. As if he were a sappy cedar tree, he was uprooted in the palace where he used to sleep. His appointed time had arrived and he passed away in his prime.

But I found it difficult to see much connection between the dead police chief and Sulgi, ruler of the great civilisation of Ur, birthplace of law and of writing. Abu Rashid's body would now be driven in a motorcade to the holy Shia city of Najaf, on the Euphrates, where he would be buried in a simple mound, among tens of thousands in the city's sacred cemeteries, not far from the grave of the prophet's son-in-law.

Sulgi's tomb was also on the Euphrates but farther south, near our twin city of Nasiriyah, four hundred yards from the great moon temple or *ziggurat of Ur.* His city was once ringed by gardens and palaces and rich irrigated soil; its streets crowded with traders from thousands of miles away; ruled by a secretive cabal of priests, there lay the royal cemeteries. There, in the winter of 1927, the archaeologist Sir Leonard Woolley found a grave undisturbed for more than four thousand years. Around the smashed skull of a woman, called Queen Pu-abi, perhaps a relative of Sulgi, was a two-foot crown of golden leaves.

"The upper part of the body," Woolley wrote, "was entirely hidden by a mass of beads of gold, silver, lapis lazuli, cornelian, agate, and chalcedony." The lapis was evidence that the Sumerians had a trade route stretching three thousand miles to the only source of lapis, the mines of eastern Afghanistan. In the porch was an inlaid lyre with a golden bull's head. And curled round the lyre was the arm of the female musician who, along with six armored guards and nine other musicians, had been killed to serve the afterlife of their dead mistress.

After two and a half thousand years of glory, Ur faltered: new peoples speaking other languages invaded. The irrigation systems were neglected; power moved up the Euphrates to Babylon and Assyria and the course of the river shifted away from the city; the marshland grew and the cities were covered in layers of desert sand. By the time that Ur's treasures were placed in a cramped and uninformative display cabinet in the British Museum, the people surrounding the birthplace of writing were illiterate tribesmen.

When I re-entered my office, Seyyed Hassan bobbed slightly on the chair, making a feeble gesture toward standing. Then he sank back into the deep folds of his woollen cloak. This was the first time I had ever been close to a senior Sadrist leader. Although I was pressing to include his colleagues in the new provincial council, we were not really supposed to deal with these men at all because they were aggressively opposed to the Coalition. I was curious to see what kind of man this was, whom our Iraqi allies in the province—both the Prince of the Marshes and his tribes and the Iranian-linked Islamist parties—wanted interned. So probably did Baghdad; an arrest warrant had already been issued against his leader, Muqtada.

The beard, which grew over his white starched collar, had tight curls as soft as adolescent down. His feet were half out of his clogs, revealing the hair around his pallid ankles. He was younger than me, and his high black turban seemed over-large. Not glancing at me but instead letting his large dark eyes drift over the cement floor, he talked quietly and slowly, as if he were contemplating not the words but deeper ideas, to which the words could only point.

He described how, when he had been abducted after the assassination and carried off to a small hut in the marshes, many times the rogue policemen had threatened to kill him and demanded to know who had killed Abu Rashid. He had kept assuring them that he was a good friend of Abu Rashid and knew nothing about the plot. In fact he wanted peace with everyone. Was there no rule of law? Why did the Coalition never act? He spoke in precise, slow, rhetorical questions, and his eyes never seemed to focus on anything in the room. "Tell me," he said, "not as a British man, not as the CPA, but as a brother, how we should deal with you and not be considered dangerous radicals."

I asked him whether he was preaching a revolution against the Coalition.

"Is it you who are saying this, or did someone else tell you to say this?" he asked.

"I am not an Iraqi. Respected people have reported against you: what have you done?" I wanted to understand why the leaders had

turned so strongly against him. I did not know if he had actually
committed a crime, or if he was a threat, or what the consequences
might be of freeing him.

"This world is nothing," Seyyed Hassan replied. "I am not concerned with politics but with God and the life hereafter. Do you think
if I was concerned with revolution against you, my people would not
protect me? That I would come and sit in your office? My concern is
with religion."

"Are you in revolution against the Coalition?" I asked.

"You say that I am in revolution against the occupation. My purpose is to study and teach the truth of Islam. I speak of nothing but
God's truth."

There was a vigor in these last words, emerging from a rich loam
of faith. He might be considered by the senior ayatollahs to be merely
a novice. But for fifteen years or more he had studied at Najaf and
watched and imitated teachers who spoke like this. It was the same
tone I heard from Buddhist monks discussing suffering, a blend of
recitation and feeling, acting a priest and being a priest. The cadences
and inward gaze revealed not only the centuries of tradition he'd absorbed at the Hawza—the great seminary in Najaf, but also his appeal to the hundreds of young men who attended his sermons and
came armed into the streets to rescue him. At the same time I wondered if he had read the New Testament and was making me play
Pontius Pilate. Ultimately I could only rule with the support of the
Iraqi leaders who wanted him interned. It would be difficult to refuse
them. My authority was after all "provisional."

Seyyed Hassan continued in his gentle voice to give a long account of Islam and the state. He spoke almost without pausing, and
I was reluctant to interrupt. He wanted a state based on Sharia law
with a strong position for the clergy. It was not clear, however,
whether he wanted the clergy to form the government or merely to
advise it. "We are not a political party," he said. "We are not a sect.
We are simply the hawza."

But as he continued, I could see that his account of Shiism, which stressed the importance of the sermon at Friday prayers and a national social network appealing to the young and the poor, reflected the influence of Sadr II. He did not mention the Coalition.

All he wanted from me, he concluded, to my surprise, was that I should occasionally take his advice. "I know you cannot always listen to me. I want, for example, for there to be no women on the provincial council and I know that for your culture and religion that is not possible. But we will form a dialogue and you will protect me from the Prince's followers." He said that people admired the jobs programs and some of the other projects done by the British military.

I was not entirely won over. Even with my poor Arabic I recognized the tricolonic asyndeton, which was the leitmotif of his oratory—three phrases without conjunctions, each beginning with the same word: *"Quwwat-al-ihtilal . . . Quwwat-al-ihtilal . . . Quwwat-al-ihtilal."* The translator rendered it as "The Coalition does this; the Coalition does that; the Coalition does the other," but whether through politeness or fear he had mistranslated. Seyyed Hassan had not said *"Quwwat-al-itilaf,"* or Coalition; he had said *"Quwwat-al-ihtilal"*—the Occupation. A word of great resonance for Arabs, conjuring the French occupation of Algeria and the Israeli occupation of Palestine.

Nevertheless, I saw an opportunity here. For the first time, the leader of the Sadr office in Maysan was frightened enough to come to our office, to offer cooperation and ask for help. We had a chance to bind into our structures the most hostile, heavily armed Islamist group in the province—a group that no one really had the will or strength to confront.

Back at the camp that evening, I went to see the new Colonel. He was still working at his desk at eleven at night and he looked exhausted, perhaps because his stomach had collapsed. He said the Prince had just told one of his company commanders to raid a house because it contained "a large terrorist arms cache." They had done

so and had found a few RPGs and a dozen automatic rifles. One of
the inhabitants had fled and they had pursued him across a muddy
field, captured him, and handed him with another suspect to the police, but the two prisoners escaped from police custody; so easily that
it seemed the police had helped them to escape. The house belonged
to Dr. Amin.

I told the colonel about the kidnapping of Dr. Amin's brother and
nephews. The colonel didn't need me to tell him that the Prince had
probably set up the whole raid to implicate Dr. Amin.

RESOLUTIONS

In desiring to defend its liberty each side tried to become strong enough to oppress the other . . . And the cause of all this is that in trying to escape fear men begin to make others fearful, and the injury they themselves seek to avoid they inflict on others, as if it were absolutely necessary either to harm or to be harmed.

— *Machiavelli,* Discourses, *Book I, Chapter 46*

Tuesday, October 28, 2003

The next day the Prince entered a special meeting with the supervisory committee and demanded to know whether it had been I or the committee who had appointed Brigadier General Sabih as the new police chief. He said that the minister of interior in Baghdad had confirmed it was entirely illegal for the committee to appoint the chief.

I replied—inventing a defense—that the provincial council had considered the case and made the recommendation, and I had appointed him.

"You have no right to do so. It is an appointment of the ministry of interior."

"In matters of grave security concerning the Coalition, the Coalition has reserved the right to do whatever is deemed necessary. In this case I exercise power on their behalf and we deem it necessary to appoint Sabih as the temporary chief." This was the most extreme claim I had ever made for coalition authority. To my relief no one challenged it.

"He will not last, the police will not accept him," the Prince replied, after a pause.

The council then told the Prince that he was responsible for the abductions because the kidnappers were from his tribe, and that if he did not release the prisoners and control his men he would be responsible for a tribal war. He replied angrily that the Sadr office was a cancer, that all the problems in the province were caused by the Iranian intelligence office, whose key representative was Dr. Amin, and that all the groups disagreeing with him—the alternative councils, the provincial council, and the clerics—were determined to destroy Iraq. He shouted that if the Coalition forces were not prepared to act against these threats he could not prevent his tribesmen from doing so. And with that, strode out.

That afternoon, Seyyed Hassan returned to warn me that the oil refinery workers were about to go on strike. He had told them to keep working while he spoke to me. I was delighted that he had come in to see me, because it showed that he was prepared to deal with us. But the news was worrying. The refinery provided 60 percent of the fuel needs of the province, and without it we would need to import forty tankers of fuel a day from Basra. There was no guarantee that we could find the tankers, get the fuel out of Basra, or protect the tankers on a road famous for carjacking and diesel theft. Lines would begin to build at gas stations, the many diesel generators in the province would fail, and Iraqis would again want to know why, with the second-largest oil reserves in the world, they were unable to get fuel. Then there would be riots.

The e-mail system was working again, so I wrote to the oil section in Basra explaining the situation, and asked if we were able to increase local salaries. Basra had written, telling us about democracy workshops and asking if we could provide Iraqi women to attend a women's conference. As usual, they had asked us two days before the conference, provided only two places out of forty for people from Maysan, and given no details on travel and accommodation.

There was a splurge of belated detail from Baghdad on the latest idea, a caucus system for electing the new government. The proposal was for "organizing committees" drawn from a balance of the provincial councils, the governing council in Baghdad, and five members from district councils. This group of fifteen would collect nominations and appoint candidates for the new assembly in Baghdad. We were told to minimize CPA participation in the whole process. The system was confusing, and none of our interpreters could think of an Arab word that would adequately convey the notion of a caucus. I suspected few Westerners outside Iowa understood it either.

And then there was an e-mail saying that Kofi Annan was "heartened," "intended to issue a report," and was reconsidering a UN resolution. It concluded with the question, "Why not have an international conference convened under UN auspices with participation by key external players?" and I thought, why not indeed, deleted the e-mail from my in-box, and went for a stroll down to the river, blinking at the still-strong sun.

On the roof, half the security multiple was sun-bathing and on a small bush by the river, forty sparrows—crowded on branches with brown dead leaves—sung excitedly. I had never noticed before how touching sparrow-song could be.

BLOOD MONEY

For this may be said of men generally: they are ungrateful, fickle, feigners
and dissemblers, avoiders of danger, eager for gain.
                              —*Machiavelli,* The Prince, *Chapter 17*

I was woken the following morning by a silver bugle playing reveille,
a reminder that the Light Infantry had now replaced the bagpipes of
the King's Own Scottish Borderers. The new colonel and his thousand men had only been in the province a week, and with the excep-
tion of the civil affairs team I was now, after a mere month, one of
the longest-serving foreigners in the province. I had just received an
e-mail saying that Molly Phee, the American officer who was supposed to take up the mantle of governor and be my boss, might be
moved somewhere else and a recommendation had gone forward
that I should be confirmed as the CPA governorate coordinator in
the province.

Meanwhile everything seemed to be unraveling at once. We
were now facing civil war between the three most heavily armed
factions in the province. The Prince's militia wanted to avenge the
death of their comrade. The Sadrists wanted to avenge the first kidnapping and the Iranian-linked groups wanted to avenge the second. Every faction saw an opportunity to eliminate its rivals. Many
citizens thought that we—the Coalition—had been too slow to re-

store order; the oil in the province was about to run out and the police were on the verge of disintegration and mutiny. I had made a dubious and probably illegal appointment of a new police chief; the Prince of the Marshes was still putting pressure on us to attack the Sadr office; the Iranian parties wanted us to arrest the Prince. Finally, there was a rumor that the Prince's brother had just resigned as ministry coordinator of our provincial regeneration committee, a move that could bring all government services to a halt. And all this had happened in just five days.

It did not seem likely that I could solve any of these things but I thought I should keep behaving as though I might. I planned a grand summit with all the provincial leadership in which I would ask them to suspend their differences and uphold the law. I spent time with the colonel to ensure that he and I were following the same line. We agreed to invite senior visitors to reinforce our joint message. The brigadier general came in from Basra and with the colonel warned that the Prince was to act within the law.

That afternoon, Sir Hilary Synnott, the senior Coalition civilian in southern Iraq, came at my invitation to join me for a meeting with three Islamist opponents of the Prince. Abu Mustafa began. "We are sorry about the death of Abu Rashid," he said, "but he is not the first man to be killed and he will not be the last. His appointment as police chief was illegitimate. You must now put pressure on the Prince to stop Abu Rashid's tribe from taking any more action and release these innocent men."

"If Abu Rashid's tribe continues the violence," said Abu Maytham, the Badr commander, "there will be civil war. There are already too many powerful tribes involved."

"But Abu Rashid's tribe will only stop the violence," added the third man, "in exchange for blood money or the death of Dr. Amin."

"Could Dr. Amin's tribe pay the money without admitting guilt?" asked Sir Hilary.

"Not a chance," said the cleric. "Unless the blame is fixed on someone the tribe will keep pursuing the killer."

"Would Dr. Amin's tribe be prepared to admit guilt?" asked Sir Hilary.

"No, because even if he paid the blood money, there would still be a vendetta against his tribe," said Abu Maytham, the Badr commander.

"You, Seyyed Rory, must call a big meeting in your own name," said the cleric, Abu Mustafa, "and invite everyone: the Prince, the political parties, the clerics, the tribes, and the Sadrists. Say that you as the CPA want to resolve the issue. Make everyone present agree that if they know anything about the murder they will hand the murderer over. If it can be proved that someone was connected to the murder, their whole people will be responsible. Finally, if anyone takes illegal action the Coalition will arrest them—anyone, that is, including the family of Abu Rashid."

The Prince was subdued when Sir Hilary and I saw him, two hours after his meeting with the brigadier general and the colonel. "Those who killed Abu Rashid want only to make trouble in Iraq," he said. "Abu Rashid graduated top in his class from military academy. He was a courageous leader, respected by all the tribal sheikhs. Only the Iranian-linked politicians who want no good for the city opposed him. They had decided to get rid of him by any means they could. The complained about his qualifications and when that did not work, they killed him."

"I agree," said the Prince earnestly when we suggested calling a meeting to control the tribes. "The cities do not belong to the tribes. Anyone who breaks the law should be excluded." But he implied that, whatever anyone claimed, he did not control the tribes. "Convene the meeting, and Seyyed Rory can act as sheikh of sheikhs to resolve this."

RESIGNATION

Since the operation of normal institutions in republics is slow . . . their remedies are very dangerous when they have to provide solutions to a problem that cannot wait.

—*Machiavelli,* Discourses, *Book I, Chapter 34*

SATURDAY, OCTOBER 31, 2003

In the morning meeting I received confirmation that Riyadh, the Prince's brother, had resigned from his post as chairman of the provincial ministerial regeneration committee. That afternoon, various senior ministry directors came in to say that the entire administration of the province would collapse unless I persuaded Riyadh to take the position of governor: the ministries would cease to function, fuel would no longer be delivered, electricity would cease. I did not know exactly what Riyadh was trying to achieve or how I should react.

I went immediately to Riyadh's house, flattered him greatly, and urged him to reconsider his resignation. In the meantime, I said, I would take his position as chairman of the regeneration committee and coordinate the ministries myself. Riyadh reminded me of my "arbitrary and illegal decision" over the police chief. I emphasized that a governor would be appointed within three weeks and certainly six and asked him to be patient. He said that he was concerned by rumors that we might be appointing a governor by election from the council. He wanted me to end the uncertainty by appointing him governor on the spot. For a moment I wondered whether everything from the assassination to the abductions had been planned by the Prince to coincide with the arrival of the new battle group and create a chaos that would force me to appoint his brother. Politely, I repeated that we would select a provincial council and they would elect the governor in six weeks. Riyadh did not escort me to the door.

Returning to the office at two o'clock to look at the final arrangements for the summit, I received a call from the battle group warning me that the Prince of the Marshes had arranged his own summit for half past two in his house and had invited the colonel to attend. This seemed to be a bid to give the entire settlement the stamp of the Prince. I asked the colonel not to attend the Prince's meeting and then I sent round more messengers to the community reminding them that the Sunday summit was still happening and nothing would be decided till then.

SUMMIT

It is always easier to convince a people to follow a proposal which seems bold and certain, even if danger lurks behind it, than to follow one which appears cowardly and uncertain, even if it contains security.
—*Machiavelli,* Discourses, *Book I, Chapter 53*

SUNDAY, NOVEMBER 1, 2003

Walking across the road to the provincial council building, I worried that the Prince of the Marshes might have told everyone to boycott the meeting and I was relieved to discover about two hundred people waiting. I recognized a clump of Sadrist clerics, the Iranian-linked parties, some policemen, the leading tribal sheikhs, ministry directors, and NGO activists. Nobody seemed to be missing. The British colonel, his political adviser, his intelligence officer, some of his company commanders, and his second-in-command were all sitting at the back of the room, not to speak but, in the colonel's words, "to show that the big guns are behind you." The Prince of the Marshes was there and had placed himself behind me with the colonel rather than in the audience. Ahmed, our Yemeni political adviser, had succeeded in gathering pretty much the entire leadership of the province in twenty-four hours.

I sat alone at a small desk in the middle of the room, facing the crowd, with an interpreter standing alongside me. "Leaders of Maysan, Sheikhs, religious leaders, political parties, independent notables, Abu Hatim," I began, trying to catch the eyes of each group as I picked them out. "Colonel and Coalition forces. *A salaam aleikum*. The events of the last week have been a tragedy for this great province." I was moving carefully now, because I did not want to take sides. "There were three crimes: first the murder of Brigadier-General Abu Rashid; second, the abduction of the clerics and later the family of Dr. Amin; and finally, the fighting in the street. This is completely unacceptable. This is a great province, a famous province that liberated itself.

"What happened on Friday was a perfect gift to all our enemies," I continued. "Of course the events were provoking. They were meant to be. Whoever organized the assassination—I am sure it was a foreign power—was trying to encourage a violent reaction. You followed their plan." I still had no idea who had organized the assassination but it seemed better to put the blame outside the room. "The only way to defeat the purposes of these cruel men is to hold together—to refuse to be drawn into this kind of conflict. You are the leaders of the province. Now I am going to ask you all—some individually—to walk up to this desk and commit to upholding the rule of law, to controlling your followers and handing over any of them who break the law. Then we will all sign a document confirming this."

I looked expectantly round the room and saw Seyyed Hassan the Sadrist cleric with his hand up. I called upon him and he got to his feet, glancing nervously round the room, recognizing perhaps some of those who had kidnapped and threatened to kill him.

"Bismillahi r-rahmani rahim al-hamdu li-illahi rabbi l-alamin," he began. In the name of God the compassionate, the merciful, praise to God, lord of the worlds. He paused, then added, *"A salaam aleikum."* There was a muttered reply from the crowd and perhaps it did not satisfy him because he tried again. *"Sallu Allah Muhammad wa Ali Muhammad."* Praise to God, Muhammad, Ali. This time he got a slightly stronger reply. "I stand here as a man of peace, a man of religion, and a man who is a victim. In this room are those who persecuted me. I will not name names, I will not point them out, you all

know who they are. Nor will I ask for justice. But let it be remembered the shameful acts that were committed. An innocent man was kidnapped, and no one has apologized to me. I have nothing to apologize for."

There was a loud murmur of disapproval because half the audience still believed he had ordered the assassination of Abu Rashid, and almost everyone blamed his militia for the violence on Friday night. There was a shout from the burly mayor associated with the Prince, and out of the corner of my eye I could see the Prince himself about to get to his feet.

I intervened. "Seyyed Hassan, we are all very sorry you were kidnapped. As I said in my speech, there were three crimes: the assassination, the kidnapping, and the fighting. Your kidnapping was an illegal act. But that does not excuse the behavior of your followers. You have in contravention of all law formed a dangerous militia and stored weapons in mosques. A mosque is for God and religion. It is not an armory." As soon as I said this, I regretted it; it was not my place as a non-Muslim to speak about mosques. But my listeners did not seem to react. I wondered whether the translator was conveying what I was saying. "Nor should you interfere in the workings of the ministries," I concluded.

"The militia acted merely to defend me," said the cleric. "I did not ask them to do so."

"You could have stopped them." We were addressing each other as though we were strangers, rather than two men who had just had a long meeting in my office.

"Not when they were fired up with the desire to save me. There was nothing I could do."

"That . . . that is simply not good enough," I said loudly. "Listen to yourself. Children were injured that night with RPGs. You cannot permit men with weapons to take over the center of the city and harm children. Their actions are entirely outside the law and damaging to this province."

"I cannot control them." We were both speaking loudly now—less for each other than for the benefit of the other two hundred people in the room.

"Have some respect for yourself and for them. You are a leader. And that is why you are here. We are all leaders. We should start taking some responsibility—"

Sheikh Rahim broke in, standing up and in his harsh voice growling, "Seyyed Rory, the murderer of Abu Rashid has been identified. It was the last British colonel."

There was a sudden silence. I leaned forward angrily.

Sheikh Rahim rushed on in his formal high-pitched Arabic: "It was the reckless policy of the last British colonel, who never listened to us or included us that is responsible for all of this. The man was an idiot—"

"The last colonel was a hero," I snapped. "He worked very hard for this province; he was a friend of mine and a teacher of mine." I wondered what the new British colonel was making of such a statement, a week after he had watched me argue with his predecessor. "He gave six months of his life to this place. How dare you say this after all the efforts he took to keep security?"

"You, Seyyed Rory, could not keep security in a girls' kindergarten . . ." I was aware of everyone watching me.

"I am disappointed in you, Sheikh Rahim. You are a mujahid and a respected preacher; you have been working for this province. And now you are talking like a child. I cannot keep security? It is you the leaders of Maysan who cannot keep security."

"Security is not our job. Security is your job. You do not allow us to act." Three or four people shouted, "Exactly."

My voice now was trembling, "Let me tell you, if we had not sent in the tanks last Friday night, you would have burned this city to the ground. All of you. It is only because of the British military that anything was saved."

"You are the government," said Sheikh Rahim, still standing and shouting. "Act like one."

I brought my fist down hard on the table, and there was silence. I could see from the reactions that this had offended most of the room but I continued, louder now, "We could have come as colonial officers, but I did not come here as a colonial officer. I—we—are not here to occupy this country. We would like to return to our families. We are doing everything we can to work for you and work with you to prepare you for the transition. I will be here with you for a year, but soon—in two years at the most—we will be gone. This is your country. Act like men, for a change."

Sheikh Rahim tried to interrupt again but I shouted over him, "No, we have had enough from you. Who will speak on behalf of the tribes?"

Suddenly I spotted in the middle row, beside the representatives of the Iraqi Communist Party, Professor Mary Kaldor from the London School of Economics, whom I had not seen since Montenegro four years earlier, and her colleague Yahya Said, a British academic whose parents had been famous communist leaders in Iraq. They were laughing like the audience at a boxing-match at my strident rhetoric about colonialism. I felt a little ridiculous and hoped it did not show.

Muhammad Abbas Muhammad Al Araybi of the Albu Muhammad stepped forward. "The Albu Muhammad will agree to cease the vendetta if proper compensation and restitution is made. I hereby swear this in front of all the sheikhs and political parties." I needed to know what he meant by restitution but I thanked him and he sat down again.

Sheikh Kadhem stood and greeted the room respectfully and said, "We the tribe of the Serai and the tribe of the Sudan agree to hand over Dr. Amin in exchange for the release of his brothers and nephews but we will not do so to the Albu Muhammad or to the police because we do not trust them, we will do so only to Seyyed Rory and the CPA."

"Thank you, Sheikh Kadhem Mushettat, I will take him."

"And on the condition he is well treated."

"He will be entirely under our protection and treated according to the law," I intoned. "Innocent until proven guilty. Treated with humanity and respect."

"Is this an Englishman's promise?" the sheikh asked.

"In front of all these witnesses," I said, "you have my word. You can hand him to me."

The sheikh sat down. Various others stood up, and to my relief I was able to recognize them all, and call on them by name. Some criticized their opponents but most asked for reconciliation. When they had finished, I said, "Now I would like you to form into groups, sheikhs with sheikhs, political parties with political parties, clerics with clerics, independents with independents. I want you each to choose representatives. Then I will invite the representatives up one by one to sign a document renouncing violence and agreeing to abide by the law. Please stand up now and gather in the groups."

No one moved. I looked up and down the lines.

"I ask you again: please stand up, organize in groups and then come forward."

No one moved.

"Please come up to my desk to sign the paper."

Still no movement. Just as I was trying to make sense of this new mutiny, Yahya from the back shouted, "Your translator is not translating correctly. By your leave—" and he launched into a stream of Arabic that brought sudden smiles of understanding to the audience. People began approaching my desk in groups. My translator muttered angrily that he had translated perfectly and couldn't help the stupidity of the people of Maysan. I wondered how much else he had failed to translate.

Finally we had a document that stated, "We the leaders of Maysan hereby express our sorrow at the death of Abu Rashid, agree to control our people, remain within the law, and hand criminals to justice" printed on two sheets of A2 paper and signed by nearly two hundred people, so that it could be broadcast on television to the entire province. I thanked everyone and walked to the door. They stood up, in respect, as we left.

It had been a strange, traditional session that relied a great deal on words and gesture, and I had put the CPA into an unusual role. Yet it was perhaps the most popular thing I did in Maysan, and it seemed to work. The next day everyone did what they had promised and the ten-day crisis was over. Much secret trading must have happened before the meeting to convince Kadhem Mushettat to hand over Dr. Amin, and Muhammad Abbas to stop the vendetta; and it struck me that I had mounted something closer to a performance than a negotiation. But in the next two months there were no more kidnappings, public vendettas, or RPGs fired in the streets.

The colonel and his staff shook hands politely at the end; they did not comment on the meeting. The colonel had said he was happy to leave political work to the CPA. The British soldiers could not have followed much of the meeting or sensed its problems because the interpreter was standing with me and whereas I could at least follow some of the Arabic—even if it was only to know that *imame* had something to do with a cleric, or that the phrase that sounded to me something like *fi nidhem-ssabiq* meant "during the old regime"—they spoke not one word. They would only have heard me asking Iraqis to stand up and them not moving or heard me shouting at Iraqis and commenting on the last colonel but they had no idea what I was responding to or what political game I was playing. They may have thought I was unnecessarily aggressive. Or they may not have cared what I thought I was doing.

The next evening, however, I was surprised to find that Dr. Amin had not yet been handed over as promised and I worried that the agreement had already collapsed. So I called the camp to make sure.

"Yes," they replied, "he walked in voluntarily to the camp with toothbrush and toothpaste eight hours ago, and we interned him and sent him to the interrogation cells in Umm Qasr."

I was enraged. This man, whom we had no reason to believe was guilty, had walked in because he had trusted my promise, witnessed by two hundred people, that I would see he was looked after. The military had not informed me when he arrived, nor given me any opportunity to speak to him. And now they had interned him two hundred miles away. I told the political adviser and the colonel that this was not acceptable. They shrugged and said they would pass the message up, but by sending him to Umm Qasr they had lost control of him—he was in the military system, and only the General could decide what happened to him next.

PART THREE

IRAQI PASTORAL

Taking the initiative in introducing a new form of government is very difficult and dangerous, and unlikely to succeed. The reason is that all those who profit from the old order will be opposed to the innovator, whereas all those who might benefit from the new order are, at best, tepid supporters of him. This lukewarmness arises partly from fear of their adversaries, who have the laws on their side, partly from the skeptical temper of men, who do not really believe in new things unless they have been seen to work well. The result is that whenever those who are opposed to change attack the innovator, they do it with much vigor, whereas his supporters act only half-heartedly; so that the innovator and his supporters find themselves in great danger.

—*Machiavelli,* The Prince, *Chapter 6*

AL-MUTANABI STREET

We will find our best helpers not in our former most obedient subjects, but among those who are now most active in agitating against us, for it will be the intellectual leaders of the people who will serve the purpose, and these are not the philosophers or the rich but the demagogues and politicians.

—*T. E. Lawrence,* The Changing East

The violence forced men to declare their loyalties. There were fifty-four political parties, twenty substantial tribes, and a dozen leading religious figures in the province. But the assassination of the police chief, the kidnapping, and the fighting in the streets brought the leaders out of the shadows. There was no longer any doubt that the three most powerful armed groups were the Prince's, the Sadrists, and the Iranian-linked parties. Each had militias; two wanted to set up an Islamist state; one was very closely connected to the secret service of Iran; all had links to criminals. This was not what the CPA intended for Maysan.

The planners in Washington and Baghdad wanted Iraq to be a democracy. This did not mean simply a fragile simulacrum, like Latin America's longest-standing democracy, Colombia, but a full liberal democracy: peaceful, rich, stable, and humane. They talked of Iraq's five-thousand-year-old civilization, insisted that Iraqis were educated, middle-class people with secular, liberal sympathies, and attempted to build the utopia of which they dreamed from units in the Green Zone dedicated to privatization, civil society, and gender

equality, a hundred million dollars for democratization, and consultants who rebranded corruption, crime, and civil war as "governance
capacity building," "security sector reform," and "conflict resolution." The apostles of this democratic revolution were to be the Iraqi
Governing Council and in particular its secular liberals—"pragmatic
leaders" such as the doctor Ayad Allawi, the statesman Adnan
Pachachi, or the banker and mathematician Ahmed Chalabi. It was
these men, not Maysan's anarcho-mafia, who were supposed to lead
Iraqis into a democratic future.

But in Amara many of the moderate, educated, middle class had
fled, and those that remained were often harassed, blackmailed, or
even assassinated for having Baathist connections. Pachachi's liberal
party had no local support. Chalabi allied with the Prince of the
Marshes. Allawi was forced to appoint the shiekh who had last been
seen on television signing in blood an oath to give his life to defend
Saddam.

I met independent figures, teachers, sheikhs, ministry directors,
and even poets, but struggled to find the leadership of which Baghdad dreamed. There was the tiny Suwaad sheikh who told me he rejected the occupation because his ancestors had fought the British
colonialists but later, after I helped a relative of his, showed me a letter in which the British representative in 1936 had praised the loyalty of his grandfather. He invited me to lunch, and the day after I
attended his house was fire-bombed, on the grounds that he was a
traitor.

The best examples of middle-class "liberal" figures with no
Baathist connections in Amara were Asad and Ali. I first met them
shortly after the assassination of the police chief. The sixty-year-old
Asad led the way into my office and slumped without a word into my
armchair. Ali, who was twenty-one, followed at a military clip in his
stiff blue jacket, shook my hand, and said in perfect English, "Pleased
to meet you."

"We are here," Ali explained, "to describe our magazine, *Maysan for Tomorrow.* We would like to see if you might contribute to the costs of running." He passed me a budget. I glanced over the figures— a few thousand dollars a month, enough in a year to refurbish ten schools. I doubted that anyone needed this magazine. I looked at Ali and was surprised when he stared patiently back. Young men who spoke good English in Al Amara were often unused to dealing with foreigners, and in their eagerness to show off their language skills could appear either obsequious or patronizing. But Ali was neither.

"What have you been doing since the invasion?" I asked.

"Last month we organized a sports day at the sports center," said Ali. "It was directed at the disabled students and the orphans. We had a number of races and competitions including a painting work-shop, and we gave some small prizes to the winners. Here, perhaps if you would like to look, is an example of our magazine."

The magazine was sixteen sheets of glossy paper. On each page was a water-color.

"They are painted by Mr. Asad," said Ali. Asad nodded.

On the third page, Asad had painted a game of snakes and lad-ders, on the fourth a man with a beret and a waxed mustache next to a map of France, and on the sixth a series of drawings illustrated the dangers of different land-mines. One woman was striding in a bonnet, with a pince-nez held in front of her eyes. The watery yellow line of her Regency dress crossed the blue corner of a picnic cloth. Different perspectives and different planes existed side by side; ob-jects overlapped and occasionally melted into each other, particularly on the page devoted to a brief history of Al Amara and its water-birds.

"We want to print four thousand copies and distribute them to all the primary schools in the province. We have never had a children's magazine in Maysan. There is nothing for children to do here, noth-ing for them to read."

Asad began to speak and Ali translated. "All the opportunity you have created for us is at risk. You have given us freedom of speech and freedom of movement but we must now move to realize it."

Ali's father was an engineer, his mother was a housewife, and his younger sister—whom he adored—spent the evenings playing chess with him. By the time he was eleven, English had become his favorite subject and it was English that he chose to study when, six years later, he graduated from high school. Perhaps he enjoyed English the most because it allowed him to get closer to Britain and America, the countries that he admired the most. At high school his reading list would have seemed more suitable for a radical of the 1930s: John Stuart Mill, Carlyle, and most recent of all, George Orwell. More modern books were mostly unavailable because they had been banned by the Baath. He memorized long and difficult quotes in English. His favorite was from the man he called "mistergeorgeebernardshaw": "This is the true joy in life, the being used for a purpose recognized by yourself as a mighty one: the being thoroughly worn out before you are thrown on the scrap heap, and being a force of nature instead of a feverish selfish little clod of ailments and grievances, complaining that the world will not devote itself to making you happy."

Ali was the only student from the province of Maysan to be offered a place to study English at Baghdad University. He chose to accept in part for the school's excellent reputation, its demanding curriculum, and its faculty, and in part for the professor who would be teaching his core course. The professor was a powerful and well-known writer whose grand public statements about international politics appealed to Ali's idealism, which had had little opportunity to flourish in his small high school or to be supported amid the quiet and sentimental rhythms of family life. Ali, who had never seen himself as an original figure, was thrilled at the prospect of acquiring a mentor, and he never doubted that he would find a noble role as a student.

Once he had settled into his cramped dormitory, Ali proved to be a good student. He listened to many language tapes and his professors congratulated him on his BBC accent, although he suspected it did not sound very English. He wrote short term papers on Dickens that focused on the misery of Victorian London. But the professor of his core course rarely raised the subject of politics, and when he did, the conversation quickly died. Ali began to see that his work, though pleasant, was not taking him forward, and his enthusiasm began to dissipate. Though naturally gregarious, he found himself increasingly withdrawn. He sensed that many of the students, like him, would have liked to spit at the picture of Saddam at the front gate: they complained about the old-fashioned cars, the vacuous local television stations, the irony of watching the regime lecture on youth and purity when Saddam's sons were nightly raping undergraduate girls. But there was something coarse about the criticisms, as though his peers had already surrendered their ideals, and he could never find anything to contribute to their discussions. This had its advantages: he did not receive a visit from the dour and bored men from the security service; the young thugs of the fedayeen militia who patrolled the campuses never stopped him; he managed to make friends with a colonel's son and thus secure a delay in his military service; although he had only a little money to bribe the professors he seemed to do well in his exams. But he was not able to express what was in his heart. He sensed that his fellow students, who were mostly Sunni, looked down on him as a dirty, backward Marsh Arab.

Occasionally his professor accompanied him to al-Mutanabi Street, where books had been sold for a thousand years or more, and they sat together in the café next to the market, while the older man discussed Paris with his friends. Ali still sympathized with the professor but he was confused: the teacher who was so unflinching in his criticism of Israel apparently found nothing to criticize in Saddam's Iraq; he spoke movingly about Edward Said and western stereotypes of Arabia but maintained that Iraqis could only be ruled by fear.

Gradually Ali began to see that he could spend his whole life in the comfortable surroundings of the university or the government, gaining slowly in status, without becoming a fragment of what he had dreamed. His fantasies about Britain and America redoubled: he woke in the mornings muttering about respect for women and human rights, tolerance of religion and traditions of dance and theater. And he began to realize that he might never get to practice the English he was learning because he might never be able to meet a foreigner.

He found it difficult to concentrate on his studies, and he was no longer at the top of his class. It was not cheap for his family to keep him in Baghdad and with his father now retired his sister was without proper support. Finally, he graduated and returned to al-Amara. He told his parents that it was only for a short time.

In Amara, he met Asad, a distant relative of his father's and a well-known painter, poet, and head of the artists' union, although he did not like the union's close association with Saddam. Asad had a wry benevolence that no one Haider's age could hope to match. His hair was long and white, which was unusual for an Iraqi, and he had a drooping goatee that reminded people of Balzac. Although short and a little overweight, he possessed a tranquility and low-voiced confidence seemed noble and otherworldly amidst the shabbiness of modern Iraq and made the students at Baghdad University seem callow and meretricious by comparison. Delighting in Asad's erudition and passion, Ali gladly settled into the role of protégé, yet Asad was no more able than the professor in Baghdad to assume a heroic persona in Saddam's Maysan, where the resistance was divided between the Prince of the Marshes' uneducated tribal thugs and medieval theocrats. Small surprise that Asad and Ali were equally delighted when British troops reached Amara.

I saw Asad at an art exhibition we had funded, reciting poetry through a microphone. I couldn't understand a word, and the translator insisted that it was impossible to translate, so I just nodded significantly and moved on. Other moderate figures—the education di-rector and some local engineers—were admiring Cubist paintings, Surrealist paintings, and a painting with geometric figures on a plain white background that seemed a parody of Kandinsky.

At the exhibition I was introduced to Dr. Kifiyah, a medical doc-tor from Baghdad who had moved to al-Amara. She had a large friendly face covered with downy black hair, and her dark eyes seemed kind. She and her daughter had recently begun to work with an organization funded by the U.S. Agency for International Devel-opment, whose aim was to establish programs targeted at women through literacy classes and some basic midwife training.

"What do you think of the paintings?" I asked.

"They are very good," she said and smiled. I did not know whether she meant it.

A burly, middle-aged man who had spent ten years in exile in the Kurdish areas showed me his paintings of the marshes, which de-picted great gray rotting fishes on parched soil—"All utterly de-stroyed by that monster," he said. Some of his canvases showed men who held missiles in their hands and screamed as their faces melted into their skulls. I was particularly struck by a portrait of a girl with long hair in a brown dress, standing in a spotlight in a dark brown room that might have been a cell, her back to the viewer. I bought it.

Ali and Asad made no comment on the painting. I suspected it was not their style. I asked them both which parties they thought should be represented on the new provincial council.

Ali muttered something in Arabic to Asad, who shrugged.

"What do you mean, sir?" said Ali.

"Well," I asked, "how many seats should we give to Dawa?"

Asad replied, and Ali said, "Mr. Asad says you must remember there are two Dawas." I glanced at Asad, who was nodding meaningfully.

"Three," I laughed.

"La, la, ithnen," Asad held up two fingers.

"Three." I counted them off. "Dawa Iraq, Dawa Islamiya, Dawa movement."

Asad shrugged and said, "I don't know. I am not interested. Actually they are no different. They just pretend to be. They are all bad people anyway, ignorant and religious. Support the moderate, secular people."

"But where are they? I don't see them. People like you don't want to get involved in politics."

"Seyyed Rory, it is not simple. It is dangerous for us. But if we did, people would support us. No one wants Islamist fanatics. Please do not appoint them."

Ali, who embodied Baghdad's ideal of a middle-class leader, was powerless: he had no armed militia, and he lacked the recklessness to confront and the ruthlessness to defeat those who did. When Islamist parties plastered posters on neighborhood walls denouncing him as a collaborator, he resigned from his translation job at the Czech NGO; his sister could not leave home because she was known to have attended a women's conference in Amman, which was considered un-Islamic. No amount of money was going to convince him or his secular friends to establish a political party.

Perhaps the only "secular" figure in Amara who was keen on politics was the Communist leader, the eccentrically named Abu Ivan. The Communist party had once been the largest party in Iraq, and was famous for its devotion to the USSR. Everyone knew the proverb, "When it snows in Moscow, the Iraqi Party puts up its umbrella." Saddam had banned the party, and the fall of the USSR had left it with little credibility, but the Shia parties still portrayed them as dangerous atheists. They operated out of shabby offices decorated with volumes of Lenin. Abu Ivan was typical of their leaders: an articulate and apparently warm-hearted middle-aged man, concerned for the rights of factory workers. But even had we chosen to support the Communists—which would have been an interesting ideological compromise—they were unlikely to win an election.

Since there was no powerful moderate leadership; we could only create it, slowly. I funded small human rights organizations, women's centers, and civic education courses. But I saw most promise in the sports clubs and trade unions, which had tens of thousands of members and a well-established infrastructure. But they had also often been very close to Saddam, and it was difficult to convince free-market theorists in Baghdad to invest in them, as they were not going to make a liberal civil society overnight.

Although the first couple of months after the invasion had been relatively quiet, the number of attacks against the Coalition was increasing. During my August visit to Baghdad the suicide bomb against the United Nations building had been followed by a huge explosion in the Shia holy city of Najaf, which had killed Ayatalloh M. Baqr al-Hakim, the leader of the Iranian-linked SCIRI party, and a hundred others. The Red Cross, which had been targeted, had mostly withdrawn. But there had been as yet no kidnapping or televised executions in Iraq, and now that we had resolved the assassination of the police chief, Maysan was quiet. I used such times of relative peace to visit the rural areas. The villages where hundreds of thousands lived had very unexpected attitudes toward government and development, and little sense of connection to either the political violence in Amara or the anti-Western rhetoric emanating from Baghdad.

RURAL RIDES

A shrewd ruler must therefore try to ensure that his citizens, whatever the situation may be, will always be dependent on the government and on him; and then they will always be loyal to him.

—Machiavelli, The Prince, *Chapter 9*

The Beni Hashim, for example, who I visited weeks after the death of the police chief, were one of the more remote Marsh Arab tribes. There were already rumors that the international agencies would give money for Marsh Arab projects, and many Iraqis who had previously despised the Marsh Arabs were now associating with them, but the Beni Hashim were authentic. Their older people had spent their first thirty years or so on floating platforms of reeds, in marshland the government never visited. But because their territory lay on the Iranian border, Saddam had dispossessed them at the beginning of the Iran-Iraq war and moved more than twenty thousand from the district into the desert. Many drifted into the Shia ghettos in Baghdad or the slum apartments in Basra, where they were lucky to find work as cleaners and servants. The invasion had now made it legal to live in the marshes again and uniquely this stretch of marsh had not been drained. Some, particularly the older people, had begun moving back though it must have been difficult for them to envisage what kind of life they were supposed to lead, with the buffaloes mostly killed, the fish stocks depleted, the huts and the floating islands broken beyond repair.

I arrived in the village to find, reflected in a pool of standing water, a barrel-vaulted building made entirely of marsh reeds and encircled by the sagging wire of a disconnected electricity pylon, concrete pipes, iron chimneys, and paving stones, half-submerged in mud. In the center of the façade was a framed portrait of Imam Ali, the cousin and brother-in-law of the Prophet. The loudspeaker draped from a column confirmed that it had a further function as a mosque.

It was bright outside, and at first when I entered the *mudhif* I could see almost nothing in the shadows. Gradually approaching forms resolved themselves into old men with checked turbans not so much tied as loosely heaped on their heads. Out of politeness they did not look into my eyes and sat, hunched over, with hands hidden in the sleeves of anoraks or arms folded, seeming anxious and uncertain. I placed myself on a homespun rug at the end of the room.

Only two men sat upright. One had a neat black beard and a military camouflage jacket and looked to me like the commander of an armed militia. The other was Seyyed Issa, the mayor. Both were young, a rarity in Beni Hashim where there was no way of making money. The bill-poster, the seller of pocket-knives, the factory worker or casual laborer would find no employment here. And the men of Beni Hashim had missed the windfall of April, when Amara was available for looting. They'd had no chance to help themselves to a small generator from a party official's house, or to gather some roof tiles, kitchen pots, or seat stuffing from a clinic. They were almost entirely dependent on money from the Coalition government.

"Thank you for having us," I said.

"Not at all," said Seyyed Issa solemnly in his one phrase of English, and then he looked up nervously and giggled. There was a silence. They were waiting for me to make a formal speech. I spoke about not raising expectations, about security and elections and the future. The older men looked at me vacantly, indifferent.

Seyyed Issa, who had been a child when they moved from the marsh regions, now began speaking on behalf of the community. He told me that he had been to Amara the previous day. With the potholes and a recent flood, the eighty-kilometer journey had taken him nearly four hours. He had called on the British military to ask for compensation: a cow had miscarried when a helicopter flew too low. He had also obtained another letter from the municipalities director supporting the residents' quest to have this area recognized again as an official district. He wanted me to follow up on both issues. While he waited for my reply, he took out a pen and a notebook and laid them carefully on the mat beside his knees. The old men watched him and nodded. They had never been to school and could neither read nor write; they had a number of reasons to respect Seyyed Issa: he had graduated from high school, the new reed *mudhif* in which they were sitting was his, he was from the most prosperous family in the village, was descended from the Prophet, and had a reputation for dealing well with the government.

The *mudhif* had, with its high vaulted ceiling, something of the form of a Norman church. The pillars, glowing as though waxed, were made from frail reeds, each a different shade of liver pâté, tightly bound, bending to their neighbor's stance, straining and splitting under the thrusting weight of the roof. On some days, the mudhif was the *mejlis,* which meant the sitting, congregation, or parliament of the people: a place to discuss events in Al Amara or even Baghdad; end a conflict with neighbors from the Albu Kheit or the Suwaad; limit the fishing; or resolve a legal case. Today, the building was not *mudhif, mejlis,* mosque, or dining hall but the audience chamber for petitioning the Dowla, or government, which in this case was me.

There was a pause. In a meeting of this sort, everyone was traditionally encouraged to speak. Seyyed Issa with his back to the far wall had to listen to the slow-witted cousin in the ragged coat on the left of the doorway. The old men asked, severally, for help with irrigation, sanitation, and so on: tap water, ambulances, modern farming techniques, electricity. "Saddam Hussein treated the people of the marshes worse than dogs," concluded Seyyed Issa. One of the old men demanded crop-dusters to spray DDT and kill the malarial mosquitoes. The other old men nodded; Saddam had done it regularly. I went through the pantomime of writing down their request but I had no intention of pursuing it; we had no crop-dusters and I thought that DDT was a health risk. I said there had been complaints that they were throwing poison into the water and then scooping the dead fish off the surface. The old men said nothing. I could not tell if they had understood.

"We would not do that," said Seyyed Issa, after a pause. "We tend to fish by electrifying the water or throwing in grenades instead. And using poisons is a traditional indigenous method of fishing—we should not be banned from pursuing our traditions."

It was true that the fish were traditionally poisoned rather than caught in nets—nets were once taboo—but I suspected traditional poisons were milder than the industrial chemicals they were now using. I made a note to ask the health department to test the fish in the market and to close any stalls selling poisoned fish.

The fire was kindled at the hearth, water was brought, coffee prepared. The men clacked their rosary beads through their fingers, picked reeds from the mats, raised their hands languidly to brush away flies, their eyes following the evenly spaced hoops arching over them like the breast-cage of a whale. A young relative carried round two porcelain cups with the coffee pot and served me first.

I offered the cup to Seyyed Issa and then to the oldest man, who returned it, so I could drain the scalding drops, be served again, shake the cup in token of finishing, and hand it to the man on my left. In some of the more remote Marsh Arab communities, people still refused to drink from a cup that a Christian had touched. They would either wash it ostentatiously or smash it. But the old man drank, had it refilled, and drank again. In the doorway stood a girl in a long brown tunic, with honey-colored eyes, a tangled mess of almost blonde hair, and a piece of plain twisted wire in her ear. She may have been eight but had a much older savvy look and a broad and thoughtful smile. The old men shooed her away. She was replaced by a group of young boys.

We had brought some soccer balls, and I gave one to the bodyguard team leader to distribute. He rolled it outside. There was an explosion of noise and violence; thirty bodies wrestled in a cloud of dust; one large boy who had been punching the others tore the soccer ball free and sprinted toward his home, pursued by the pack.

After lunch we were invited to go out in the boats. The bodyguard team and the police stepped carefully into the rocking canoes with their weapons. I lay on my stomach in the sharp prow. The boats were a mixture: some of wood, caulked (or more strictly "paid") with bitumen, and some of fiberglass and aluminum, apparently taken from the military after the Iran-Iraq war. Each was more than twelve feet long and had a shallow draft like a punt. The rowers sat on the back transom edge of the boat or in some cases stood, handling the oar like a sweep.

We floated out on water much darker and more metallic in sheen than the cloudless autumn sky. We floated past the reeds that grew from yellow roots up green stalks, eight feet long, to thick gray seedheads. In the channels between the reeds you could see very little. A few shards of pollen floated on the surface, the water was so still that it seemed thick and heavy. Some birds—far fewer than earlier travelers described—flew overhead. Not far into the high grass we reached a small circle of open water, in the center of which some men were sitting on a floating bed of reeds. Their island was twenty feet in diameter and on it they had a hut, some green sedge, a buffalo, and a large diesel generator. Once, Marsh Arabs lived on floating platforms year-round; but this was a temporary home for harvesting and fishing. Like almost all of today's Marsh Arabs these men lived on dry land.

Later in the day, we entered another *mudhif*. The structure can last, they say, half a generation, and this was approaching that age. The exterior was bleached like rope in a tropical dockyard. The interior columns had become gray like old sheaves of barley, and the woven walls were splintering so that the space felt like the interior of a threadbare tent, drafty and punctured by sunlight. The sheikhs here were mainly from the Albu Ghenam tribe, and since they had almost all been in Iran, living for fifteen years within a sprawling refugee camp, none of them had proper identity cards, so they could not collect food rations. Their sheikh asked for our support. I told him to give me a list of the people who needed cards. But his nod of agreement was too hasty. I sensed that—because he was illiterate, or because it was too complicated, or because he did not trust us or any government—he wasn't going to produce such a list. So I just undertook to tell the Ministry of Trade representative to be helpful. This earned a grateful smile. Then we returned to the vehicles.

Once the old men had shaken hands and seen us depart, their day was largely over. They would walk slowly back to huts or small reed shelters in mud courtyards. There they would wait out the day until the evening meal, which might be little more than bread and perhaps rice, with no meat or fruit or vegetables. Some would listen to religious sermons and the news on the radio. The older men did not and often could not read, and there was no electricity in the village to power a television.

At dusk, the water buffalo would return to the compound, thrusting out their hairy lips and loose, bristled necks, lowing for fodder, their horns gray, cracked, and mud-caked like ancient pottery. The women would push them toward the corners of the yards and squat beside them, running their fingers down each teat in turn and sometimes dropping a little of the milk on the cow's flat black nose as a reward. Families now had only one or two buffalo each. But that was enough for a glass of the strong sweet milk for dinner.

The women did much of the work: operated a loom if they had one, fetched water, washed, cared for the children, and swept the thick layer of sand that accumulated daily in their huts into the street. But they were almost entirely excluded from education and the political life of the village. Often they were not welcome in the mosque. They were frequently victims of honor killings, forced marriages, and domestic violence. I never met them. But when not looking after the buffalos they were known for composing and reciting poetry—oral poetry, because almost all the women were illiterate—which after ten years of exile in the silent desert now competed with the cacophony of Marsh birds.

Shortly after dark it was time to sleep, since everyone would wake early for ablutions and the dawn prayers. Only in a village with an active mosque did evening prayers provide a firm excuse for the men to gather a second time in a day.

Perhaps a quarter of the province lived in this fashion—though in many cases growing wheat and keeping sheep, rather than relying on fish and buffalo. They did not pay taxes and they received little from the state. Legal punishments were meted out by the elders in the *mudhif;* people seldom used the courts or the police.

I had visited the community in order to learn about their political influence. I concluded that they had next to none. They were too poor and too remote. It was not their young men who were battling in the streets of Amara. If they voted, they were likely to vote for the Islamist groups because they were endorsed by the Ayatollahs and re- flected their conservative social values. The people of Beni Hashim were no more likely than Ali to lead a democratic revolution.

If the villagers would not confront extremist politicians in the capital, we could at least protect them from extremism's worst effects. The villagers were the majority and, although poor and uneducated, they could be strikingly pragmatic and moderate. We introduced a program designed to empower local communities, modeled on a program I had seen in Afghanistan, which was in turn derived from Indonesia.

We asked each village to elect a development committee and gave it five thousand dollars to spend as it wished. The money was given publicly, often on television, so everyone in the community knew how much had been given and to whom. Money still went missing, but it did so at a local level rather than lining the pockets of city contractors and civil servants or padding the salaries of foreign development workers. The development committees were supported and advised by the teams of young Iraqi graduates and monitored by RTI—an international NGO. But the projects the villagers chose reflected their own priorities. They could build clinics, schools, and roads quickly, cheaply, and sustainably, using local labor. And their elected bodies could represent and defend villagers against the politicians in the capital.

But the project—now called "the Maysan rural development program"—would only change rural power structures over years. And it was unpopular in Amara. The education director and other civil servants preferred to build slowly and expensively rather than delegate to villagers; tribal sheikhs wanted the money and patronage; local politicians argued that they needed the resources to develop their own power and popularity. I doubted the program would outlast us.

DEPUTY

*He considered it necessary to introduce efficient government, because he
wanted the region to be peaceful and its inhabitants obedient.*
—*Machiavelli*, The Prince, *Chapter 7*

THURSDAY, NOVEMBER 5, 2003

Five weeks into my time in al-Amara, Molly Phee, a U.S. State Department officer, arrived as governorate coordinator of the province
and I became her deputy. I had been hearing about her for weeks,
first that she'd be my boss, then that she would be transferred to another province while I remained as governorate coordinator. Now
she was again coming to Amara, apparently because the U.S. administration had now decided that a strong U.S. presence was needed
there.

I met Molly in an office in the Green Zone on her way from New
York to Amara. She had been in Iraq for two days and like all new
arrivals was weighed down with body armor. She was slightly shorter
than me and younger than I expected—perhaps only five years older
than me, Chicago-born, with pale Irish skin and amber-colored hair.
Like Bremer she wore a pair of U.S. Army desert boots beneath a
crisp jacket of good leather and black trousers.

She had just been briefed by my predecessor, Major Edward
Melotte. I did not know what he had said—hadn't indeed known he
was going to brief her—and when I tried to describe the province, it

seemed that she had already been told a great deal. She asked me to get hold of a generator from one of the ministries and went on alone to call on senior officials. There had been a great deal of violence in the week of her arrival: there had been a rocket attack against the Al Rashid hotel, our accommodation and disco in the heart of the Green Zone; the Red Cross office had been bombed, killing twelve; the deputy mayor of Baghdad was assassinated; Spanish diplomats had been murdered. Some of Molly's State Department friends had recently decided not to extend their tours in Iraq, shaken by the attacks or disillusioned with the lack of resources for reconstruction. At the monthly meeting with Bremer and the generals that afternoon, Molly took Maysan's seat next to the wiry General Petraeus, who had led the reconstruction of the Kurdish areas. I took an empty seat behind her.

"When are we going to get salary payments for our provincial councils?" asked a Coalition governor. "We are supposed to be supporting the Iraqi government."

Bremer looked down the table and growled, "I thought I already said, 'Make that happen.'"

"Yes, sir," replied the colonel responsible for municipal salaries.

The colonel was a reservist in his late fifties from the rural Midwest. After the meeting I followed him past a table topped with a marquetry picture of the Dome of the Rock, along the upper corridors of the palace. I told him that our treasurer had accepted the salary authorization letter from Baghdad and had acknowledged that there was a line item in the budget but was now insisting that there was no cash in the account. We had informed Baghdad and had heard nothing back. I emphasized that we were already facing assassinations, abductions, and riots and that we would be unable to control the province if the leadership remained unpaid.

The colonel replied that he had passed our salary questions to the Ministry of Finance a few weeks ago. I suggested we visit Finance. We passed the room of the British captain in charge of Iraq's Olympic bid—I guessed it had once been a small bedroom—and arrived in the converted marble bathroom that housed a finance adviser. He was in his mid-twenties but looked fifteen. The colonel explained my request.

"Yup," said the young man, "it's sitting right there on my desk. I'm just kinda busy right now but I'll try to get round to it when I call on the minister next week."

I interrupted. "I am sorry to push this. But you are going to have to take this sheet of paper, you yourself, and walk it personally through every office and stand at people's desks until they sign it, because we cannot wait any longer."

Molly and I rode together in the back of one of the armored vehicles on the three-hour drive along the Tigris, back to Amara. I learned that she had studied on the East Coast and worked on Capitol Hill before joining the State Department; had served for ten years in embassies in the Middle East—Amman, Cairo, and Kuwait—and spoke good Arabic. She knew many of the senior U.S. officials in Baghdad and Washington. She had been trapped in New York working on UN resolutions for weeks after her appointment to Maysan.

I did not know what Molly expected of her new job in Amara, arriving to find the police chief recently assassinated and no governor or provincial council in place. I reported that we had to make decisions on the budget of the local ministry of finance; on altering Marsh Arab fishing methods; on privatizing the sugar cane factory; on choosing a new police chief; and on placating a violent Islamist militia. And that that was only the work of a single day. But I did not think it was my job to emphasize how unsuitable our experience—mine and hers—could be for this kind of administration. We knew something about the region—Molly much more than me. But diplomats like us were normally based in a comfortable embassy compound, rarely managing anything more than a couple of embassy secretaries. We had been trained in an institutional culture that emphasized prudence, compromise, and careful drafting; not the bold executive decisions required to govern a semi-war zone. Fortunately for her posting to a British-dominated team, Molly turned out to have a very British sense of humor.

Ten days later, Bremer announced that we would transfer sovereignty to the Iraqi government on June 30, 2004. The CPA was growing larger, more idealistic, and more bureaucratic. So far, I had been a lone administrator, shepherding some development projects, maintaining security through compromises, and managing local crises. I had imagined this would continue through a long and gradual transfer to an elected Iraqi government. No handover date had been defined. But now I was to be part of a much larger team, implementing a plan from Baghdad, and handover would be in seven months.

Our overall objective was becoming less and less clear. Baghdad was still determined not "to bring back Saddam's Iraq or to create an Iranian-style theocracy" and talked about a democratic state that represented the majority and protected the interests of minorities. But we no longer had time to hold elections before we left, and we were less and less comfortable imposing our values. Although we had colonial powers, we were not colonial officers. A mid-nineteenth district officer on the northwest frontier of British India might play chiefs off against each other, manipulate, cajole, plead, and bluff, and open fire on rioters and looters, and if the chief challenged his authority he could lead a raid or bribe him with bags of gold. But the new breed of administrators disapproved of such methods, and it was not clear what we were supposed to do if the Coalition's interests and objectives clashed with those of our Iraqi successors.

Within a fortnight Molly and I had settled into an almost invariable routine. Each morning we met on the path that led from the showers blocks to our accommodation. We collapsed together into the back of our armored vehicle and, if we were awake enough, discussed what to say in the morning meeting. Usually we just sat there, staring through the inch-and-a-half-thick bulletproof windows at the drab winter scene: the tall, smoke-belching minarets of the brick factories and the workers crawling over the tar-stained roofs. Most of these men were in debt slavery to the factory owners, and the fumes cracked their teeth and wrecked their lungs. Their life expectancy was rumored to be twenty-five.

In the office, we woke to fresh coffee that Molly had imported from Kuwait. A.J. the finance officer, wearing under his linen jacket a curious faded drill shirt that appeared to be almost First World War issue, would open the 8:30 meeting peering through tortoise-shell spectacles at sheaves of paper. The rest of the team growled, blaming him for contract delays and lack of money. The real fault lay in Basra.

Molly—who had taken on the burden of running an office that was now, with the bodyguards and the civil affairs team, approaching a hundred people—brought order to our idiosyncratic and sometimes arbitrary procedures. She told the team about debates in the UN and programs for senior visitors, explained our legal powers, chased requests from local politicians, publicized scholarship schemes, tried to acquire and produce pamphlets on civic education.

After the meeting, at nine, Molly would open her office door and step back at the sight of dozens of fat flies lazily circumnavigating her desk. We tried air-conditioning and a commercial spray and daily swept the black carcasses off her window sills. But in the next meeting in her office, our Iraqi guests would again be moving their hands gracefully through the air to brush the flies from their faces. We tried blue bowls of poison paste and, when that failed, military fogging spray sent by the British Battle Group. These methods made us sick but had little effect on the flies.

At ten on most days, we crossed the road to the provincial council building for a two-hour meeting with an Iraqi council or committee. Molly would sit at the tiny table and in quiet but precise Arabic rebut complaints. I had tended to focus on local issues; she emphasized general principles and the international and legal context and used her background at the UN and in Washington to lay out the exact status of the occupation, explained why decisions were not coming from Baghdad, and offered insight into the political discussions at the center. She stressed that the invasion was an opportunity for the Shia to take power in Iraq for the very first time, and emphasized that they should do so with respect for minorities.

Because Molly spoke good Arabic, she was not beguiled by the equivocations of the translators and could hear disagreements without mediation. Thus when the translator suggested Abu Ahmed wanted a "legal government," she heard that he was in fact pushing hard for a *"Wilayat-e-faqih,"* or theocratic government. She adjusted quickly even to the Marsh Arab dialect and because she carefully read Arabic publications, she found things that I missed—for example, that an Arab translator had inserted into a USAID-sponsored pamphlet on democracy, "Iran is the most perfect example of democracy in the world."

At the end of her first ten o'clock meeting with the supervisory committee, the cleric Sheikh Rahim approached her and growled, "Miss Molly, we are delighted you are here. This is a Muslim province and we prefer people to dress respectably. Can I please suggest that in future you cover your head?"

"I am a respectable woman." Molly replied. "My father would be insulted to hear you suggest otherwise. I am a Christian from another culture and in our culture respectable women do not cover their heads." There was no law in Iraq making women cover their heads. And she knew that if she covered her head every woman in the province would be made to do so because their men would say, "See, even the American governor covers her head." Nevertheless, Maysan was becoming more conservative. In September, there were still women who wore bright scarves in the streets, but by November almost all went out covered from head to foot in a full black *abaya*. And Seyyed Asad, the once-kidnapped Sadr cleric, refused to meet Molly unless she covered her head.

During the afternoon we received individual Iraqis. At six, the last visitor would leave for evening prayers and we would spend three or four hours working on e-mails, missing the evening meal in camp. The thousands of foreigners in the Green Zone in Baghdad and in Basra, who worked in everything from the police to tourism, kept being replaced. Each new appointee sent e-mails to the provinces asking for support for their pet projects. Molly picked up on an e-mail from the U.S. Marines who were running the Iraqi Army recruitment, convinced them to provide a thousand places for soldiers from Maysan, and invited them down to site one of their recruitment centers in the province. She found that hundreds of millions were available for the Marsh Arabs and that foreign experts were discussing reflooding the marshes, but that few Marsh Arabs had been included in the discussions. So she formed a Marsh Arab council to represent their interests, and she pressed to create a micro-credit scheme for small businesses.

We worked fourteen- to sixteen-hour days and were seldom able to take a day off. I no longer had time for a run with the soldiers every evening. I was concerned that we would become stale if we kept up this pace for the next seven and a half months. And although our operations were becoming more orderly, we were still not entirely in control. The bodyguard team often seemed to be on weapons training when Molly wanted to go somewhere; Baghdad refused to acknowledge or respond to our increasingly detailed requests for information; Basra still delayed contracts for weeks. And although Molly emphasized again and again that she did not "like surprises," all the other parts of our rickety system—Washington, London, the Battle Group, Baghdad, our own team—still failed to tell us things we needed to know. Again and again, locals knew about new initiatives, rulings, or operations before we did. Our staff continued to complain that the laundry stank of kerosene and the cleaners washed the dishes in industrial floor bleach.

In the vehicles on the drive back, Molly and I were almost too tired to speak but often, as soon as we reached camp, Molly would go into a meeting with the British colonel. Sensing that as an American civilian and a woman she could be shut out of military issues, she insisted on dealing directly with the colonel rather than with his political officer. She got to know all the company commanders. She controlled her temper when a British major told her that women were a waste of time on local councils. If she thought the Battle Group was shirking its duty by failing to disarm a militia group or by ignoring the looting of electric pylons, she never failed to tell them. None of this was easy in a masculine, military British environment. But the colonel also grasped the importance of the relationship and Molly's approach produced results.

The military had been threatening, when I arrived, to remove our civil affairs team and "civilianize" development. They had ignored my complaints that we had nobody to replace them. I had taken it up to the director of operations in Baghdad and the general, and when that failed I had told the team to aim to close their portfolios by the end of December. Molly reopened the issue, and convinced Baghdad to keep our team and to increase it till we had one officer covering each ministry.

THE PATHS THAT LEAD TO DESTRUCTION

Men never do good except through necessity; but when they have the free-dom to choose and can do as they please, everything immediately becomes confused and disorderly.

—Machiavelli, Discourses, *Book I, Chapter 3*

We had money. The civil affairs team continued to reconstruct schools, clinics, prisons, and youth centers. Iraqi ministries and district councils were more involved in our decisions and the provincial council had more autonomy. The temporary police chief was increasingly confident; the agreement after the assassination had held, and there had been no more killings. In short, things were improving. Some of this was the result of our policies but it was mostly due to the people of Maysan. Our influence was always limited: the CPA staff was small, the police much too weak to impose security, and the Coalition forces were few. Molly and I could not map, predict, or control social change. Yet from a thick clay of custom, Shia faith, historical opportunity, and leadership, a new kind of citizen was emerging: a citizen who was not too delusive, aggressive, or self-sacrificing; who was making choices and getting on with others; who showed a willingness to work within the law; who found ways not to know about the paths that led to disintegration; who chose to overlook the fecund potential for anarchy.

But not long after Molly's arrival in Amara, at the end of the morning meeting with the civil affairs team, we heard the sound of chanting in the street. The door to the conference room opened and police Sergeant-Major Hassan beckoned me out. I made my apologies and walked down the path with J.D., our large British gate commander, in step beside me. He had dealt with a number of demonstrations before my arrival, sometimes by laughing people out of their grievances and once, it was rumored, by walking out swinging a big stick, and I had grown fond of hearing him joking with visitors in a cockney-Marsh Arab argot.

At the metal gate the policemen were jostling to peer through the little sliding window. The chants were much louder. J.D. said that a couple of bricks had been thrown earlier but none in the last ten minutes. The crowd were probably Sadrists. I briefed the bodyguard leader, asked the policemen to open the door, and walked out, with four of the bodyguard team.

The green banners of the demonstrators were as large as sails. I could not read the zinc-white calligraphy that ran from right to left. There were perhaps fifty people in the front row and a couple of hundred behind them; despite the sun, many wore thick anoraks and heavy plastic sandals on their feet; their trousers were frayed, their hair slicked back. They looked as though they came from the worst areas of the city. They stopped chanting when they saw us, and a young cleric standing to one side, in full turban and robes, turned away from me. I did not want to stand around too long.

"A salaam aleikum," I said loudly. "I am Seyyed Rory from the CPA. I would like to take three of your representatives to discuss things. Please choose three."

Someone shouted, "Don't trust him." Four people were pushed forward.

"How about four? We are the leaders," said one of them.

"Fine. You four, come with me." We turned round and walked briskly back into the compound, followed by the four men. The gates slammed shut behind us and there was silence. I explained to the men that they would have to be searched. An unshaven man with a dark face, bloodshot eyes, and large pupils waved his hands and refused and seemed from his erratic hand gestures and unfocused gaze to be using opium, like many of the urban poor. I told him that if he refused to be searched, he would be sent outside again. A short man in a shell-suit asked me to be patient, then he huddled with the group and emerged to say, "Okay, we will be searched." They were carrying nothing.

I took the short man by the hand and we walked up the path in silence. The Tigris was on our left, the water muddier than usual, sluggish and brown. There were some small orange flowers on the bushes. I always enjoyed the two-hundred-yard walk to and from the gate, a rare opportunity to get out of the office and walk in the sun.

Since the morning meeting had ended, I sat them in the main room and asked whether they wanted tea or coffee.

"We are not here to drink," snapped the unshaven man with the bloodshot eyes. "We are here to have our demands met."

I told the interpreter to bring tea and sat down. I had not slept well and I wondered if I looked exhausted. I was hoping the tea would wake me up.

"I am looking forward to hearing your demands," I said.

"We will only talk to the new head of the office," replied the unshaven man.

"I am afraid the head of the office is otherwise engaged. I am the deputy head of the office."

"We will talk to no one except the head of the office."

"In which case I am afraid you will be waiting a long time. She is about to go to Baghdad."

There was another quiet discussion and the short conciliator said, "Okay, we will discuss with you if you agree to take our opinions to the head of the office and Mr. Bremer."

I agreed.

The unshaven man began to read from his notebook. "The occupying forces have proved that greed, cruelty, and ambition are their guiding ideals; that insensitivity and stupidity are the only qualifications for your administrators; cowardice and pusillanimity for your soldiers; stinginess and prejudice for your development workers. Large and small puppets on the hands of the grasping fists of the elders of Zion . . ." It was clear that, despite his opium-shot eyes and shabby jacket, he had received some kind of education.

"Will you excuse me," I said. "I must see what has happened to the tea." I smiled and walked out the door and, to wake up, went for a walk around the yard.

A British officer asked if I had a moment to talk. He wanted to discuss a British rear-gunner who, half an hour earlier, failing to duck when the Land Rover he was standing on passed under a low bar in town, had been knocked out of his vehicle. The officer had been in our compound when he heard the news, and upon learning that there was no transport available, had cast procedure aside and run alone out of the gate, where an Iraqi driver had given him a lift to the scene. The soldier was lying on a carpet of blood, and the other soldiers were staring at him, paralyzed, as a crowd gathered. The officer confirmed that the medics were on their way, posted sentries to block the road, and tried to resuscitate the soldier, but it was clear that he was going to die. He asked the other men what the soldier's first name was because he wanted to reassure him, but the rear-gunner was an eighteen-year-old who had been in Iraq only a few days and had just been assigned to the platoon, so no one knew, and he died. It was the first casualty of the battle group's five-month tour. The officer remembered with gratitude the Iraqi who had given him a lift and with anger an Iraqi in the crowd who had spat at the blood.

When I returned to the room the unshaven man continued where he had left off: "Enslaving our women; sucking red mercury from our ground like leeches on the arteries of the Iraqi nation: impious, impertinent, insane . . ."

"I am so sorry," I interrupted. "I do not have much time. I have a meeting with some clerics at nine. I wonder if it might be possible for you to tell me your demands."

The unshaven man looked irritated but he flipped through the notebook.

"Number one. The Coalition has done nothing for this province. It is stealing the oil revenue of Iraq. There is enough revenue to provide for everyone yet we are in penury."

I explained that Iraq was exporting one and a half million barrels a day and at current oil prices that was about fourteen billion dollars a year, of which ten billion was spent on subsidies and ration cards. He quibbled on the figures and I conceded that the revenue would be more if the oil price rose.

"Number two. We demand construction, basic services. There is no work in this province." He sounded increasingly angry.

"We have done a great deal of construction in the province."

"You have done nothing. Everything is lies." And then he shouted some more things that the translator did not translate. I asked what he had said.

"He is talking about a Jewish conspiracy."

I led them into the corridor where we had pinned up the balance sheets of 240 construction projects. I took them down the list of schools. "Al-Uzeyr primary, complete, seventeen thousand dollars. Al-Amara Girls Secondary, complete, thirty-four thousand dollars." I kept them there till they had seen the prisons and the law courts, the youth centers, the pontoon bridges, the clinics. They didn't seem to care.

We went back to the main room and Karim entered with the tray of tea. But the demonstrators refused to touch the cups he set down, and demanded they be put back on the tray. This was an insult. I took two of their cups and drank them myself.

"Number three," continued the unshaven man, "there is no employment. We demand jobs. Number four, you must give back our red mercury." Red mercury was believed to be a substance worth more than gold. We were supposed to have built our offices over the deposits and when we were not smuggling Iraqi women into the international sex trade we were smuggling out red mercury. I never met anyone in the Coalition who had ever heard of red mercury before they came to Iraq. I later learned that it was a mythical ingredient for a new generation of nuclear weapon. I didn't believe it even existed.

"Number five, you are planning to appoint an entirely undemocratic provincial council. We demand that Mr. al-Musawi is appointed to the provincial council . . ." I had never heard of al-Musawi.

"Number six . . ."

"Can I answer these one by one?" I asked.

"Not yet," said the small man who had so far acted as the conciliator. He said that he would never cooperate with the Coalition or take money from them; they were an evil force. He was an educated man, he had graduated from high school, and now look at what he was wearing. He gestured to his track pants, which had "Reeboock" printed on the side. He said that without immediate full employment the entire province would go up in flames.

"Can I answer your complaints now?"

"No. We have heard enough from you," said the unshaven man.

"In which case," I said, sounding angrier than I felt, "perhaps you should leave." I stood up. And so did they.

"We will gather ten thousand in the streets," the unshaven man shouted. The others took him by the arm.

"Thank you," said the short conciliator.

"You are Hitler," added the unshaven man.

The short man asked me if we could have a private word. I took him aside into a room. He sat down opposite me, fixed me with his dark eyes, and began to mutter something quickly in Arabic. As he did so, he stroked the knuckles of his right hand down his cheek and twitched his hand in front of his crotch, loudly sucking in his breath and groaning. I said I didn't understand. Again he stroked his cheek, gestured at his genitals and made what I took to be a sound of pain, this time miming taking off his pants. I told him to wait and called in an interpreter.

"He says, sir, that when he was shaving his pubic hair this morning . . . *na'am* . . . *na'am*" the interpreter said, nodding and waiting for the next phrase, "with the razor blade . . . he cut his penis . . . the tip of his penis. Off. And he wonders what he should do."

"Has he tried the hospital?"

"He is going to take down his trousers. He wants to show you his penis now."

"Thank him for the offer. Tell him it would be better to go immediately to the hospital."

"He says he has no money. Can you give him money for the doctor?"

"Tell him the CPA is not authorized to provide money to individuals. Our funds are for communities." I took a twenty-dollar bill from my wallet. "Tell him it is a present. And tell him in return to make sure everyone goes home."

The short man took the money with a smile and walked outside. Within ten minutes the crowd had gone.

IMPORT SUBSTITUTION INDUSTRIALIZATION

When difficult times put you under pressure you will not have enough time to take harsh measures, and any benefits you confer will not help you because they will be considered to be done unwillingly, and so you will receive no credit for them.

—*Machiavelli,* The Prince, *Chapter 8*

We had, as the demonstrators said, failed to solve unemployment: perhaps 70 percent of the province was unemployed and unless we created economic growth there would be more political unrest. But how could we create growth in a monstrously contorted and corrupt economy, muddled by Saddam with tariffs and subsidies, monopolies and wage-support, credit and exchange controls, and dominated by state-owned enterprises employing tens of thousands in the manufacture of a few expensive and shoddy goods to be scattered on the shelves of state-owned department stores under the care of obese and insolent shop assistants in uniform?[4] Saddam had gained popularity by handing lucrative jobs to his allies and had consumed the national budget by giving free food rations to the people and subsidizing electricity, power, and gas. Iraqi diesel had become so cheap from

---

[4]We were never formally briefed on the Iraq economy so it was difficult for us to know why in Maysan—which had a fertile soil and excellent climate—Saddam had not introduced new crops and better irrigation but had instead built factories. Perhaps he had been worried about markets, foreign exchange, security, and sanctions. Or perhaps he believed that industrialists ploughed their profits back into their industries, whereas peasant-farmers had spare time on their hands and land-owning sheikhs wasted their income on new silk robes. Or perhaps he was just copying what almost everyone else was doing in the developing world in the seventies.

subsidies that black-marketeers made a handsome profit smuggling it even into the other oil-producing Gulf States. All the defenses of the planned economy—the border controls, the customs office, the statistical office, and the penal codes—had been destroyed by the Coalition invasion, and it was no longer possible to protect Iraq against foreign imports. The factories could not sell their goods, the workers stopped turning up, and the plants were looted: every generator and machine had been removed and either smuggled to a neighboring country or sold as scrap.

The ministry directors were little help. That they blamed everyone else was not surprising: what was astonishing was how quickly they seemed to conclude that there was nothing they could do, as though their responsibilities as senior officials, their heroic efforts to maintain the decrepit infrastructure of the province through decades of sanctions and arbitrary terror, had been only a distraction from their true desire, which was to abandon their thousands of employees and detailed plans and take on the role of bewildered witnesses. We were often forced to perform tasks that belonged to the ministries. In November, for example, when an electricity shortage left Amara with only four hours of power a day, the ministry director confessed helplessly that according to the national dispatch center, Maysan was receiving a steady sixty megawatts—more than it had under the old regime—and he could not convince Baghdad that there was any problem at all.

The civil affairs team made an hourly record of power in the substation, and proved that we were lucky to receive sixteen megawatts and that the dispatch center had conspired with Nasiriyah and Basra to steal our electricity. With Molly's permission, I sent a deputation to Baghdad, paid for ministry officials to sit in the substations in Nasiriyah and Amara, bought them satellite telephones, and told them to report whenever the power dropped below sixty megawatts. Within four days we had a steady supply for twelve rather than four hours a day. But not everything could be solved so easily.

In September, the civil affairs team in Maysan had tried to restart the state-owned factories. They sent a proposal to the international donors' conference for Iraq, held in Madrid, consisting of a single sheet of paper that asked for "3 to 5 million dollars" for the local plastic factory and "4 to 8 million dollars" for the paper and pulp factory. Their aim was to "improve security by creating employment and," they added, in a phrase that implied they shared some of Saddam's economic theory, to "reduce the need to import from overseas." The donor conference understandably refused to give ten million dollars on the basis of a single sheet of paper.

The civil affairs team then considered the sugar cane factory that stood near Majar Al Kebir. Once the employer of thousands of people with overseas subsidiaries, processing units, sugar export agencies, and thousands of acres of plantation; it was now a half-looted shell: generators broken, camels grazing in the fields and destroying what remained of the crop. Refurbishing the machinery would cost a million dollars.

A consultant on a visit from Basra announced that world sugar-cane prices had collapsed in the face of sugar beet, that the plantations would take years to recover, and that the plant would never be competitive. My military predecessor, therefore, proposed converting Maysan's farmers to high-value fruit "such as Kiwi" and making the sugar-cane factory into a fruit-packaging plant that could sell direct to British supermarkets. He presented this idea to Andy Bearpark, who had worked with Mrs. Thatcher and supported privatization. Andy referred to the Major as a "bloody Stalinist."

A million dollars was a great deal even for our bloated budgets and I understood that only a specialist, working for months, would be able to come up with a serious plan for reinvestment or privatization. In the meantime, we continued to pay the salaries of the three thousand workers and the factory remained closed. But I never quite escaped the impression that I ought to have been doing something more radical, and our local confusion was echoed in Baghdad.

The American economists in the Green Zone wanted dramatic reform. Bremer had plans to privatize the banking system and all the state-owned enterprises. He had already abolished customs tariffs, and introduced a new currency and a new central bank. He intended to save five billion dollars a year by "monetizing the food basket"—giving Iraqis cash instead of food and getting the government out of supplying rations—and another five billion by cutting the oil subsidies. Cutting subsidies on diesel would eliminate the black market that financed most of Iraq's crime.

But none of the reforms were ever implemented. Ninety percent of Iraqis, in every poll, refused to give up their ration card system, and every attempt to raise fuel prices resulted in riots. Taxes were not collected, utility bills were not paid. Privatization did not occur; the ration basket was not "monetized," and the fuel subsidies were left in place. Iraq was considered too unstable for radical economic reforms.

Our economic policy, therefore, was little more than tinkering: supporting the few surviving industries, repairing buildings, and inventing jobs. We hoped such activities would be enough to reconstruct the province, win popularity, and stop political extremism. But it was rare to find a project that fulfilled all three objectives. Many of our most expensive ventures, though beneficial, won us no thanks: water purification projects cost millions but were mostly underground and produced water that, although safer, looked the same as the old water. We were blamed for the disrepair of schools that Saddam had taken the credit for building, and got no credit for refurbishing them; no one saw the equipment we bought for ministry offices or thanked us for providing a municipal rubbish dump. Even the most popular projects—large bridges, rural regeneration grants, or mass employment schemes—seemed to have little influence on whether people voted for armed militias.

In November, we were delighted to hear that the U.S. taxpayers would provide 18.3 billion dollars for civilian reconstruction: nearly a thousand dollars for every man, woman, and child in Iraq. This, Bremer said, was the largest single foreign development investment ever made, exceeding in annual terms the Marshall plan for post-war Europe. The ministries had already made provisional allocations. We in the provinces were given less than three weeks to suggest how to spend the money. Baghdad needed the proposals in early December so they could clear Congress and be signed by the President at the beginning of January, with a view to dispensing the money by spring. Admiral Nash, who had been in charge of naval procurement, was brought in to run the program because, as Andy said, "He buys aircraft carriers and is the only man in the world who really understands spending billions of dollars."

Only 60 percent of the population in Maysan had access to drinking water and sewerage, so I asked George Butler to produce a thirty-million-dollar draft plan for water in a week. George, who was a water engineer, said that no sensible plan could be drawn up in less than six months and refused to try, so I turned to a visiting civilian engineer for the task and asked for similar drafts from the civil affairs officers dealing with electricity and roads. A week later I sent a glossy document to the Green Zone outlining our ambitious projects. When we received no reply, Molly suggested I travel to Baghdad.

In the Green Zone, discovering that our province had been allocated only 2 percent of the total budget, I called on all the senior foreign advisers in the ministries, whom I had met a month earlier, and told them that Maysan, which none of them had visited, was the poorest and one of the least stable provinces in Iraq and convinced them to let me see the breakdowns of their budgets; they may have regretted this later. I returned to Amara after three days of meetings, having increased our allocation to 110 million dollars, mostly by diverting money from neighboring provinces. I had received a pledge from Andy Bearpark's office that our per capita allocation would be tripled to three hundred dollars. I had also extracted promises from the departments of irrigation, police, electricity, and oil for another 98 million dollars. The triumph, however, was partial: new management, congressional inquiries, fresh tenders, arcane subcontracting, and extravagant security meant that a year later Maysan had received almost none of the money it had been promised.

In November, the refinery workers went on strike, just as the kidnapped cleric Seyyed Hassan had warned, because they had learned that the CPA was erroneously paying Basra workers twice their normal salaries. There was no money in our budget to increase our salaries to the new Basra level and CPA Basra refused to reduce for fear of unrest. The workers were illegally picketing the factory, and if the strike continued there would be no more fuel in the province and all the needs would have to be met by importing fuel from Basra. Shortages and riots would follow. At this point I took my first leave, returning home to Scotland.

I returned a week later on a plane to Kuwait with some middle-aged Irish and Scottish engineering consultants and CPA South's new tourism adviser. These men, who were based in Basra and had worked in many countries, were steady, slow-moving, and phlegmatic. They were good at telecommunication technology and electric networks and urban planning but not very interested in sheikhs and politics. In accordance with CPA instructions, they went by bus to spend a day and a night at the Kuwait Hilton beach resort, but because our Amara office was tiny—a tenth the size of the Basra office—and we were short of time, I took a taxi to the border, persuaded a Humvee to give me a lift across no-man's land, and met my bodyguard team at the other side.

Kuwait's neat bougainvillea and clean desert colonnaded with electricity pylons gave way at the border to craters filled with stagnant water, burnt-out trucks, and a leprous morass of rotting garbage. Just before the confluence of the Tigris and the Euphrates we passed a village demolished by artillery fire and an abandoned school in whose ruins lived two hundred families, recently returned from Iran. The electricity pylons by the roadside had been bent like paper clips by looters, and what remained of their copper wires trailed along the ground: various security companies had employed tribal sheikhs to protect the lines but since they invariably chose the wrong sheikhs, the number of attacks against the pylons had increased. As we drove through Al Uzeyr, someone threw a stone at the side of the car.

At the outskirts of Amara there were no lines at the gas stations and everyone in the office seemed cheerful. I asked them how they had solved the strike. They said they had sent a company of British troops to the refinery and asked for support from the Prince of the Marshes. The Prince had arrived and ordered the strikers to return to work. When their leader refused, the Prince knocked the man down with his fist, his men laid about the principals with their rifle-butts, and two of the strikers were dragged away in the Prince's pickup trucks.

"Miraculously," I was told, "everyone has now returned to work."

The Prince had clubbed and abducted while a company of British soldiers stood by and the public would interpret this as support for the Prince and his arbitrary methods. I was furious with this decision. It was true that the strike was creating a security problem, that the pickets were technically illegal, and that without fuel there would have been riots and criticism from Baghdad. I had always been prepared to be polite to tribal sheikhs, give money to prominent clerics, and cut some complicated deals. But this latest incident was unacceptable. We wanted to be remembered positively in the province; we should have been setting an example and accepting the consequences of the strike. But perhaps I felt this more strongly because the Prince was involved.

JOBS

If one wants to keep up a reputation for generosity one must spend lav-
ishly and ostentatiously . . . You can be much more generous giving away
what does not belong to you or your subjects.
                    —*Machiavelli,* The Prince, *Chapter 16*

The next demonstration at our gate was against the existing employment scheme, theoretically run by the Ministry of Municipalities and
Public Works but in practice through a tense collaboration between
the Prince of the Marshes and the Sadr office. The demonstrators
believed that, of the thousands of jobs, only a few hundred actually
existed; that the civil servants collected salaries for ghost individuals
and the few genuine slots went to their political supporters. This
was true. The demonstrators claimed that the Coalition was the
only trustworthy body in the province and begged us to start a new
scheme and run the whole thing directly. This would test our capacity, take more authority away from the ministry directors, further
undermine our successors, and generally run counter to all good
development practice. But political unrest was spreading and we
needed to calm the streets, create employment, and win back credibility for ourselves so I told the demonstrators that we would announce our plans in a fortnight and produce the first jobs in six
weeks. They insisted on a note. I wrote one. Everyone stood up, smiling broadly and shaking my hand; it was as though we had just closed
a Wall Street deal.

The province was now waiting for us to deliver. Since all our officers were busy we gave the task to Chris, a forty-five-year-old British major. Chris had never run an organization of this size before and he had only been in Iraq for a few days; he would have to process thousands of applicants and could offer only twenty-five hundred jobs to ten or even fifty times as many unemployed. If the process went wrong or did not produce results within six weeks, we could expect more riots.

Everyone wanted the patronage power over twenty-five hundred families: the tribal sheikhs told us to let the tribes (by which they meant the sheikhs) decide whom to employ; Seyyed Issa, the district council leader from the Marsh Arab area of Beni Hashim, insisted we should leave it to the district councils; and the union of unemployed laborers suggested we choose from the union. The brother of the Prince of the Marshes, the alternative councils, and the Ministry of Municipalities, who were theoretically already controlling seven thousand casual laborers, were furious not to be able to control more.

The work was unskilled, so qualifications were irrelevant, but jobs given to the wrong people would be worse than no jobs at all. If we gave too many jobs to the Albu Muhammad tribe, the Beni Lam would muster; too many jobs in the villages and the urban poor would riot. I therefore proposed that we enter the applicants' names into a computer and select the workers at random.

We wanted projects that required little equipment. I suggested planting trees but Chris said that there was no irrigation. When I pushed to refurbish the souk, he convinced me that this was specialist work, better undertaken by a contractor. He decided instead to demolish the buildings that had been bombed during the war. He would get the workers to take them down brick by brick and the rubble could be used for filling roads. By the end of the second week he had ordered hundreds of spades, sledgehammers, and wheelbarrows.

This project would cost us millions and we would be paying the workers directly, not through contractors. Molly was not permitted to sign off on more than fifty thousand dollars at a time and the CPA required elaborate tender and bidding procedures so she and Tony, our finance officer, designed a new financial management system and, with considerable rigor and charm, convinced Basra to let us run it. Eric, our newly arrived IT specialist from a quiet town in the Midwest, stayed up to build a computer database for the lottery. Kyle, a twenty-five-year-old administrative officer from Virginia, called in the newspaper editors, and, two days before the date of the job registration, put advertisements in the local papers and on television, telling people to muster at a site on the southern edge of town.

The night before the registration, I was summoned to the base and was gestured to a plastic chair at the end of the colonel's office. Facing me in a line were the colonel, his adjutant, and his company commanders. The company commanders were usually based a couple of hours' drive outside the camp—one covering the north, one the south, and one in the bandit town of Majar—so it was unusual to see them gathered together. The colonel looked angry and so did his officers.

"This is an Orders group," he began, "to talk about the job registration tomorrow. I don't care about politics; I am just a simple soldier." He was not: he was an Oxford graduate whose officers kept him well informed about local politics. "But it seems to me there has been a stupid decision and we are going to have to come up with a workable new plan. Ideally we would cancel it but I understand you have briefed the population that this is going to happen?"

I nodded.

"So we better find a way of doing it without too much loss of life."

The ops officer—a young captain—began to read rapidly from his formal briefing, nervous perhaps at being surrounded by so many senior officers. Everything had been worked out, down to the grid points on the map: the registration point would now be moved from the southern part of town to the stadium in the northwest. I did not like the idea of an angry mob of unemployed men marching through the center of town to the new site, and I was furious that the colonel was trying, on the final night, to change a scheme that the Battle Group had known about for weeks, and that we were funding with two million dollars. I said all this but there was little that I could do. He had over a thousand soldiers, including his own infantry battalion, companies from two armored regiments, and a raft of military hardware including helicopters, which made him, as he often reminded me, the sheikh of "the biggest tribe in the province." Without his support I was powerless.

I reminded the colonel that there would be riots if we did not provide jobs and asked how we were supposed to inform everyone twelve hours before the event that the registration site had been moved.

"Not our problem," he replied.

I explained that with people on leave, I had a staff of eight. I didn't see how we could reprint hundreds of fliers and posters and distribute them all over the province before the next morning. I was prepared to provide hundreds of dollars to find and pay extra Iraqi assistants—although I wasn't sure how I would account for this—but he would have to provide at least two platoons to assist in printing and distribution.

When the colonel replied that the scheme was misconceived and that Chris was out of his depth, I became angry and defended Chris. The company commanders glared at me but said nothing. Finally, we agreed that the registration would proceed, the site would be moved, and the colonel would support us in publicizing the new site. Back at the office, I told the staff to start rewriting, printing, and photocopying new leaflets and posters. It rained all night. The two platoons turned up to distribute the fliers, a group of Iraqi street children helped to plaster them up, and we were able to get the new information out over most of the province by dawn.

The winter morning was damp; the gray sky was low, seeping into the fabric of the tents. Fresh drops hung on the metal struts of the military vehicles and settled in a thick mist over the camouflage paint. The heavy two-propeller Chinook, with its thumping rhythm as it crossed the fence on patrol, was a black silhouette half-dissolved into the fog, and my shadow was hardly visible. Outside the stadium fence, clutching the bars, were hundreds waiting for the registration. I ran up the banks of seats in the arena with the bodyguard team behind me and, emerging on the roof, saw, beneath the cloud that shrouded the tops of the one-story houses, hundreds of men in flip-flops, with their trousers rolled up, splashing through silver patches of groundwater toward the stadium. British troops in riot gear, visors on their helmets; sticks in their hand; rifles over their backs, marched out to meet them and made the Iraqis squat in three large groups some distance from the gate. We needed to protect against suicide bombers who were now targeting job registration lines elsewhere but we did not want to anger the crowd by being too aggressive.

Two young British snipers were leaning over the wall beside me, watching boys playing knee-deep in a puddle. One of the snipers fiddled with the loose end of the Hessian bandage that he had wrapped round his rifle, and the other stroked the top of his telescopic sight as though it were a lucky charm. A loud "good morning" rang through the air and I turned to see Chris running his hand over his cropped hair. He was the only soldier without a beret on, perhaps to show that he was not entirely controlled by the colonel's orders, and, despite his solemn expression, his mouth kept twitching with excitement.

The sniper passed me his telescopic sight, through which I could watch the soldiers dragging queue-bargers out of the line: some Iraqis, as they dodged the soldiers, lost their shoes in the mud but everyone seemed good humored. Haider was standing outside the perimeter, waving, and one of the organizers of the demonstrations was marching up and down in a shiny three-piece suit, carrying a clipboard, ostentatiously monitoring the registration. A British ser-geant told him to step outside the perimeter. He protested for a mo-ment and then he turned his back, returned to the road, and stood watching from a distance. As the growling sergeants continued to

The author in a meeting of the provincial council.
Guardian Newspapers Ltd. 2004

Community leaders in a district council meeting in Maysan.

The headquarters of the CPA (formerly Saddam's Republican Palace).
Courtesy of Edward Melotte

Meeting of the governorate team leaders in Baghdad. CPA Chief Paul Bremer is in the foreground; Barbara Contini, governorate coordinator of Dhi Qar, is on the far left; Molly Phee, governorate coordinator of Maysan, is in the second row wearing sunglasses; the author is immediately to her right; CPA Director of Operations Andy Bearpark is behind Bremer's right shoulder. *Courtesy of Rory Stewart*

Captain Lovell of the Maysan civil affairs team cuts a ceremonial cake.

Charlotte "Charlie" Morris of the Maysan civil affairs
team meets with local representatives.

The author with Seyyed Issa in front of his *mudhif*.
Guardian Newspapers Ltd. 2004

Marsh Arab children.
Courtesy of Edward Melotte

The author, Molly Phee, and Charlotte "Charlie" Morris at a meeting in a *mudhif* in the marshes. *Courtesy of Rory Stewart*

In a Marsh Arab canoe near Musherrah.
Courtesy of Rory Stewart

Crowds being controlled by British soldiers during
the job registration in the Amara stadium.

The covered souk in Amara.
Courtesy of Edward Melotte

A crowd of
demonstrators at
the gates of the
CPA in Amara.

British military Land
Rovers drive into the CPA
compound in Amara after
a day of riot control.

The director of archeology
in Dhi Qar with Sumerian
pots confiscated from looters.
Courtesy of Micah Garen

Italian troops at the handover ceremony at the Ziggurat of Ur.
Courtesy of Micah Garen

The handover ceremony at Ur. (From second on the left) Italian General Corrado
Dalzini; Barbara Contini, governorate coordinator of Dhi Qar; Sabri Badr
Rumaiath, governor of Dhi Qar; and the author. Behind Governor Rumaiath
is Major General Andrew Stewart. *Courtesy of Micah Garen*

keep the columns apart, Chris, watching the soldiers doing something they had never done before in an alien country with no common language and doing it well, finally allowed himself a full grin. The light glowed on the left cheeks of the applicants. I counted three times: it seemed there were a thousand in two columns lining up at the entrance and twice as many sitting down in the wedges. One group began a song and then stopped, perhaps at the sight of a passing *mullah*.

"There we are, that's the platoon, opening the gates," said Chris. As he spoke the first six Iraqis entered along a duckboard. "And those six lads are the search team." The Iraqis, who were being searched, lifted their hands willingly and laughed. "And then they proceed to the registration." They marched slowly forward, bright ration cards in their hands. "And that's them done and they leave." As the men walked out the far gate, Chris looked at his watch in satisfaction: "We can do about a thousand an hour."

Ten thousand people registered that day without incident. And within three days, two thousand five hundred began work. I mentioned this in our weekly report to Baghdad, adding that we had now refurbished more than half the schools in the province and all the clinics and that the new electric generating station was due to open in a fortnight. But the job scheme was not really economic policy: we were transferring money to win political support; it was doubtful whether the work would be productive or sustainable: our successors would be landed with supporting a scheme they would find difficult to discontinue. Seven thousand people who applied did not get jobs. We needed to do much more.

Meanwhile, we learned that there was activity in the ruined sugar-cane factory. Men gathered in the factory late every night, arriving in conditions of great secrecy and leaving singly. It was on the edge of the neighboring city of Majar, which, surrounded by shanty towns of displaced Marsh Arabs, had been a hotbed of resistance against

Saddam and was now one of the most extreme, anti-Coalition communities in the South, dominated by extremist clerics. Six British military policemen had been caught and murdered in the center of Majar in the summer: the largest number of British troops killed in a single enemy attack since the Falklands War, twenty years earlier. There were reports of an al-Qaeda cell.

Some intelligence analysts suggested that the factory had been adapted for the manufacture of bombs; others thought that since the narcotic trade was flourishing it had something to do with the manufacture of heroin. The general was consulted. The covert observation team of the battle group—which had been trained to watch IRA safe houses, hiding for days in hedgerows, sleeping, eating, and performing all other bodily functions where they lay, with the help of plastic bags—was deployed, with expensive night-vision sets.

Just after dusk the team observed Iraqi vehicles arriving with their headlights off. Some men entered the factory. The soldiers advanced with their image-intensifying equipment. And then suddenly the net was filled with rough voices saying, "Extract, extract." For a moment it must have seemed to the operations room as if they had stumbled on a Martian landing.

It was only the next morning that word began to spread that what they had seen, highlighted in the green glow of their night-image goggles, was men gathering for gay sex.

MUTINY

Maysan remained relatively stable but across the rest of the country the insurgency was gathering strength. In the week after Molly's arrival, sixteen U.S. soldiers were killed in a single day; the UN and the Red Cross formally announced the withdrawal of their international staff; and an opinion poll was released in which two-thirds of Iraqis now described us as an "occupying power." The next day, November 10, there was a mutiny in our local police: some said it had been orchestrated by the Prince; others blamed the Islamists and Iran. Molly and I sat in the base alongside the colonel, facing seven senior police officers, including Seyyed Faqr, a middle-aged man with a pock-marked face, a heavy black beard, and a black turban to signify his descent from the Prophet, who had been appointed police chaplain by the previous British colonel. As far as I knew, ours was still the only police force in Iraq with a chaplain. There was a rumor in town that the chaplain was an impostor who had bought his black turban in the market, but he had the authentic swagger of a self-satisfied preacher.

"*A salaam aleikum"* he began and paused, and then with a smile at the room announced, "we have decided that Brigadier General Sabih, the acting police chief, will step down. The new chief will be

Brigadier General Hussein Hatu." He gestured to a florid, portly man who smiled smugly. "Here is a diagram showing the new structure." Nadhem, the reckless Marsh Arab who had led the hunt for Abu Rashid's killers, was going to take over the Amara city police and his deputy was to be Abu Rashid's twenty-eight-year-old brother. This proposal was signed by everyone in the room including Brigadier General Sabih, whom they were sacking. The chaplain and his Marsh Arab allies—supported, I guessed, by the Prince of the Marshes because they were from his tribe—were challenging a police chief appointed by the Coalition. We could not allow this to happen. The British colonel spoke first, saying that "the supervisory committee approved the appointment of Sabeer," his English drawl transforming the short Arabic vowel of the policeman's name.

"The post of police chief is empty," snapped the chaplain. "General Sabih exists only to do paperwork." The chaplain's voice and demeanor as he explained this to us was abrupt and dismissive. Since politeness seemed only to encourage his rudeness, I said bluntly that what he proposed was impossible and illegal and that Brigadier General Sabih would remain the acting chief until a new provincial council, governor, and public safety committee chose a new chief in a month's time.

"General Sabih does not want to be the police chief," replied the chaplain. "He has signed as much on that paper. He is going to step down. Now."

"Is he?" I asked. "I have heard that from you but not from him. General Sabih?"

The Brigadier General looked uncomfortably at his silk socks and muttered something about overwork.

"Do you want to step down?" I insisted.

"He will step down when I tell him to step down," interrupted the chaplain. "General Sabih will resign on the spot." His voice was getting increasingly loud.

"Does this have your support?" I asked the others. No one replied. None of the Iraqis in the room were comfortable challenging the chaplain perhaps because of his status—represented by his black turban—as a cleric and a descendant of the prophet. I was aware that Molly and the colonel might feel I was doing too much talking. "Seyyed Faqr," I continued, "under the 1969 law and the first order of the CPA only we the Coalition have the power to appoint a police chief. You do not have the power. You never have and you never will."

"Since you the Coalition are the leaders of Maysan," suggested the chaplain, now baring his teeth in an ingratiating smile, "and you are in a position to make a decision—make it now."

"We work within the law," the colonel interjected. "This is a legal process."

"What matters is not the law," argued the cleric. "What matters is God, children, possessions, lives. These things are more important than the law. Forget the law. God is above the law and I represent God."

I replied that as a religious man, he was obliged to respect justice, which was sacred to God.

"If no one will do this," continued the cleric, "I will make the sacrifice of becoming the police chief myself."

I could only laugh.

"I resign," shouted the chaplain, leaping to his feet.

The cleric drew his cloak around him and walked to the door; the other Iraqis scrambled to their feet, begging him to stay, grabbing his arm, pleading. To my disappointment he sat down again, reiterating, "Our only duty is to protect the province and the sons of the province."

"Anyone who breaks the law," I snapped, "—anyone—will be punished under the law."

"Are you threatening me?" roared the chaplain. "I will resign. Do you want me to resign?"

"I am not threatening."

"I am a man of honor. You cannot talk to me like this. I am a major in the police," the cleric shouted.

"You are a major shouting at a British colonel and insulting your own general in public—is this the kind of discipline and respect you wish to introduce into the police?" I said. "A policeman indeed?"

"I was appointed by the last British colonel. I am a registered policeman."

"Then where is your police hat?" I asked, taking a risk by mocking a cleric. "You'd better decide whether you are wearing a police hat or a turban." There was a pause and then Nadhem, who presumably like me had heard the rumor that Faqr had bought his turban in the market, broke into his familiar, deep laugh and everyone else laughed with him.

"The British military appointed me to the police as chaplain," Seyyed Faqr said defensively, aware that he had just lost. "I am going. I resign from the police. I offer my resignation."

"Well I am sorry to hear that," said the British colonel languidly, and then after a pause, "but I suppose since you are so insistent we will have, with sorrow, to accept."

There was silence and then the cleric stood, gathered his robes about him again, and without any farewell stormed to the door. This time no one attempted to stop him. If Molly was surprised to confront a mutiny in her first week, she did not show it. She made a speech reminding people of the new legal procedures and asking for understanding and patience. At the end of the meeting Nadhem hugged me. And the mutiny, such as it had been, was over. But Brigadier General Sabih clearly no longer had the confidence to run the force.

We needed a strong and credible police chief. Baghdad's ministry of the interior wanted to appoint police chiefs themselves but we believed they lacked the knowledge to pick the right man. We therefore proposed that a local police committee of Maysan residents and politicians should interview and appoint the chief and then oversee his operations. This was a new idea from the Irish senior police adviser. There was nothing like it in the other provinces or in the law but we had convinced the military, the regional coordinator in Basra, and Baghdad that this was the best option. We announced that we would appoint a new provincial council and through them a governor, a public safety committee, and an effective police chief by the end of December. We had six weeks.

SHEIKHS

The state which becomes free makes enemies for itself not friends. All those
who profited from the tyrannical government, feeding upon the riches of the
Prince, become its enemies; since they have had their privileges taken away
from them, they cannot live contented and are each forced to try to estab-
lish the tyranny in order to return to their former authority.
—*Machiavelli*, Discourses, *Book I, Chapter 16*

We were forbidden to hold elections for the new provincial council
because the "democracy experts" in the U.S. believed Iraq was not
yet ready: it lacked the necessary measures for registration, monitoring, and voter education and "the lesson learned" from Bosnia was
that "elections held too early lead to the domination of extreme sectarian parties." We were therefore forced to play the role of king-
makers in our new democracy and choose the councilors ourselves.
Since no standard model was given, each CPA team was left to in-
vent its own council system and our choice of forty councilors from
eight hundred thousand people was, at the very least, controversial.

The only election I tried in Maysan was for the "half-mayor" of
the shrine town of Ali Al Sharji, a large, smiling man in elaborate
tribal dress and a favorite of the British military. Rather than having
rival councils, Sharji had two mayors from different tribes who alter-
nated weekly: a situation that the mayoral election was intended to
solve. The smiling man was elected. Three days later he was ambushed on the road between Sharji and Amara and killed.

Otherwise we chose people for the council through interviews, conducted six hours a day over two months, in which we met hundreds of Iraqis—trade union leaders and university professors, businessmen and guerrillas—each with different views on the province and its appropriate leadership.

Those we did not invite for meetings often forced us to meet them by organizing demonstrations at our gate. A young turbaned cleric came with two hundred men and told me in a high-pitched voice that he had been a leading bomb-maker in the resistance movement; that ninety-seven of his relatives had been killed by the old regime; that the local Saddam hospital, newly named the "Sadr" hospital, was only intact after the looting because he had put guards around it; and that my only choice was to put him on the provincial council.

I asked him what he thought about the current situation. He answered that he was sorry that we were not cutting the hands off thieves. It was ordained in the Koran.

"But even Imam Khomeini did not encourage people in Iran to cut off hands," I said.

"Imam Khomeini has his opinion and I have mine," the cleric replied.

Young Shia clerics were normally deferential toward the age and wisdom of a Grand Ayatollah like Khomeini. I asked how long he had been in the *hawza*, the seminary in Najaf.

"Two years," he replied. It was normal to study there for fifteen years or more.

I asked which Grand Ayatollah he had followed.

"I followed myself," he replied. This disregard for learning and authority appeared increasingly typical of young Shia politicians and their religious opinions seemed fractured, less controllable, and increasingly militant.

Another demonstration on the same day demanded that we include Seyyed al-Musawi. The demonstration leader assured me he did not belong to Seyyed al-Musawi's party: he was simply a neutral citizen who appreciated the wonderful qualities of Seyyed al-Musawi. I told him that Seyyed al-Musawi could come to see me at three. He wrote this down laboriously on a flyer with a thick black border, which I signed, and the crowd drifted away.

Seyyed al-Musawi came, a little after three. I had never seen any-one in Maysan wear a waistcoat with a suit before, or with patent ankle boots and a silver tie. He introduced himself as the leader of the "Shabaan revolutionary movement" party (so-called after the 1991 Shabaan uprising against Saddam). I had never heard of them. He returned the flyer and produced a certificate confirming that he had attended a meeting with the pretender to the Iraqi throne and a let-ter under a crest of a warrior riding a rearing blue-winged horse. The letter ran:

28 April 2003

Mr. al-Musawi has helped 16 Air Assault Brigade in construc-tion and procurement activities in Amara, Maysan. We trust him. He is effective and vigorous. We would recommend him,

Signed, Major—

I ran my fingers over the piece of paper—it was the first trace I had seen of this major, who like half a dozen other military officers over six months, must have done a job very like mine. I had never even heard of him from either our local staff or the military and I wondered if I would be forgotten as quickly.

Seyyed al-Musawi said his father had been a well-known business-man in Al Amara whose assets had been confiscated by Saddam and his brothers killed because they had joined him in the resistance. He too had saved a number of public buildings from the looters. He had recently returned from Baghdad and had newly refurbished an office in the center of town.

"You know, I am in a unique position," he continued, smiling as he relaxed into the conversation. "You see, I am one of the few people who can really control the unemployed poor in Amara. I understand them and they follow me. I can give you much intelligence on Baathists and fedayeen. If we are working together there will be no more riots and demonstrations." He thought he could be the governor or police chief and he was ready to serve on the public safety committee.

I asked him to wait while I went to get him some tea.

In the kitchen I saw our longest-serving translator. He turned over the flyer, which I was still carrying. Surrounded by a black border were the words ISLAMIC FRONT. THE OCCUPATION FORCES. RED MERCURY. WHITE SLAVE TRADE. CORRUPTION. JIHAD. INFIDEL. THE COALITION ARE ENEMIES OF ISLAM.

Jihad has a number of meanings—some quite mild and introverted—but the translator was in little doubt that the flyer said it was a religious duty to kill the occupation forces. It was signed by the young cleric who had sat in my office two hours earlier, angling for a position on the public safety committee. I was tempted to brush this off as empty rhetoric but the translator was much more worried. I asked him if he remembered al-Musawi.

"Yes, he stole too much money. I told the Major at the time but he would not listen to me. This man is a very corrupt man."

"What about the 'Shabaan revolutionary party?'"

"There is no such thing. He has just made it up. He played no part at all in the Shabaan uprising."

"And his support in the street? These hundreds of people with banners for him?"

"They are criminals—the most low criminals—we know them—he pays them each to come out in the street."

"Where does he get the money from? And the money for the office?"

"Probably from some foreign country—it is easy to get money to set up parties and organize demonstrations at the moment. As the proverb runs: 'the failed businessman becomes a conman.' Throw him out of your office. You should not even recognize him by seeing him. He is sick in the head—unbalanced."

As I walked back into the room with the tea, al-Musawi stood up smiling warmly to greet me. "Seyyed Rory, not only have you called me your friend but you have made me tea with your own hand. Now we will be like brothers. You would have liked the Major—a very good man. I have sent him an e-mail in the United Kingdom and he has replied—he comes from Macclesfield, his wife's name is Judy." He sipped his tea and continued. "We did very good work together—the Kumayt school we built it together in three weeks." He put down his glass and smoothed his trousers over his boots. "I am so pleased you are here. I have had trouble with gate guards for the last few months. They have not been letting me in the gate. Now you have invited me in. We can do so much good work together. So, how about it, will you put me on the public safety committee and the Provincial council?"

It was vital that we selected the right councilors, for they would have to guide the province through the first few months of independence with very little support from the center. Baghdad was weak and chaotic and rarely communicated with the provinces and all its constitution-drafting, UN resolutions, and tinkering would be irrelevant if the provincial governments could not restore order and security. We needed, therefore, to find councilors who were popular, legitimate, well-informed, honest, democratic, human-rights respecting, effective, friendly toward the Coalition, and powerful.

No individual had all those qualities. Liberals such as Haider, who were interested in human rights, had no power. Strongmen such as the Prince could be violent and intolerant. The most popular factions—the Iranian-linked groups and the Sadrists—were often conservative, dismissive of minorities, and opposed to the Coalition.

Throughout November and December some of the hundreds that we met emphasized their human rights credentials, some their power, others their popularity. One group stressed the traditional leadership of paramount sheikhs and the senior Najaf clerics. Another group imagined Maysan to be a secular, nationalist province that had thrown off "medieval traditions" and wanted technocrats, whom it dubbed with the emotive Arabic words, *mustaqalin, muta-alami'*—independent, educated. Others, perhaps more realistic, saw Maysan as a society in flux, increasingly influenced by new and unpredictable forms of popular, political Islam.

As we discovered different elements in society and tried to find the best leaders, we began to realize how every faction had dozens of potential chiefs, each with an involved and often controversial history. The traditional Baathist ruling class had gone, and Iraqis struggled to guess who might best replace them.

Even the tribes, who were the most clearly defined and long-established group, were difficult to incorporate because their structures were collapsing. In 1900, Maysan had been almost entirely tribal and the sheikhs had been the wealthiest and most powerful men in the province. Social change and government policy had eroded their power, however, and Saddam's support had only slowed an inevitable decline. Most urban Iraqis perceived the sheikhs as illiterate, embarrassing, criminal, powerless anachronisms who should be given no official recognition. The sheikhs could no longer, despite their claims, raise ten thousand armed men—perhaps they never could. I never observed them raise more than a couple hundred. Their daily visits to our office to request building contracts, clinics, and the chance to form militias proved how short they were of money and patronage power, and in the struggle to sustain themselves some tribes relied on theft, kidnapping, smuggling, and looting.

This did not mean, however, that the sheikhs were simply an irrelevant feudal remnant. They were still the most powerful men in the rural areas, where about half the population remained; they owned much of the land, and agriculture was the only half-functioning element of the shattered economy. Almost every crime in the villages was tried and settled by the sheikhs; the police barely operated outside the capital and we could not afford unnecessary enemies. Even, therefore, when sheikhs were little more than small-time rural gangsters, setting up extortion rackets under the pretense of security or skimming from contracts, I generally paid them the respect they thought they deserved. We decided to give seven of the forty council seats to the largest tribes and excluded three major sheikhs who had been too close to Saddam. This decision brought the excluded sheikhs into our office.

They entered, in fine woolen cloaks and crisp white robes, with gold bands on their headdresses. They were accompanied by the Prince. "If you put my cousin, Muhammad Hattab, on the council, I will slit his throat," began the oldest sheikh, flicking his finger over the white stubble on his neck. The finger was fat and jewelled. His toe-caps, despite the dusty path, were black mirrors like his sunglasses. And his voice was a harsh half-whisper.

Molly asked if he was threatening us, in which case, she said, we could arrest him now.

"No one is threatening anything," said the Prince of the Marshes, "the translator made a mistake."

The translator broke in angrily. "I did not."

I could see why people called the sheikh a gangster. But perhaps like all gangsters he did not, in fact, control all his gang. And this was presumably why he was so angry that we were representing his tribe on the council with his cousin. It was less obvious why the Prince supported him.

Ten years earlier, this sheikh had put his tribe at the disposal of Saddam. It was a powerful group that lived on both sides of the Iranian border, and he claimed to control the Iranian faction as well. While the Prince of the Marshes was in hiding and fighting the Baath, the sheikh hosted dinners and commissioned poetry; held televised tribal war dances in support of Saddam; and handed dissidents to the government. In return he received medals, epaulets, certificates, money, rank, guns. People noticed that when the police arrived to stop him shooting in the air at a wedding, he showed a particular warrant that made the police give him ammunition instead of arresting him. The Baath had classified him as a "Category A: Sheikh of Proven Loyalty." He ran an extensive information network for them and he had been made a major in the intelligence service.

Then, in April, came the invasion, and most people associated with the Baath fled. This sheikh, however, did not abandon his Amara villa but instead placed armed guards around it and retreated to his tribal heartland. He probably kept the money he had been given by Saddam to finance an insurgency against the Coalition, but he continued to appear in public and claim the allegiance of his tribe. Meanwhile the invasion opened the offices of the intelligence services to the looters and brought the files to the people, and made the members of the secret service known. And this was as true for the director as the clerk; for the operative as for the analyst; for the executioner as for the store man; for the sheikh as for the cleric; for the collector of information and also the provider of information to him.

Those who had stolen the intelligence files read them and noted the addresses and sold the contents door to door. Documents started at a few dollars a sheet. You could collect the manila files like stamps and see who had reported on you at school and at work, or which neighbor's report had led them to take your father away; and where he had been held and for how long; and what he had said in that time, on the official record; and what were the grounds for trial; and who sentenced him; and who carried it out; and where he was buried. And if a family wouldn't pay you enough for revealing the contents, another family would pay you for the opposite.

But the sheikh escaped his fate, although in three provinces people hearing the name of this ignoble, ignominious nobleman, said, "The sheikh was very close to Saddam." He sat in his tent in his tribal area and his tribesmen brought cases to him based on the files. For weeks, he and the other sheikhs determined how much compensation the victims of the old regime were entitled to—so much for the death of a relative; so much for a missed promotion at work—and ensured that those who were still around paid. But no one brought a case against the sheikh himself.

I had been prepared to include the Albu Muhammad Sheikh, although he had been close to Saddam, because he was the undisputed leader of the largest tribe in the province and no one had connected him to particular crimes. But this sheikh and the others in my office had committed such crimes that their very presence would make mockery of the new council and drive all Islamist parties into open opposition. Perhaps this was the Prince's aim, or perhaps he thought he could make them vote for his brother.

"I will not speak for my tribe, but why have you not included the Bazun?" asked the second sheikh, who did not need to remind me that he had helped us by handing over Dr. Amin, the suspect in the assassination of the police chief.

"Why have we not included the Issa?" I replied, mentioning the traditional enemies of the Bazun. The Bazun sheikhdom was in dispute between two main families, one of which had stolen all the heavy digging equipment from the ministry of municipalities and public works. "Or," I continued provocatively, "the Fartus." One of the sheikhs cleared his throat noisily. The Fartus were perceived by more "aristocratic" sheikhs such as these men as marsh bandits. "We can go on for ever. But there are only seven places for the tribes. And we need to choose."

"Let the tribes themselves choose—don't choose for them," said the Prince of the Marshes.

But sheikhs were not elected by one man, one vote. I had four people in a day disagreeing about the paramount sheikhs and there was no reason for one tribe to vote for another tribe, and no formula for weighing the big tribes against the small tribes. Everyone agreed that we should include the three largest tribes that had represented the province on the king's councils in the 1950s—the Beni Lam, the Albu Muhammad, and the Al Azerj—and also the Suwaad, a large Marsh tribe from the Iranian border.

"Let us add in your tribes," I nodded to two of the sheikhs from the Beni Kaab and the Albu Deraaj. "And you in particular do not need to worry," I said to the third sheikh. "Your son will have a seat on the council anyway, as the mayor of your local town council."

"I do not care about councils concerned with municipal sewerage," snapped the sheikh.

"Which leaves only one space," I continued. I listed a number of very large and prestigious tribes: the Serai, the Saada, the Bahadil, the Saadun, the Morean, and the sub-clans such as the Albu Kheet. "Which tribe," I asked, "would you like excluded?"

There was silence. And then the oldest sheikh snapped, "Our tribe dominates al-Amara and we have relatives in Iran, ten thousand of them. Things have been easy for you because we have cooperated so far. If you do not give me a seat on the council but instead represent our tribe with my cousin, we will withdraw all cooperation from the Coalition."

At this point, Molly and I jumped in to tell him that if he did so it would go badly with him.

There was silence again and then the second sheikh spoke less stridently. "Of course we will not turn against you, but why just us, why have you excluded us?"

They were challenging me to say that they were Baathists. I replied, "This is a political council, not a tribal council. No one disputes that you are the heads of your tribes. And in recognition of the tribes," I continued, "we will build a tribal mudhif and set up a council of the tribes where you can be represented in your proper places. Although you will not serve on the provincial council, it is only a temporary interim body and you will have an opportunity to stand for election in a year's time."

"Let me tell you—if you do not give us seats," snapped the jeweled sheikh, "our cousins will never sit for us."

Molly told them sharply that the meeting was over. These men had crossed a line. Neither Molly nor I would consider including them in the council. They strode out of the room. And we could only wait and see whether the sheikh would try, as he had threatened, to work with Iran and turn ten thousand men against us, or whether this was only the machismo of a leader who was leaderless and impotent. In the meantime, we needed to redouble our focus on security. Attacks were increasing.

PRECAUTIONS

When the river is not in flood men are able to take precautions, by means of dykes and dams, so that when it rises next time it will neither overflow its banks, or if it does its force will not be uncontrolled and damaging.
—*Machiavelli,* The Prince, *Chapter 25*

The friendly Japanese diplomat I had met, with a towel round his waist, on my first trip to Basra airport had been dragged from his car and murdered, while traveling in Central Iraq. A Fijian working as a bodyguard on an infrastructure project had saved his life by shooting one carjacker through the windscreen and clubbing the other to death with the butt of his rifle. A British civilian adviser to the CPA had been killed by a bomb fixed to the underside of his armored vehicle. The British Treasury adviser with whom I had breakfasted on my first morning in Baghdad had somehow survived when a rocket passed straight through his bedroom, killing the man next to him. Men had been killed in mortar attacks as they walked to the café in the Green Zone. And on November 12, in our neighboring province of Nasiriyah, a truck bomb had killed nineteen Italians in an instant. The terrorists were looking for soft targets.

We needed to think not only about the economic and political roots of the violence but also about immediate security measures. When I next climbed to the roof to watch the young men holding up pictures of Muqtada al-Sadr, I was reminded that, as the Prince had warned, a sniper in the date palm grove could pick us off from the riverbank. He could also, I saw, get out of a car on the new highway bridge and fire a rocket-propelled grenade at us; the wasteland across both branches of the river was a perfect place from which to launch mortars or rockets; and a car or truck bomb could be driven very close to our compound walls.

Security measures were ugly; our lives were cramped and the view of the Tigris was one of the few pleasant aspects of our site and a real contribution to morale. When people had first suggested sniper-screen—a plywood wall between us and the river so that we could not be seen from the far bank—I vetoed it. But looking down at the compound from the roof I concluded that I had underestimated the dangers. This brought me into one of my first serious disagreements with the British military.

I wanted to stop the construction of the large prefab cabins with plywood walls that were being assembled for us in Kuwait and instead build in brick with steep-pitched roofs, so that if a mortar hit, it would detonate far above the bunks. I was able to do this, although it was difficult at first to convince the Coalition to pay for the new materials and accept the delay in installation. I also wanted to take the advice of a visiting security adviser and mount watch-towers, create a chicane approach to prevent truck bombers from having a straight run at the front door, cut off half the lanes of traffic, and position a company on the far bank. Although the CPA would be paying for the construction, military engineers would be undertaking the work and they had many other commitments. Only the Brigadier could agree to create a new company base on the other side of the river. The major in charge of security in Amara believed that increasing our defenses might actually encourage attack, by making us look less like a humanitarian outfit and more like a military camp. When I continued to insist that terrorists would not hesitate to target humanitarian offices, this normally mild man exploded. "You have your talents, Rory," he said, struggling to control himself in front of the other people in his office, "but security is nothing to do with you. Back off," he spat. "Just back off." I had to ask him to continue the conversation outside on the balcony.

The major had disappointed me and I had enraged him. He knew I was no military expert and he thought I was getting above myself. I knew that security measures were often wasteful and unnecessary and that security was his responsibility; and because I needed good relations with the military and liked the major, I would have preferred to back off. But he was blind to how quickly the insurgency was spreading and how soon we would be attacked with truck bombs and mortars. And so, having failed to convince him of my position, I briefed Molly, then went round and behind and above him in Basra and Baghdad and London and got the scheme through at considerable expense. The security measures were complete before the attack on our compound began.

THE ISLAMIC CALL

It is the duty of the rulers of a republic to maintain the foundations of the religion that sustains them; and if this is done it will be easy to keep their republics religious and as a consequence, good and united. And they must favor and encourage all those things which arise in favor of religion, even if they judge them to be false.

—*Machiavelli,* Discourses, *Book I, Chapter 12*

Our weekly "situation reports" to Baghdad imposed a structure on our actions—job schemes, the police, the council—but my note-books consist of fragments: glimpses of rough hands, a flung net shattering the Tigris, the brittle casts of mud scattered beneath military boots. We did not only think about politics. George Butler commissioned a local artist to paint his daughter from a photograph and wondered whether his tour—twice extended—would be over in time to share Christmas with his family. Molly and I gossiped about the new American IT specialist and a political officer and wondered whether they would survive life in the compound. They did, and gossiped with us in turn about newer arrivals. In the late evenings, my colleagues called their husbands, ex-wives, and children, waking them on dark winter mornings in the West. I was relieved that I did not have to think about a family as well as the job.

A puppy had been left in a cardboard box at the compound door before Molly's arrival. His belly was pink, he had short white hair, fawn ears, a fawn tail, and two fawn patches on his coat. Kyle, our newly arrived twenty-five-year-old administrative officer, asked if she could keep him and I—muttering a little about Muslim sensibilities, which required someone who had touched a dog to perform elaborate ablutions before prayer—let her. He peed in my office and when we scratched him gray mud rose up from his coat.

I taught him to sit and we fought to play with him but he was not popular with everyone. When Kyle called him Tigris, the colonel said that that was where the dog was going. He objected to his soldiers being used to babysit the dog—although they enjoyed it—and according to the quartermaster the animal contravened health and safety regulations. I thought I could laugh them out of this. I couldn't. When Molly arrived, she announced that it was entirely inappropriate to keep a dog in a compound where Muslim visitors were received, and she told me to tell Kyle to get rid of it. Kyle hid the puppy in her room and I agreed not to tell Molly. But since it was a small compound Molly soon noticed the dog being smuggled out for its evening walks. I won a second delay by asking the Salvation Army if they would consider taking Tigris and commissioned a kennel and run for him in the compound. A month later, after a day in which there had been demonstrations, unpleasant allegations from Baghdad, and a threat to boycott all our political structures, I found Molly cuddling Tigris on her lap. The dog stayed.

Outside the compound wall, most Iraqis ignored us. Our meetings with the council were televised, so they knew that there was an American governor called Molly, but even our own staff struggled to tell the difference between the functions of the CPA and the military. Some canny citizens, who saw us as a potential source of salaries for their families, formed NGOs dedicated, at least on paper, to "human rights" and "sewing for women" and submitted very detailed requests for filing cabinets and Pentium 4 computer processing units. Most of the men, however, whom I glimpsed in the kebab shops or walking two paces ahead of wives on country lanes had no direct contact with our office and experienced the Coalition only through Arab television stations, which made the American military look like the Israeli army in the occupied territories.

Even in the stable context of our office, with good translators, it was often difficult for us to understand Iraqi guests and for them to understand us. Molly joked that the family pride, vendettas, genealogies, and avarice of the sheikhs echoed my home life in the Scottish highlands and made them easy for me to communicate with, but the truth was that the most basic concepts, like "civil society" or "Sharia law," meant very different things to each of us. What was a lived experience for one side was often an abstract concept, learned in a textbook, for the other. Too often, the sophisticated and controversial points that we imagined we were making were experienced by our listeners as sonorous platitudes. This was particularly true when we tried to select councilors from the Shia political parties.

There were more than fifty Shia political parties in the province, most only two months old, and it was nearly impossible to distinguish between them. Saddam had made membership in these parties a capital offense, so each party was defined by exile and violence. There were three major established groups: the first, SCIRI, had been based in exile in Iran; the second, the Sadrists, had largely remained in Iraq; the third, Dawa, had been largely based in other countries, including Britain. The founding leader of SCIRI had been martyred; the founding leader of the Sadrists had been martyred; the founding leader of Dawa had been martyred. All fifty were splinters from the original Dawa (the "Islamic Call" party) and even the rump of Dawa had split between Dawa Iraq tendency, Dawa Islamic, and Dawa Movement (whose subleader was also martyred).[5] This bewildering array included the most powerful and fastest-growing groups

_____

[5]This is only one example from dozens stretching from faded old parties, such as Ayatollah Taqi Modaressi's Islamic Labor and its cousin Talia to the many new parties with resonant names—such as "Hamas," which was no relation to the Palestinian Hamas and consisted of only two men and a briefcase. Iraqis were as confused as we were by Harakat Hizbollah (the Movement of the Party of God)—an armed offshoot of the Iranian-linked SCIRI—which was quite different from Hizbollah Iraq (which belonged to the Prince of the Marshes) and from Hizbollah Lebanon (which was an offshoot of the original Dawa).

in the province, and I wanted to give at least twenty positions, half the council, to them if we could only find the right candidates.

Abu Muslim, the provincial leader of Dawa Movement who came to my office to explain the parties over many cans of Coke— or rather Diet Coke, for he worried about his heart—was the son of a Marsh Arab sheikh and had spent fifteen years in the Iranian holy city of Qom, swimming in the dangerous waters of Iranian-linked anti-Saddam politics. Although he had studied for years in theological seminary, he did not wear a turban or clerical dress but a baggy Western suit, and the only sign of his piety was a bruise from continually pressing his forehead in prayer against a sacred tablet of Najaf clay. He sat with his short legs twisted sideways, his broad thighs straining at the seams of his suit trousers, clacking his rosaries through his hands and pausing only to stroke his four-day stubble as he wove his rhetoric.

"To the right levels and in the correct way," he began, "must people be educated; for the religious culture is perverted, suffusing minds with sundry weaknesses, just as the pride of the scientists too has tainted our thoughts with wantonness. And they have forgotten to read, though the sustainer, the most bountiful, has taught man the use of the pen, taught man what he did not know." He muttered the last few words, a quotation from the Koran.

Abu Muslim described the leaders of each party and their masters and their masters' masters in a golden chain of succession that stretched back to the prophet Muhammad; rattled off the names of the nine martyred brothers of the SCIRI leader, specifying their theological publications, imprisonment, exile, arguments, and the place and manner of their deaths. For the sake of the interpreter and me, he simplified and repressed his allusions and images and, when he saw us losing the thread, stopped listing his theological influences ("al-Ghazali, al-Amadi, Ibn Ashu al-Maghbadi . . ."). But even with my very limited vocabulary it was clear that almost every sentence contained a new trope and figure of speech or even more striking figures of thought. He emphasized by understating and asserted by seeming to ignore. All of this reflected his formal training in rhetoric, which he had studied along with grammar and logic in theological seminary.

The conclusion of all Abu Muslim's oratory, labyrinthine reasoning, and Muslim patristics was that government should be based on the popular vote, not on Sharia law; that clerics should play no role in politics; that Sharia was just a general encouragement to love the cosmos; and that Iraqis should cooperate closely with the Coalition. He campaigned for these unusual views indefatigably, propagating them through his new creation, a large "advisory council" that included both the Badr militia and the Communists, and since everyone from the Prince to the Sadrists seemed convinced of his intelligence and goodwill, Molly and I readily agreed that he should be the first Shia politician included in the new council.

It was, however, particularly difficult to assess the views and personalities of potential councilors when we were locked in our offices. In Afghanistan, forty nights of sleeping in village houses and watching men fiddling with their rosaries, greeting their guests, and reprimanding their cousins had allowed me to take some measure of them in their less guarded moments. But new security regulations meant that any movement outside the compound needed to be justified: I required a bodyguard of six just to walk in the souk, and Molly thought traveling around the province wasted time we badly needed to deal with the growing political problems and incessant e-mails.

Here in the artificial context of our Maysan office, our exchanges were short and carefully shaped, charged with dialectic and equivocation and woven with ruses of self-defense and self-promotion. The only man who seemed at all natural in this environment was the second Shia leader whom we selected. Abu Mustafa would stride through our civil affairs room, smiling and greeting everyone as cheerfully as though he was in his own *mudhif.* On many occasions he brought along his six-year old son, a quiet, well-behaved boy in long French

shorts and a neat cardigan—only the miniature bow-tie was missing—who spent the hours surfing Google Arabic in our office while
his father talked. It was hard to guess that it had been only three
months since the boy first saw the Internet.

Abu Mustafa was the most charming figure among the moderate
politicians. A cleric of forty, he was part dilettante, part salesman,
part mystic. His father, the grandson of a paramount sheikh from
neighboring Nasiriyah, had moved to Amara as a preacher in the
1960s. From him Abu Mustafa had inherited a small mosque in the
market and the grand manners of a tribal aristocrat. His face was
framed by a neatly trimmed black beard and his large eyes were
warm. He was slim, and his very upright bearing made him appear
taller than he was, and athletic, an impression that sat oddly with his
sedentary profession. He spoke in a light, unhurried tenor, his manner teasing, playful, allusive.

At first meeting he could seem a very Western man: he talked
often about Europe, appeared more concerned with his new Internet
café and gas station than theology, and, unlike the many visitors who
were embarrassed around our female staff, seemed untroubled when,
one evening, Charlie Morris stopped by my office in a T-shirt. But
when I asked him what he thought of the many young Iranians who
violated the restrictive dress codes, he replied, "They are bad people.
In Iraq we must ensure that women are properly covered."

He was most in his element dandling his son or plaiting his
four-year-old daughter's hair while he chatted with Molly or me,
and his long, easy, digressive talk seemed to suggest a certain indo-
lence. Yet his simple anecdotes, accessible to the illiterate in his congregation, and without any of Abu Muslim's exuberant vocabulary,
were strangely elusive and metaphorical.

"In the past," replied Abu Mustafa when I asked him about violence in the province, "Iraqis used to go on exchanges with Western
families. One day, an Iraqi man who was staying with a German
family went to buy a gift for his hosts. He could find nothing suitable

in the shops except a small toy battle tank, so he wrapped it and gave it to the family on the day of the Christian festival. The children opened it and saw it and then the German father asked gently, 'Why did you buy this? Do you want my child to be infatuated with tanks?' Iraqis must begin to remember their civilization; they have forgotten what to know, love, or fear."

As he finished, Abu Mustafa lapsed into silence, waiting for the significance of the anecdote to sink in. His most straightforward words contained more than I could grasp. Thus when he talked about memory he used the word *dhikr*, which had resonances of invocation or ritual remembrance, and his tripartite distinction between "knowledge," "love," and "fear" echoed that of Sufi mystics. I did not know how much to read into any of this.

In politics, he seemed always to be failing on the verge of greatness. His position as a cleric from a well-known family, his quick tongue, and his good relations with the Coalition gave him many advantages, which he asserted through his dress: a neat white turban and robes with a crisp starched collar from the best clerical outfitter in the Iranian holy city of Qom, where he had lived for fifteen years. He had credentials as a resistance fighter, could rattle off the details of every weapon available in the province, and had inherited some respect from his brother who, having been a leader of the 1991 uprising against Saddam, had served as the revolutionary governor of Amara for a week until he was caught and executed.

Yet Abu Mustafa was never entirely trusted. The Prince had once said that both he and I were Iranian spies, so Abu Mustafa always made a joke of talking to me in Farsi. This was a strange joke, for although the Iranian parties were wary of him and professed not to know what he had done in the resistance, Abu Mustafa had certainly once worked for the Iranian secret service and continued to meet their case officers. Nevertheless, we included him as the second Shia political councilor because he had a strong influence over his immediate congregation, positive views about the Coalition, and, despite being both cleric and politician, a belief that religion should be separated from politics.

As we continued our search, the rhetoric and mannerisms of the parties remained much easier to grasp than their policy positions. I fully saw how elusive the policies could be only when I called on Abu Akil, the national head of Dawa Iraq tendency, a middle-aged man in a gray suit and wire-rimmed glasses, but no tie. Unlike Abu Mustafa or Abu Muslim he was a famous man with a country-wide reputation and worked from a shabby office in Basra, with flimsy plastic chairs, pious posters, and cigarette butts on the concrete stairs, illegally requisitioned from the Baath and guarded by bearded private militia men. Like the other Shia leaders, he favored more conservative social codes; his sugar-coated glasses of tea rested on saucers depicting bare-armed eighteenth-century women, which in turn rested on a party newspaper insisting that women cover their heads. When I asked him to define the differences between the parties, he replied:

"It is necessary to consider the government of the Islamic jurists from a scientific, not a political, point of view. As Muhammad Baqr al-Sadr said in the founding document of Dawa, democracy is the basis of the power of the individual and the community." His long, elegant fingers moved through the air as he sketched out theories of government. I felt as if I were back in a university seminar. But I was also confused. I knew that Abu Akil wanted a theocracy, so why was he presenting himself as a democrat?

"So is God and Sharia law the ultimate authority in the state, or is it the people?"

He paused and said very slowly, "The two are the same . . . Power derives from the law which is based on Sharia, which comes from the Koran and God. But it also derives from the constitution which is created by the legislature elected by the people."

As he went on spinning distinctions between power, authority, law, and legislative actions, I felt more and more as if I had fallen into the story of Alexander the Great and the ancient gymnosophist who says, "Trying to explain my philosophy to you through your interpreters is like trying to drink clean water out of a mud bath." Abu Akil referred to works by three different ayatollahs, drew distinctions between Islamic theory and policy, and concluded that the clerics should direct the religious, moral, and social actions of the people but not their politics. Whatever that meant. The other men in the room looked at him with a disciple's patient admiration, recognizing the wisdom in the familiar phrases. The conversation continued as follows:

> **RS:** "Abu Akil, I understand the differences in leadership and in the history of your groups, but what differentiates you today from the other parties?"

> **Abu Akil:** "Of course, Seyyed Rory, the parties are different because they look to different clerics for guidance: different *mujtahid* [clerics qualified to interpret the Koran]."

> **RS:** "And these different clerics have different opinions?"

> **Abu Akil:** "Different interpretations but not different opinions. We are all Shia. We perform emulation toward the Grand Ayatollahs, *ijtehad from the faqih; taqlib to the mirja.* And because they are all Muslim, they all agree."

> **RS** (desperately): "How about economic policy?"

> **Abu Akil:** "Islam teaches all of us that there should be a pragmatically regulated free market. All agree on that."

> **RS:** "So would I be right to say that there are no substantial differences between your parties?"

> **Abu Akil:** "No. There are many differences. We agree in fundamentals, differ in policy."

> **RS:** "Give me an example."

Abu Akil: "There are theoretical differences, intellectual differences, conceptual differences."

RS: "Can you give me an example, please?"

Abu Akil: "Well, for example, in Britain you have a Labour party and a Conservative party—it is like that."

And that is all I got in a two-hour conversation. We later confirmed that Abu Akil was closer than anyone to the Iranian government, believed strongly in a theocratic state, and had split away from his rival parties largely because he was paid sixty thousand dollars to do so. We did not, therefore, include his party in the council.

At about this time I began to provide the more moderate Shia politicians, including the rhetorician Abu Muslim and his friend Abu Mustafa, with some financial support. Politics was not a level playing field. The Iranians and Syrians were pouring money into more extreme Islamist groups, sometimes encouraging them to preach against us, sometimes to attack us, aiming thereby to create instability and deter us from invading them next. More moderate Islamists such as Abu Muslim, who were most likely to support human rights, tolerate minorities, oppose terrorism, and cooperate with the Coalition, received no foreign financial support. They had lost property and suffered greatly under the old regime: our third inclusion in the council, the gravel-voiced Sheikh Rahim, had lost a car showroom and had been imprisoned for ten years; two of Abu Mustafa's gas stations had been taken from him, and his brothers had been killed by Saddam. Men like these wanted to travel the province and communicate their vision of the future but they could not afford cars or bodyguards, rent meeting halls or microphones, nor print pamphlets. The moderates could not hire a tea-boy; the extremists could hire an entire rioting crowd.

Finally I gave them each six thousand dollars, a decision that presented bureaucratic as well as ethical problems. I said the money was

for "refurbishing their mosques" because even though our contracting regulations had been relaxed to reflect the realities of spending in
a semi-war zone, our funds were still really intended for "bricks and
mortar" and it was difficult to track the clerics' use of the money. The
clerics produced copious receipts, in triplicate and signed, from local
firms for building materials. Molly asked me to visit the mosques and
photograph the work.

Abu Mustafa showed me an antechamber in his father's mosque
and said that was where the money had gone. Sheikh Rahim drove
me out to a football field, on the edge of which was a large pile of yellow bricks and some girders.

"There it is," he said.

"It doesn't look like very much," I replied.

"I know," he said. "I have the site and you have bought me this
but I am still collecting money from the public to build the whole
mosque."

"All you got with our money was this?" I asked.

"No. There was a lot more. But you remember I asked you for
money for guards and you said you could not give them to me. So
the people who live in the houses round here have stolen most of the
building materials." I photographed the pile of bricks. Molly was
unimpressed, and I never found out what happened to the bricks or
whether the mosque was completed.

Sheikh Rahim continued to be very rude to us in public meetings, and later he lost his job in a corruption scandal. But I didn't regret my decision to support him. Months later, when we were under
attack, Sheikh Rahim was almost the only man prepared to face an
angry Sadrist mob and tell them the Coalition was doing a good job.

SADRINES

The strength of the disease should be well estimated and if you see you are able to cure it, set yourself to doing so without reservation; otherwise leave it alone and attempt nothing.

—*Machiavelli,* Discourses, *Book I, Chapter 33*

The most troubling Shia group, however, were the Sadrists. Even the largest Shia exile parties struggled to understand them. The senior Shia leaders—the *mirjajiya,* or "sources of emulation"—such as the great Ayatollah Sistani were traditionally chosen for their ability to answer intricate theological questions. But the founding leader of the Sadrists was never a particularly impressive theologian. Seyyed Muhammad Sadeq al-Sadr (Sadr II) was instead a paradox: an old man from a grand lineage who appealed to the marginalized, radical young; a conservative thinker who revolutionized religious practices and made preaching more important than theology. By promoting Friday prayer services and attracting young, emotional preachers to his mosque, he attracted huge crowds of the often illiterate urban poor, funded them, and encouraged them to dwell on the emotional cult of the return of the Shia messiah, or hidden Imam. When Saddam killed Sadr II, he completed the cleric's transformation of Iraqi Shiism. Hundreds of thousands of Shia Iraqis no longer deferred only to the great theologians of Najaf but instead—and almost blasphemously—regarded the dead Sadr II as their "source of emulation" and even followed his radical twenty-eight-year-old son. Muqtada had not even the slightest pretension to theology, but he sent young,

like-minded clerics to all the provinces, created his own armed militia, assassinated clerical rivals, declared an alternative government,
and called for the immediate departure of the infidel Coalition.

Bremer—perhaps refusing, like many Iraqis and foreign com-
mentators, to believe that a young, violent, under-qualified cleric such
as Muqtada could ever command serious support among the Shia; or
perhaps simply underestimating his poor and illiterate supporters—
decided to confront Muqtada and in October gave a secret order for
his arrest. We were instructed to cease contact with the Sadr office.
Molly had already told me to stop meeting Muqtada's local representative, Seyyed Hassan, who had been keen to meet me after his
kidnapping.

I believed it disastrous to confront the Sadrists. Muqtada's supporters were numerous, radical, and far more powerful than we acknowledged. They included the whole network of alternative councils
in district towns as well as the professional and middle-class members
of the Fodala party established by Sadr II's old Chief of Staff. Even if
we could fight Muqtada and win, the Sadrists could still take seats in
the forthcoming election, leaving us to face a recalcitrant and duly
elected enemy. The Sadrists were not as yet attacking us, and I preferred to make them share in the responsibility and errors of the new
council rather than criticizing it from the outside, and I preferred
them to conduct their fights in the council rather than on the streets.
I also believed that we could influence men like Seyyed Hassan. I
therefore pushed to include Sadrists in the council by sleight of hand.
We brought in their "more moderate" Fodala faction, even though
they were illegally occupying the city hall. We convinced the alternative councils to join by promising to merge them with the official
councils in the district towns, and negotiated their demand for every
seat on the council down to three of the forty seats. Finally we convinced Seyyed Sattar, the Sadr chief from the troublesome town of
Majar, to join.

———

One evening at eight, when I had been in Amara a few months, I slipped out of the compound alone, leaving the civil affairs team to watch an Indiana Jones movie. It was the tenth day of the Shia holy month of Moharram. On this day 1,324 years earlier and two hundred miles from Amara, Imam Hussein, the grandson of the prophet Muhammed was betrayed, fought with his seventy-two followers against an army, and was killed. A procession had formed to commemorate this martyrdom. Saddam had banned such processions, and this was therefore the first in Amara for decades. It was organized by Muqtada's office and was guarded by their militiamen, who in defiance of Coalition orders had lined the streets with guns. That morning, nine suicide bombers had struck the procession in Kerbala itself, killing a hundred and wounding three hundred.

The electricity had as usual gone, and it was so dark that I could not see the faces of passersby. I walked quickly along the road toward the souk and slipped into the thick crowd on the pavement on Baghdad Street. Some were weeping. Slowly, a cart, lit with oil lamps, was pushed into view, pasted with an image of Hussein in a green turban with blue eyes and a neat beard: the standard picture I had seen in villages in Afghanistan and Pakistan, apparently produced in Iran. Thousands, from boys to their grandfathers, in tight bandannas, bare-chested, were chanting in harmony their love of the martyr and beating their palms on their breasts. As they chanted they swayed and, in rhythm with the chants and the slap and hollow percussion from the chests, some flung high flails tipped with sickle knives that snapped down over the sharp edge of their collar-bones and snagged like crampons in their flesh. At each step and with difficulty, they dragged the blades from the scars again, and the bright blood bubbled and ran.

I had last attended an Ashura procession at midday in the fierce April heat near Multan in the Punjab, where there had been police with heavy machine guns on each street corner to prevent a Shia-Sunni riot. My Pakistani host, who was one of the flagellants, had allowed his eldest son—just turned twelve—to join him. As I watched them march, a friend walked beside me, explaining each chant and pointing out the prominent flagellants. The son put little energy into the swing and winced before it struck. The older man had an easy, confident manner with his flail and he was expressionless. Like many of the others, he was a prosperous businessman and his large stomach suggested that this was the most exercise he had taken in months. A few of the flagellants—young men in black beards—overdid it, and were taken off to hospital. One died from infected wounds. The procession finished in the central square and at the end my host, his metal whip in his rear pocket, smiled broadly and said, "It was marvelous, a real spiritual experience, it is remarkable." Then he rubbed away the sweat and the blood with his black shirt and invited me to tea and cakes.

On this occasion in Amara, there were no police. It was too dark to see very much, and I recognized no one. I guessed that the man with the microphone was telling the story of the final tragic battle, and I heard the chants of *"Ya Hussein."* I noticed the Sadr "army of the redeeming Imam" with their Kalashnikovs, and the thin bearded faces of the flagellants in the lamplight. But I learned little from the blood and shadows. Someone beside me, turning, caught my face in the lamplight and asked, "Are you an Englishman?" I denied it and worked my way back through the crowd and into the compound.

MAJORITY AND MINORITY

Apart from those he has chosen he should refuse to listen to anyone, but
pursue his aims steadfastly and not waver about decisions he has taken.
                                    —*Machiavelli,* The Prince, *Chapter 23*

My desire to give half the council to the more moderate clerics and
Islamists was frustrated by three things. The first was opposition from
Baghdad, which insisted we had "not invaded to create a Shia theocracy" and still wanted councils dominated by secular liberals. The
second was the behavior of the parties themselves. While the Islamist
leaders made elegant distinctions between metaphysics and virtue
and constructed careful arguments about religion's place in politics,
their followers in Amara firebombed or closed all the Internet cafés,
cinemas, video shops, musical instrument sellers, liquor stores, and
riverside cafés. No women, even Christians or Sabians, could now
appear in public with bare heads, and very few women were daring
enough to wear the colored scarves and coats favored in metropoli-
tan Iran. Almost everyone wore the all-enveloping black *abaya.* Women
would no longer eat in public with young men who were not from
their family. Dr. Kefiyah, the head-scarf-wearing Baghdad-trained
doctor I had met at the art exhibition, began to receive letters that
claimed her family was immoral. Then posters were put up in her
neighborhood saying she was an Israeli spy and threatening to kill
her if she did not leave Amara.

Finally there was the Prince, who hated any influence from Iran and knew these groups would not vote for his brother as governor. He shifted from simply intoning, "Exclude them, they are bad men, trust me" to more fashionable development jargon: "Seyyed Rory has not included the poor, vulnerable, and marginalized groups; you must represent women and religious minorities."

There were only twelve Christian families and perhaps a hundred Sabian followers of John the Baptist in a province of nearly a million, and their representatives on the previous council had said nothing in meetings. I thought that the Coalition forces—who had taken an interest in the minorities and frequently visited them—would be sufficiently strong to protect their interests, and my October draft for the council had, therefore, included only two women and no religious minorities. I preferred to use the new council to accommodate, balance, and appease the armed groups.

But Molly, who did not want an Islamist monopoly and wanted to protect minorities, decided to include three women and three religious minorities—a Christian, a Sunni, and a Sabian—thus deciding six seats out of forty. These new groups would never vote for an Islamist candidate because they were opposed to conservative Islamist social codes, so we had in effect given six votes to the Prince's brother. We had so far included, in addition to the "moderate" Islamists (the diminutive orator Abu Muslim, the mystical businessman and cleric Abu Mustafa, the gravel-voiced Sheikh Rahim, and a young politician from "Dawa Islamic party"), two Iranian-trained and linked militia commanders from Badr/SCIRI,[6] and five representatives from the various Sadrist elements.

The Islamists came in to protest a large and surprisingly unified deputation, which included parts of all these factions, called "the Islamic Front." My notebook records their spokesman saying:

[6]Khaled (Abu Ahmed) from Badr/SCIRI and Abu Miriam from Harakat Hizbollah.

There are 120,000 prophets in Islam and they are all equal. We respect Jesus and remember his advice to turn the other cheek. We are sorry about September 11. We wish to thank you for freeing us from dictatorship. Particularly we, the Islamic parties, come to thank you for freeing us from this nightmare. But when the children of Islam saw the names for the new provincial council we were very sad. We see that people from the tribes and the Islamic movements are missing, while the Christians and Sabians—and we don't ignore their role but they are just a minority—have seats. If you gave those seats to Muslims it would benefit Islam. And you are obliged to serve the country under the Geneva Conventions.

Their suggestion, in coordinated speeches from the various leaders and culminating in the crisp rhetoric of Abu Muslim, was to drop the minority religious groups and one woman and replace them with the Islamists. The SCIRI militia leader said that if their demands were not met, all the Islamist parties would boycott.

The group had prepared themselves carefully with practical solutions, imagined our religious, political, and legal agenda, and responded to what they guessed were our concerns: radical Islam, terrorism, the Geneva Conventions. Their language, however, did not connect with ours and Molly was particularly irritated at their continued rejection of women and minorities. We would not give them as many seats as they had held on the old "supervisory committee" and when they refused to choose among themselves, we excluded not only the representative of Abu Akil's Dawa Iraq (on the grounds that they were controlled by Iran), but also Abu Maytham, the burly Badr commander. We hoped that neither man would protest with his armed supporters.

Molly concluded the meeting by saying, "Please remember, you turned away from political power in 1920 and you have suffered for it ever since. Now is your chance to participate. Do not miss it."

By the first week in December—two weeks before the final announcement of the council and a month into Molly's time in the province—we had agreed who would be on the council and the consultations ceased. In countless meetings with other groups—writers and union leaders, shopkeepers and civil servants—we had traded human rights for security and security for democratic popularity and all three for a government that was friendly toward the Coalition. We wanted to build a strong, independent Iraqi province, by giving leaders money and weapons and not undermining their decisions; we also wanted to protect human rights. The choices—as with an interim government after a war anywhere from Maysan to Afghanistan—were of lesser evils. Since I believed that there could be no future without security and no security without strong government, I fought to include the most powerful men in the council. Others, believing that support for strongmen was only a dangerous short-term measure and that lasting security could only emerge from liberal values, preferred gentler but more enlightened representatives. I insisted that there could be no long-term state without short-term security. But such theoretical debates were rare; instead of deliberating over moral sacrifices or intricate paradoxes, we tended to mix groups more or less intuitively: some with power, some with popular support, some with liberal values, and some who supported us.

In the nearby province of Muthanna, the CPA had composed a council from four groups of ten. In Maysan, forty was made from four times seven: seven tribal sheikhs; seven district mayors—chosen by my favorite method, a lottery—seven political parties, seven religious representatives—and some more that we wanted. These were included in the opaque category of "educated and experienced" representatives and encompassed the head of the teacher's union; the aged Sheikh Ismail, who had been such friends with Mr. Grimley; a very ambitious young activist and lawyer, Ali Hammod; and Riyadh Mahood, the brother of the Prince of the Marshes. This category was supposed to provide seats for some respected local figures who did not fit any clear group and balance the factions. But would this council hold the province together and elect a good governor?

POET

Men should be either caressed or crushed; because they can avenge slight injuries but not those that are very severe. Hence any injury done to a man must be such that there is no need to fear his revenge.
                          —*Machiavelli,* The Prince, *Chapter 3*

There were two main candidates for governor Kadhem, the scruffy, balding Islamist Badr commander who had spent a decade or more in Iran, training with the revolutionary guard; and Riyadh, the Prince's brother. We had weakened Riyadh's family position over the previous three months, blocking the Prince's attempt to appoint the police chief and the governor; preventing him from filling the council with his supporters; openly empowering his Islamist rivals; ignoring his advice on contracts; and taking away his patronage control over the job scheme by running it ourselves. Riyadh now saw us—and apparently me in particular—as his main obstacle to power. One of the Islamist politicians hinted that if Riyadh became governor he would exact a terrible revenge. But his appointment was out of our hands—the council was electing the governor.

One afternoon, I drove out to the *mudhif* of one of Riyadh's friends, Sheikh Hatem, the chief of the Bahadil. Rather than being built of marsh reeds, this sheikh's *mudhif* was a long cement bungalow, surrounded by date palms, a hundred yards from the national highway. The sheikh, though in his eighties, moved almost at a trot to the gate to greet me, trailing a Najafi wool cloak woven into a transparent gauze. His nephew, the seventy-year-old Sheikh Ismail, stood smiling beside him in a perfectly tailored plain stiff camel-hair cloak. "Today," the old sheikh said, greeting me, "is not the day to complain that the British military have built their camp on my land or the fact that I have no bodyguards to protect me—although I have often been threatened because of my friendship with the Coalition. Today I am only your host."

My host had been alive before Iraq existed, when Amara was simply a provincial town in the Ottoman Empire. He remembered the day of duck shooting with the British explorer Thesiger in 1953— during which his good friend Faleh had been killed. It was the second tragedy for Faleh's father, the paramount sheikh of the Albu Muhammad. The sheikh had just disowned and withdrawn his protection from his other son because the boy had killed his stepmother; that son was later assassinated in the date grove opposite our office. The paramount sheikh had wept while the street sellers sang, "How can you weep for the death of the son you disowned?" They still sang the song, fifty years later.

At that time of these deaths, my host was already a grandfather. Whereas his nephew, Sheikh Ismail, only remembered Mr. Grimley, my host had been alive in 1916, when the British political officers for the twin provinces of Maysan and Dhi Qar had included Thomas and Philby, the first foreigners to cross the Empty Quarter (the powers behind the throne in independent Oman and Saudi). He had also been alive when the British sent Leachman, Aubrey Herbert, and Lawrence of Arabia from Amara in 1916 to negotiate surrender terms for the starving garrison of Kut. Herbert was the great-grandfather of my predecessor, the Irish Guards' Major Melotte, spoke fluent Ottoman Turkish, and was twice offered the throne of Albania. Leachman, the political officer in Amara, was famous for traveling alone among the Bedouin: "He could shoot a tribesmen dead for misdeeds in front of his own tribe and no hand would be lifted against him." But their mission to Kut was a failure and the Kut garrison surrendered the following day. Many of the 38,600 British soldiers who died capturing and then losing Kut were buried in the Amara cemetery. I asked my host what he knew of these events.

"Nothing, I was only a baby," he said.

"But surely your father told you something . . . ?"

"No, I'm afraid I am not as old as I look."

No one in Amara talked about the First World War. Nor did they talk about the Iran-Iraq war of 1980–88, where the front line was Maysan and in which many of the modern political leaders had fought against their own country on the Iranian side, and in which the hundreds of thousands of casualties—including young boys seeking martyrdom by marching through minefields and conscripts struggling through clouds of gas—were much more recent and personal. But everyone still talked about Colonel Leachman, who had been the British political officer in Amara and was killed in Fallujah at the start of the uprising of 1920. The sheikh who shot him in the back became a national hero, his grandson was now one of the leading figures in the Sunni insurgency, and Fallujah was still a central symbol of resistance.

Sheikh Ismail, my host's nephew, said gravely, "Do not leave us, Seyyed Rory. If you leave things will collapse. We need you." Perhaps because he was so old and dignified, his flattery almost convinced me. I felt guilty because I had just heard that I might be transferred to Nasiriyah. Maysan was now an increasingly well-run province with a good relationship with Baghdad. Nasiriyah had more than twice the population of Maysan, a tiny CPA office and an Italian military presence that largely stayed out of local politics, and the Foreign Office thought I would be more useful there. I had an irrational nostalgia for my early days, in reality fraught and burdened with responsibility, but in my memory simpler, less bureaucratic, and more personal. Perhaps, too, my vanity suffered from the realization that Molly could run the Amara office very well without my help. In any case, the autonomy and challenge that awaited me in Nasiriayah appealed, but I worried about letting down the sheikh. I hoped we had chosen the right people for the council and that they would be able to improve things after we left.

The uncle then recited some love poetry in the Marsh Arab tradition, which appeared almost impossible to translate, unless in doggerel:

> *Two gowns has she and a third of red;*
> *So sheer are they that through*
> *Their folds I yet can see*
> *Her waist's tattooed*
> *Broad band of blue.*

I assumed that there had once been more tattooing on ladies' waists in Maysan. I was assured, however, that if my classical Arabic had been good I would have heard dense ambiguity and ambitious references. The sheikh had not written much poetry since he had turned eighty, but in this one he seemed to say he preferred girls to war and politics. I said that it reminded me of one of Yeats' last poems: "Why should I that young girl standing there my attention fix/On Roman or on Russian or on Spanish politics?" I mangled the poem and the sheikh probably no more than sensed the theme, but he was laughing politely when Riyadh appeared.

Riyadh glanced briefly at me as though surprised to see me there, and then scrubbed his arms at the basin before entering. He was with his two sons and I asked after their health. He replied curtly and beckoned his children to his side. After we had eaten the bright oranges, he said, "So, Sheikh Hatem, I see you are trying to make friends with Seyyed Rory. But his occupation will be over and he is going soon. Forget him. Forget the British. It is we who will remain." And then he laughed. No one else did. Sheikh Hatem, ignoring Riyadh, came forward to me with bottles of Parisian scent and said, "We will never forget the British here." He splashed cologne over my face and arms and then over my suit jacket as well.

OUR SUCCESSORS

Though one man alone is fit for founding a government, what he has founded will not last long if it rests upon his shoulders alone; it is lasting when it is left in the care of many and when many desire to maintain it.
—*Machiavelli,* Discourses, *Book 1, Chapter 9*

In the last days before the first meeting of our new provincial council, the sheikhs repeated their threat to kill their rivals, the alternative council network avoided meeting us, and the Iranian-linked parties threatened to resign in sympathy with their two excluded friends. Nevertheless, as Molly and I entered the council chamber, there were thirty-nine new councilors present, and as we sat down, the last— Seyyed Sattar, the Sadr cleric—walked through the door. I had already greeted everyone but him individually, shaking the warm, dry hand of Sheikh Rahim and hearing the nervous courtliness of Sheikh Muhammad Abbas, the whispered suggestions of the three female representatives, the chuckle of the bear-like mayor of Maimuna. I was pleased at the solemnity that masked their excitement.

On our right was the Prince's faction; the Islamist leaders sat on the left. In the front row were clerics and sheikhs; young mayors, women, and technocrats sat at the back. This seating arrangement, which had not been planned, echoed both Western parliamentary divisions (conservatives on the right, radicals on the left) and more traditional Iraqi codes of precedence. I knew these people well. Most had killed others; all had lost close relatives. Some wanted a state

modeled on seventh-century Arabia, some wanted something that resembled even older, pre-Islamic tribal systems. Some were funded by
the Iranian secret service; others sold oil on the local black market,
ran protection rackets, looted government property, and smuggled
drugs. Most were linked to construction companies that made immense profits by cheating us. Two were first cousins and six were
from a single tribe; some had tried to assassinate each other. This dubious gathering included and balanced, however, all the most powerful political factions in the province, and I believed that if anyone
could secure the province, they could.

When we had each drunk a small cup of scalding coffee, the
gravel-voiced cleric, Sheikh Rahim, made a long speech about the
nature of liberty, Shia Islam, and sovereign government; the last two
hundred years of Iraqi history; and the importance of public service.
The alternative council chairman followed with a long speech about
harmony. There were three cameras recording the meeting, and although the sheikhs continued to chatter and one let his mobile phone
blare out some mournful dirge of Lebanese pop before answering it,
the speakers presented themselves as founding fathers, suffusing their
oratory with a gravitas that might have suited an address by Thomas
Jefferson.

It was Seyyed Sattar, the Sadrist representative, who finally silenced the chatter of the sheikhs. He began with a verse of the Koran
and then in a trembling voice announced: "This council is illegal. It
is poisoned by the presence of the Coalition. You are forbidden to
take your oaths."

I looked around the room, hoping that someone would answer
him. No one did.

"Seyyed Sattar," I began, "you must be patient."

"Mr. Rory tells us to be patient," he continued. "He boasts of all
the Coalition has given us. All? They have done nothing. Let me remind you of his promise to spend twelve million dollars on electricity

generation. Lights for the whole province. And look at this room. We are the provincial council and we are speaking in the dark." A couple of people laughed. Some, nearer me, clicked their tongues as though they thought this was a cheap shot. "Not twelve hundred or twelve thousand, twelve million dollars. But what has he done with it?"

Three members of the alternative council, led by the alternative council leader from Al Qala, who was in a brown suit and polished crocodile-skin shoes, nodded and looked at me as though I had blown the millions intended for electricity on a big night in Vegas. Two other men were shouting at the same time, and I could hear fragments of their speeches: "Rules and procedures . . . the office of the martyr . . . the occupation."

I said, "We have refurbished two hundred and twenty schools out of four hundred . . ."

"Where?" shouted the Sadr cleric. Sattar, whom I had hoped would bring Sadrist support to the council, was instead trying to destroy it.

I raised my voice over him. "And outside the window is a one-million-dollar irrigation barrage project we have completed. And the Buzurgan electricity project would have been finished . . ."

"This is lies . . ."

Abu Mustafa, the businessman and mystic, stood: *"Sallu Allah Muhammad,"* he intoned, his light voice rising to a gentle crescendo, then after a pause, *"wa Ali Muhammed."*

This salute was the traditional way of calming an argument. There was silence and then in unison forty voices chanted, *"Allah huma salli Allah Muhammad,"* paused, and in staccato finished, *"Wa Ali Muhammad."*

Silence. The "moderate" Sheikh Rahim, who had taken money for his mosque and often supported us, now stood and I had hopes he would restore some of the solemn harmony of the opening addresses. "I would like," he said, "to register my objection to Bremer's statement that Sharia law should not be the basis of the constitution.

This is an Islamic country." Today, it seemed, he was being an Islamist, not a democrat. Molly caught my eye. She had never trusted him.

"Yes, it is an Islamic country. But it is not Iran," shouted a large man from across the room. The people beside him laughed.

"What are you suggesting?" asked the speaker.

"He's suggesting nothing," drawled the cleric, who like everyone else had caught the insinuation that the Islamists were Iranian spies.

The sheikhs did not make public speeches. They were old men, and most had not completed a high school education. Because they overrated their social position and underrated their eloquence, they did not want to expose themselves to debate with educated, middle-class politicians. When the judge on my right called Abu Miriam, the Iranian-linked militia commander, to take the oath of allegiance, he rose slowly to his feet and looked down the room at Sattar, the Sadrist cleric who had said that the oath was illegal. Sattar muttered something. A man shouted at him to speak up. Sattar said nothing. Abu Miriam strode down the carpet to the podium, put his right hand on the Koran, and in a clear voice read out a promise to serve the council and the people. When the moderate Sadrist leaders from Fodala and the alternative council also walked down the aisle to take the oath, Seyyed Sattar left the room; the other thirty-nine councilors were sworn in. Molly and I were pleased: We had included every major political faction, tribe, and religious minority; no leading credible figure had been excluded; we had split the Sadrists even if we had not won them all; the different factions who had fought after the police chief's death were now inside the council, balanced against each other.

Abu Mustafa appeared in my office after the meeting, greeted me with a quick smile, but more quietly than usual, and sat, arranging his elegant robes around him. He wanted to talk about our successor—the new council.

"The only problem," he observed, "is that you and Molly chose the council—we did not elect it."

"Did we fail to balance the different factions?"

"Balanced? Oh yes, you balanced well," he said, studying me thoughtfully. *"Hafiz te shayan waghabit anka a'shia."*

The interpreter, to protect my feelings, translated, "You memorized some things and you forgot some things," but Abu Mustafa's words were a fragment from a poem that begins, *"Kul li'men ye'dai fi'elmi felsafetan."*

> *Tell him who claims to know philosophy*
> *You memorized one thing but you missed so many things*

DEPARTURES

The people make better choices in electing magistrates than does a Prince, for one can never persuade the people that it is good to elect to public office an infamous man of corrupt habits—something that a Prince can easily be persuaded to in a thousand ways.

—*Machiavelli,* Discourses, *Book I, Chapter 58*

At the next meeting we asked the new councilors to vote for the officials of the province. Most of the speeches for these posts ran something like this: "My name is Ali. I am from a well-known family in Amara. You know my father. Thirty of my family were martyred by Saddam Hussein. I fought as a *mujahid* against the old regime. I am a high-school graduate and I want to serve the province. I ask for your vote."

Abu Mustafa was elected deputy chairman of the council, Sheikh Rahim as deputy governor. There were six candidates for the position of governor. The most experienced was a retired major-general who was immediately rejected as a Baathist. He was followed by a tiny old man who made a short speech, mostly in English, saying, "I am grateful to the Coalition, yes, and I love London and Winston Churchill" while winking at Molly and me.

The votes were by secret ballot. The judge began by showing the empty box to prove there had been no tricks. Each councilor was called up in turn and disappeared into the side room, put two crosses on the ballot paper for governor, and put the ballot in the box. The papers were unfolded one by one and then read out: there was one abstention and then four votes for Riyadh, the brother of the Prince of the Marshes, and then five for the SCIRI leader with the comb-over. Then another for each; then, to my surprise, two votes for the old man who liked Churchill. It became a close race between the Prince of the Marshes and the Islamist parties. Presumably, the women and the minorities and the tribal sheikhs were voting for Riyadh, and the clerics, Dawa, and SCIRI were voting for Kadhem.

In the end, Riyadh was elected governor, his small margin ru-mored to be due to Sadrist support. If we had allowed the Iranian-linked parties to have six seats or pushed back on the number of women and minorities, he would probably have lost. Riyadh was now our successor and responsible for leading the province for the next twelve months, rebuilding the economy and preventing civil war in this poor, shattered, and fragile region. We wanted him to forge a government that was not only strong—Saddam had run a strong government—but democratic in the widest sense: better for Iraqis and stable and friendly toward us.

Riyadh marched up to the desk and with a slightly dismissive smile waited for Molly and me to make way for him. To my relief, Kadhem, the defeated SCIRI candidate, met my eyes and smiled, apparently accepting the result.

It had been a curious method of producing a governor, consider-ing that we could simply have appointed the governor ourselves, or held a full election. Instead we had constructed a "representative" council and allowed them to elect a man who was neither our choice nor the people's. The ideal governor would work with all elements in the fractured society, calm the tribes, enlist the Sadrists, make al-liances with the Iranian-linked parties, and by careful judgement and tact gain authority, transcend the factionalism, and create a unified identity for the province. Riyadh was not such a man—perhaps there was none such—but Molly and I hoped he would be at least an ad-equate partner and a strong successor. He was a competent adminis-trator, with twenty years' experience in the civil service, the respect of ministry directors, the support of the majority of the councilors, great power through his brother's militia, and excellent connections in Baghdad. His outlook was secular, modernizing, and technocratic; he was not going to hand the province to either the Islamists or Iran although he would have to compromise with their strong representatives on the council. Like us, he wanted security and economic growth; we had acknowledged him publicly as our successor. He knew we would leave for good in six months' time and that in the meantime we had the resources to help him.

I did not agree with the governorate coordinators in neighboring provinces who felt fatally wounded by poor planning, ill-defined missions, insufficient resources, and little support. I believed that our small teams, fluid identity, and relative isolation were inevitable consequences of the invasion and, indeed, advantages. I was pleased to work without interference from Baghdad or London; our team was by now experienced, flexible, and energetic; we had good relations with other parts of the system and were able to acquire more money than we could manage and spend. If we now failed to help Riyadh build a functioning state, this would not be the fault of poor organization or grand planning at the center but rather a failure of local relationships.

I invited the newly elected governor to the office. I wanted to congratulate him and to show him, for the first time, all the details of the CPA budgets and programs in Maysan, explaining that from here on out we would work together to determine projects and try to follow his wishes on expenditure. I emphasized that I was trying to get him a large and entirely independent budget. Riyadh looked at me searchingly and stroked his tired, lined face, and then, to my surprise, he smiled and said, "At last we can begin." Then he reminded me that security was at the heart of all our problems, and slowly revealed that he intended to take full control of the police, establish a secret intelligence service, ban demonstrations, arrest a journalist who had criticized him, and expel his Sadrist opponents from the council.

I listened in horror to these illegal proposals, and when he finished, suggested gently that we focus on economic development, not
security. His face became impassive, his eyes suspicious. Perhaps he
remembered earlier disagreements. He insisted vehemently that there
was no point in being governor unless he could establish security. He
rebuffed all my counterarguments, interpreting them as a personal
insult to him or an attempt to undermine his authority and promote
his enemies.

TRUST

But if you disarm your subjects, you begin to offend them for you show that you do not trust them, either because you are weak and cowardly or because you are too suspicious.

—*Machiavelli*, The Prince, *Chapter 20*

I hoped that things would improve at the first joint meeting of the new governor, the new provincial council, the ministry directors, and the mayors. Coalition governors were inventing different political structures in different provinces because Baghdad had not yet defined the legal powers or budgets for local officials. In my first weeks alone I had told officials to follow the 1968 municipalities law. John Bourne in Nasiriyah had issued an early draft of Baghdad's new proposal on interim powers, even though it was being radically revised.[7] Molly preferred the council to be an advisory body until Baghdad issued the law on interim powers. Whatever their formal powers, however, I was determined to lend the officials our authority and money until they became fully autonomous.

---

[7]All the leaders were new to their jobs and needed to gain experience and learn responsibility. The Green Zone wanted to give local councilors the power to sack ministry directors. I had long opposed this, believing that it could only lead to confusion, counterorders, corruption, and nepotism. The ministries—the only the functioning element of government—were federal services, run from the center. Baghdad's proposal would, therefore, have given the councilors sporadic power over ministries which did not report to them—in effect power without responsibility. I preferred to give the councils independent budgets for municipal projects. Baghdad seemed to be coming round to this idea but they had not yet given us the money, and in the meantime they continued to draft ambitious reforms of the structure of local government.

Molly and I intended the joint meetings of the councils and ministries to represent the people's problems to the government. The first
meeting was devoted to education, and the education director made
a presentation on the two hundred schools we had refurbished and
showed maps and copies of all our future programs. I was attending
only as an observer and, to show that the new Iraqi government was
now in charge, I sat at the side of the room, ceding the head of the
table to Riyadh.

I had expected the mayors to argue about the exact locations of
schools and to press for areas we had overlooked. But the mayors sat
in silence, and when the presentation was finished they stood, one by
one, to demand weapons licenses and control of the local police.
They had disappointed me. I guessed that because their main income
came from controlling the black market in diesel and gas through
their local filling stations, they preferred guns to schools.

They then began to make speeches criticizing the Coalition. The
new mayor of Ali Al Sharji, who had replaced my friend (the alter-
nate mayor) after his assassination—and may, indeed, have been responsible for it—roared, "You have done nothing for us. We do not
even have any oil in this province." The governor turned to me and
asked me to reply. I said that they should no longer address complaints to me but rather to the oil ministry.

"But what have you done?" the mayor persisted.

I replied, reluctantly, that we had just imported new pumps, from
Switzerland.

"As always Seyyed Rory promises," he replied. "But when will
they be installed?"

"They are installed and the refinery is producing more usable
fuel per gallon than any refinery in Iraq . . ."

"Oil was just an example," snapped the governor. "Councilors, I
promise that when Seyyed Rory and the CPA go we can get something done."

"Seyyed Rory, the twenty-five-hundred jobs-program is not enough," said Sheikh Rahim. "Many people are still unemployed."

"How about more police?" asked the cleric, Abu Mustafah.

"More schools in Al Kheir," said the mayor of Al Kheir.

"Pavements in Beni Hashim—people are rioting in Beni Hashim—you do nothing for us," said Seyyed Issa, the young mayor from the Marsh Arab *mudhifs* in Beni Hashim. The day before he had been sitting in my office talking pleasantly and thanking me for the employment program in Beni Hashim and for commissioning his people to build a new *mudhif* in the center of Amara. "Our salaries are insulting," he said now. "We should not be volunteers." Although they were now receiving salaries, district councilors received only sixty dollars a month—less than we were paying for our unskilled jobs program.

"I agree," I said, "I have raised it with the ministry. We are waiting for an answer from them."

"That is a lie," said Sheikh Rahim, my sometime-ally. "I have spoken to the ministry. They say they are waiting for you."

"You give us no power," said another mayor. "No ID cards, no weapons licenses. You don't define our authorities, or that of the governor, you give the streets over to looters . . ."

When the meeting ended, the governor invited me for coffee. This was the first such invitation. He pointed out the crowd at the gate and asked why I did not clear them. I said it was primarily an issue for the military and suggested that since the British general was visiting today, he should raise it with the general.

"I have made my point," he said contemptuously. "If you want to ignore it that is your problem."

After the meeting, the leader of the alternative council took me aside. He said that he had refused orders from the Office of the Martyr Sadr to leave the council and had broken all links with Muqtada. "I told them if I must choose between Seyyed Hassan and Miss

Molly, I will choose Miss Molly." He had been involved in a scam with the Sadr office to skim off government money but he now regretted it and would make a public confession. He assured me that the Sadr office was losing support and that, following his defection, they would be powerless. I was delighted that we had managed to get him into the council but wondered whether he would really be able to deliver his supporters or whether he had, by joining us, lost all credibility. And what would the council itself do?

In the evening Riyadh asked me for fifty dollars to repair his window, which had been destroyed in a recent demonstration. Although he was the governor, his salary was only four hundred and fifty dollars a month, and Baghdad had still not agreed to give the governors an independent budget. Not only could he not undertake projects or employ staff, he could not even buy pencils. For the sake of a tiny sum of money—a couple thousand dollars a month from the hundred billion we had spent on the invasion—we were alienating our key partner and successor. If it had been October, when I was on my own, I would have been tempted just to give him an allowance of two thousand dollars a month from our own funds and say, "You don't need to come to see me about that. You are the governor. Take the money; do whatever you like with it: buy sweets for visitors, mend your car, fix your windows." But I was not alone any longer. The CPA financial regulations did not allow us to provide salaries or budgets for officials; money was supposed to be used for construction and equipment. And it was Molly who would have to bear the responsibility if we were investigated for financial impropriety.

On this occasion I knocked on the financial controller's door. He glanced up irritably from the keyboard. "Yes?"

"Could I please have fifty dollars to fix the governor's window?"

"Does he not have a budget for that?"

"No," I replied, "under the 1968 law on municipalities . . ."

"Fifty dollars seems an awful lot for a window," he said. "Are you sure that's right?"

I went outside and found an Iraqi engineer and asked how much a window cost. "Thirty-five dollars," he said.

I walked back inside. "I have asked an Iraqi engineer. He said fifty dollars is right for a window."

"Well he's not having it now. The governor was very rude to us last week. Tell him he can have it next week." And he looked down again at the keyboard.

I walked back to my office, took fifty dollars from my own pocket and gave it to the governor. Riyadh pocketed it angrily.

An American democracy expert came from Baghdad to do "capacity building" with the local council. On a white board he drew an oblong on its side, to represent the council, and then beneath it four vertical oblongs, to represent its subcommittees. "He is drawing a dog," said a sheikh. "Are we back in primary school?" asked another. "We are an ancient civilization," said one cleric, "and they treat us like Congo cannibals."

"Welcome to your new democracy," said the democracy expert. "I have met you before. I have met you in Cambodia. I have met you in Russia. I have met you in Nigeria."

At the mention of Nigeria, two of the sheikhs walked out.

A NEW CHIEF

Just as good customs require laws in order to be maintained, so laws require good customs in order for them to be observed.
—*Machiavelli,* Discourses, *Book I, Chapter 18*

Nothing, however, made the governor as angry as the quest for a new police chief. Under the old regime the governor—who was usually a general and a cousin of Saddam—appointed the police chief and ran security. The assassination of Abu Rashid, however, had taught us the dangers of imposing a controversial chief supported by only one faction. To ensure a wider base of support, we had designed with the British police adviser a more "progressive" system, whereby the police chief would be chosen, appointed by, and remain accountable to a local public safety committee.

We received a hundred and twenty applications for the public safety committee and Molly and I sifted them with the colonel. We were able to include an eminent sheikh of the Sudan who had been left off the council but we failed to persuade the representative from Dawa Iraq tendency to take a seat. We offended the demonstration leaders Seyyed al-Musawi and Seyyed Wathiq by not selecting them, offended the Islamists by insisting that the governor, not Abu Miriam, chair the meetings, offended the governor by saying that the committee as a whole and not he as an individual should appoint and control the police chief, and offended the committee by restricting their powers. We did not even try to include the Sadrists.

This whole public safety committee system had, as the new governor never ceased to point out, no basis in law. The provincial council had no constitutional authority over the police. Baghdad wanted police chiefs to be appointed centrally, by the Ministry of Interior. And there was no such thing as a public safety committee in any other province. In short, we had made it up, on the curious model of a British police committee.

Fifteen men, all with military or police experience, applied to be chief of police. Each wrote a lengthy police plan for examination, and six were interviewed by the committee. The final vote produced three candidates: Brigadier General Sabih, the old silk-stockinged police chief, who now to our surprise had the support of the Prince of the Marshes faction (the Prince had apparently forgotten opposing his appointment two months earlier and calling him "a weak Baathist"); a middle-aged judge who had been a police officer in his youth and who had a reputation with some people for bold integrity and with others for prodigious corruption; and Abu Maytham, the habitually black-clothed Badr commander, whom we had excluded from the provincial council.

The latter, an Islamist who had spent more than a decade in Iran, working through Badr with the Revolutionary Guard, claimed to have been a special forces officer in Saddam's army, sacked for his political opposition to Saddam. An examination of his army record showed he had been in the logistics branch and suspended for insubordination and going absent without leave. The colonel called him "a special forces G3 pencil supply officer." He was, nonetheless, the most charismatic and self-confident candidate. People sympathized with him because we had excluded him from the provincial council although he had played a leading part in the province, and because his son, while playing recently with his father's pistol, had killed himself. They were also ready to have a counterbalance to the governor and the Prince of the Marshes faction. Abu Maytham, therefore, received more votes than anyone else.

We sent all three names to Baghdad with letters from the committee, explaining the voting results, and heard a week later that the Interior Minister had approved the Badr commander and former pencil supply officer as police chief. Abu Maytham's formal letter of appointment from the Minister of Interior was endorsed by the provincial council and announced publicly. This meant, as the governor screamed, that the Iranian-linked Badr brigades had now taken control of the security apparatus. Molly was worried and pointed out that we had excluded Abu Maytham from the council two weeks earlier partly because of his Iranian links, but she agreed that we had no choice but to support the appointment. If Abu Maytham had been vetoed, his militia groups, already more powerful than the police and angry at Riyadh's election, would have challenged the state; now the new chief might be able to channel Badr's strength through official channels to restore security; while the governor, the Coalition, and the public safety committee provided a counterweight to the police chief's activities.

It took some time for Abu Maytham to get a uniform—he was too large for the standard uniform and had to get a tailor down from Baghdad—but he went immediately to work and at the end of the first week had mounted a successful raid on the weapons market in al-Amara. Meanwhile, Riyadh and the Prince told the interior minister that Abu Maytham was an Iranian spy and persuaded the minister to reverse his decision and issue another letter of appointment for a new police chief from Baghdad. This decision was a direct challenge to the Shia political parties, to the provincial council who had endorsed the police chief's appointment, to the Coalition forces, and to us. Molly wrote immediately to Bremer's deputy, whom she knew well; I wrote to Sir Jeremy Greenstock, the British representative in Baghdad. Bremer arranged a meeting with the interior minister.

When the would-be chief came from Baghdad and attempted to enter the main police station, he was immediately surrounded by policemen who threatened to kill him. Abu Maytham magnanimously

offered him safe passage, but not his office. The would-be chief took
refuge in the British military camp. I walked with him in the evenings
and learned that he was an educated Baghdadi with deep prejudices
about the Marsh Arabs and "wild provinces" like Maysan. He had
accepted the job with strong reservations and was desperate now to
go home. He said Abu Maytham was welcome to the position, cursed
everyone from the Prince of the Marshes to the Islamists, and returned to Baghdad.

The British general announced that under his security powers
he was confirming Abu Maytham. Bremer's deputy, encouraged by
Molly's telegram, called in the interior minster and ordered him to
drop his opposition to Abu Maytham—a strong step at a time when
we were transferring power to the Iraqi government. The interior
minister backed down but refused to send another letter of appointment to Abu Maytham, so for the next twelve months Abu Maytham
acted as police chief without any formal appointment and the governor, who felt increasingly impotent and betrayed, refused to deal with
him.

I gave one of the civil affairs officers the task of renovating the old
Ottoman covered bazaar in the town center. He surveyed the area,
consulted shop-keepers, and proposed street leveling, draining, and
replacing modern façades in the market with traditional brick. I
wanted to build a gate for the souk as a permanent gift from the CPA
to Amara, so that there would be at least one enduring trace of our
presence. We discussed this with the governor, showed him photographs of traditional souk gates from Egypt to Kuwait, and suggested
a competition for the design. The governor returned the next day
with a design for a concrete arch, to be faced with bright modern
bathroom tiles and fairy lights. Again we had to choose whether to
empower the governor. We overruled him. The gate was never built.

The Prince was spending more time in Baghdad on national politics.
One night, however, when I stopped by Ahmed's house for dinner,

the Prince strode in. Smiling gracefully, he brought the whole room to its feet while he asked in his gentle voice after people's health.

Later there was some dancing, and after I had danced, he beckoned me to him, took the silk, gold-embroidered cloak off his back, and presented it to me. I put it on, then he sent to his house for a full set of clothes and presented them to me as well. We spent the rest of the evening sitting side by side in robes.

When the Prince heard I was being transferred to Nasiriyah, he threw a party to celebrate my departure. He did not invite me. I heard that he told the guests that I had been the main impediment to his power in Maysan, that when I left he would have a free rein, and that my departure would save the province from the Iranians. At the time, I was flattered by his complaint and proud of having counterbalanced the Prince.

But when I think back to my time in Amara, it is not the projects that I remember: not the two hundred schools refurbished, the ten thousand jobs created, the rural regeneration program, the dams, the electricity, the cooperation with the ministries, the balancing of different factions on the new provincial council, or the appointment of a strong police chief. Instead I remember how we handled the January demonstration.

DEATH BY THE OFFICE WALL

If a ruler can keep his subjects united and loyal, he should not worry about developing a reputation for cruelty; for by punishing a very few he will really be more merciful than those who over-indulgently permit disorders to develop, with resultant killings and plunderings.

—*Machiavelli,* The Prince, *Chapter 27*

JANUARY 9–11, 2004

In early January, a mob gathered in the street that divided the governor's office from our compound, waving placards and chanting, "Death to the Governor." Many people in the crowd were from the Beni Lam—rivals of the Governor's tribe, the Albu Muhammad—protesting with some reason that Riyadh was giving jobs to his relatives. The leaders also said that they had been promised eight thousand jobs in the new Iraqi civil defense force. It seemed like a larger version of previous demonstrations. Some in the crowd smiled and waved at us; most directed their attention to the governor's building. There were journalists at the edge of the crowd.

The police had no experience in crowd control and were still weak from the assassination and abortive mutiny and tussles over the police chief. Riyadh, who had surrounded himself with a break-away faction of the police—into which he had put tribal relatives to supplement the hundred cousins of Abu Rashid—insisted that we clear the square at once and impose a curfew. This was almost exactly what a British colonial administrator would have recommended; it was exactly what we did not want to do. We had some sympathy with the crowd and our sympathy with the governor was ebbing. Every encounter with him was now a confrontation. He was no longer interested in visiting us to talk about development, his accusations against journalists and rival politicians sounded increasingly paranoid, and he took every public opportunity to say that we were a waste of time. The demonstration was a semi-legal gathering, and we had no wish to disperse it violently, particularly in front of journalists. To our relief the crowd faded away that afternoon without incident.

The next day a crowd gathered again, and again Riyadh came to ask us to clear them away. We said to him: "This crowd has a right to freedom of association and freedom of speech—we have not come to bring back Saddam's Iraq." To which we added, pompously and idiotically, "Mr. Governor, in Britain there are often ten thousand people demonstrating outside the parliament."

"This is Iraq, not Britain," replied Riyadh. "They do not understand about peaceful demonstrations—you must clear them away." We refused. He returned to his office.

Some of the boys were now beginning to throw stones. An old man was standing with his bicycle between the crowd and the governor's guards, clearly neither with one side or the other, just watching. The crowd was giving the traditional ululation and chanting and whistling. One man raised a picture of Saddam, another knocked him down, a third shouted that they should attack the political parties, someone knocked him down.

The governor had begun to construct a brick wall around his office and the bricks were lying loose on the street, providing a convenient source of missiles. Some of the crowd had their faces wrapped, but most made no attempts to conceal who they were: Seyyed Wathiq al-Battat was walking pompously in front of them in turban and clerical robes, the ex-fedayeen block leader was using a mobile phone, and I recognized a man with a neat beard and a red *keffiyah* around his neck from one of the Sadrist alternative councils. We locked eyes and he gestured angrily at me: we had clearly not silenced the alternative councils by giving their leaders three seats on the provincial council. There were, fortunately, none of the tribes we had offended and no one from the Iranian parties. When Molly asked the Iranian-linked politicians to tell people to go home, they tried but were pelted with bricks. Riyadh insisted, however, that the Iranians had paid for the crowd.

A junior British soldier who had served in northern Ireland was standing next to me. "I'd just open up from this tower and slot them," he said angrily.

I brought in some of the demonstration leaders—poor men in gym shoes—to hear their complaints. One called for the governor to step down, another congratulated "our brothers in Ramadi" for killing Americans. I replied in a rhetorical flurry: "Who would you have as governor? You? Or you? And for how long? Till another mob comes tomorrow?" As the translator was stumbling through my speech, there was a harsh crackle of machine-gun fire and I shepherded the demonstration leaders into the safer center of the building, where they stood a little embarrassed, surrounded by the rest of our civilian staff.

Outside, I learned, a demonstrator had run forward, thrown an object, and sprinted away as it exploded behind him. The governor's security force pulled back, the crowd surged forward, and the governor's private police opened fire, some shooting straight at the crowd. About twenty men had been hit and two demonstrators killed at the gate of our office. These were the first deaths in a demonstration since I had been in the province.

Molly and I met immediately with the colonel and told the governor and his forces to go home. We were horrified that he had opened fire on the crowd. The British troops agreed to guard the governor's office. Occasionally the British soldiers trotted forward in a phalanx of riot shields to push the crowd back toward the junction, moving awkwardly, weighed down by their body armor and the webbing on their

hips. Usually they just stood still through the long afternoon. I watched
three young soldiers standing alone behind their plastic shields facing
what might now have been a thousand people, many of whom were
flinging rocks at them. They stood there patiently for minutes as the
pile of stones grew around them, not stepping back an inch.

Then some young men at the corner of the souk began to throw
improvized grenades again. A boy in a red parka and a man in a
shabby singlet with a white turban waved their hands a great deal in
the air and whooped after each explosion. Two of the soldiers were
injured by the grenades. One Iraqi in a blue coat, who was not waving and whooping like the rest, kept coming round the corner and
flinging grenades. I saw him shot though the head by an army sniper
and killed.

For a moment after the shot, the men scattered into side streets.
Then they reformed in greater numbers. Now the military was firing
plastic baton rounds, three hundred and fifty of them. I never saw
them lose their tempers or lash out. But at least five Iraqis were killed
during the day—most close to our gate.[8]

By evening the crowd began to wander home and the military
"de-escalated the situation" by reducing their presence on the ground.
They were thinly stretched over the province and the soldiers needed
to get back to the camp to rest. Shortly after dusk Molly and I began
to receive calls. Abu Mustafa said that a mob had got into the governor's building and was looting. Molly asked me to call the colonel and
tell him. He assured me that I was wrong and that his men were firmly
in charge of the building. Half an hour later Abu Mustafa called again
to ask what we had done to protect the building and to add that the
mob was ransacking the pharmacy on the adjoining street. British
soldiers were apparently standing by and giving the thumbs-up as
they carried out the furniture. The colonel said he would check with

---

[8]Two years later, however, in 2006, a video was released, apparently from the day of the demonstration, showing British soldiers dragging Iraqis from the crowd and beating them. The pictures were
shown worldwide and the soldiers were court-martialed.

his company commander and called back to reassure me this was nothing but rumor.

When I received a call from the electricity substation on the outskirts of town to say that they were under siege from a group of gunmen, I rang the operations room. They said they had just flown a helicopter over the substation and there was no gunfire to be seen. Then I was telephoned again from the substation to say that gunmen had broken into the outlying buildings. I asked one of the company commanders to send a patrol. I was irritating the military with my calls.

When I returned to the camp in the evening, a cold rain was flying past the cement block accommodation and hammering against the plastic walls of the portable toilets. Leaning against the wind, clutches of soldiers in waterproof coats were quick-marching toward the cookhouse.

CREDIBILITY

What will make [the ruler] despised is being considered inconstant, frivolous, effeminate, pusillanimous and irresolute: a ruler must avoid contempt as if it were a reef.

—*Machiavelli,* The Prince, *Chapter 19*

The next morning, we found a 62 mm mortar shell lying outside our perimeter wall. I wrote an e-mail to Head Office and explained that Molly, the colonel, and I had been meeting with the crowd leaders. I concluded, "A crowd of at most five hundred people is not indicative of the views of the 850,000 in the province."

After this optimistic sentence, I walked across to the governor's building with Molly and some majors from the battle group. Daylight revealed that the windows had been smashed, the doors had been kicked in, and all the computer equipment and furniture had been stolen not just from the governor's department but from the clinic across the road and from the new offices of the provincial council.

I asked the company commander how this had happened when the British soldiers were guarding the building. He reminded me that his soldiers had been seriously injured during the afternoon and that he had no desire to get drawn into a squabble between the governor and the people. Nor did he want to escalate the situation, create unnecessary enemies, and cause more resentment against the Coalition by killing Iraqis. He added that he thought the British public and politicians would not think it was worth losing a soldier's life to protect a piece of empty property. He had no more to say; he was not interested in justifying a military decision to a civilian.

We found the governor in his private office, sitting at his heavy desk, which had been presumably too large for the looters to take, and staring at his newly broken windows, surrounded by most of the provincial council. The Prince's group and the Islamists were for once sitting together. But the alternative council leaders were not in the room.

Someone was reading aloud from a pamphlet produced by the demonstrators and signed by the alternative councils:

> We condemn the crime by Baathists, who killed innocents on a peaceful demonstration for their legal rights . . . we will expose the names of the people who committed this cowardly crime and give them to justice. The Coalition has usurped all rights . . . we will make with our bodies explosives which will shake the Old British kingdom.
>
> We demand jobs, electricity, the dissolution of the Prince of the Marshes' militia, a new election to appoint a new governor, and that the following people are handed to justice.

It named the Prince of the Marshes and the governor.

"These people talk randomly," said the governor in a tense, quiet, tired voice. "Even among themselves they agree about nothing. It is impossible to get a consistent demand from them. I have declared a state of emergency," he said. "I have fired the current police chief and will be taking over. I have called the Iraqi Civil Defense Corps into the city to help restore order. No crowd will be allowed to gather again."

Chants from the courtyard confirmed that about a hundred and fifty demonstrators had again gathered at the gate and we were probably stuck inside. The calls and chatters made it difficult to concentrate on the governor's quiet voice. We waited till he had finished and then Molly and I reminded him that he did not have the power to fire the police chief, call in the ICDC, or ban demonstrations.

"Then I resign as governor. What is the point of being governor? I have no powers." He was very angry.

My military colleagues still believed that the governor had overreacted by opening fire on the crowd and that we had given a model display of restraint and de-escalation. But the Iraqis in the room disagreed. From their perspective we had failed in our duty to clear the crowd and were, therefore, directly responsible for five deaths and the ransack of the town.

"The demonstration is a deliberate conspiracy," said Abu Muslim.

Abu Ahmed claimed someone he knew was bribed with five hundred dollars to join the demonstrations by an agent of Saddam Hussein. Abu Mustafa called for the arrest of the young cleric Seyyed Wathiq, as "a dangerous revolutionary"; a fortnight earlier he had sat with him in my office.

Sheikh Rahim shouted, "The British military are deliberately trying to bring the provincial council into conflict with the people and stir a civil war. The British are responsible for everything that happened. The looting was done by the British military—they themselves have kicked down the doors. And they have stolen the computer equipment."

It was now my turn to make a show of anger. I did so partly for the benefit of the British major, to prove that despite my criticism of the previous day I was still on the military's side. "You saw the honor and restraint that the military displayed all afternoon after your police had opened fire on the crowd. And you suggest we are thieves?" The whole room was angered by my tone of voice even if they did not understand what I was saying.

"How do you explain the boot marks on the door then?" asked

Sheikh Rahim. "I can show you the marks and I can show you pho-tographs—they are British military boots."

I had no idea but I guessed, "If this happened, and I have no reason to believe it did, the soldiers were searching locked rooms or looking for observation points. They did not steal the equipment."

Sheikh Aziz shouted, "Seyyed Rory by behaving angrily thinks he can frighten us. We will not be intimidated. We reject this occupa-tion." Sheikh Aziz had long seemed a supporter of ours.

The council was enraged that we had failed to protect the build-ing. The authoritarian response they wanted—as instinctive to them as to an old-fashioned colonial administrator—was not instinctive to us. Certain measures were difficult for us even to contemplate. How many unarmed people were we prepared to kill to defend a ministry building? Were we prepared to lose soldiers to disperse a demonstra-tion? Or to defend a governor's office against looters?

It was ten months since the looting in Baghdad had badly damaged the reputation of the Coalition—a disaster that most com-mentators blamed on poor planning, insufficient troops, and bad command. In Amara, however, where we had planned, had months to prepare, and had many soldiers, well-trained and experienced in crowd control from Northern Ireland, looting had occurred again, partly because we thought property less important than life. And be-cause we could not define the conditions under which we were pre-pared to kill Iraqis or have our own soldiers killed. Occupation is not a science but a deep art that can only be learned through experience.

Finally the governor came to the point. "And why did your soldiers not protect this building from the crowd? You sent home my security force, dissolved the police line, and took responsibility for the building. How did you then let the crowd get in and steal everything?"

One of us replied, "Governor, maybe it is better that a little com-puter equipment gets stolen than that more people get killed."

And he said: "What are you talking about? Would you let the mob go stampeding into your office and loot your computer equipment?" We had no answer. Of course, we would have shot anyone who tried to break into our compound. The governor left that meeting certain that we were not prepared to give him the level of protection we gave ourselves. And from then onwards almost any hope of cooperation was lost.

PART FOUR

NASIRIYAH

Many have imagined principalities and states that have never been seen, nor known to exist. However, how men live is so different from how they should live that a ruler who does not do generally what is done but persists in doing what ought to be done will undermine his power rather than maintain it.

—*Machiavelli,* The Prince, *Chapter 15*

ARRIVALS

A stranger is leader in a foreign city.
                    —Sumerian proverb from Ur, c. 2000 B.C.

TUESDAY, MARCH 9, 2004

I set off from Amara for Nasiriyah on a dry, hot March afternoon, determined to apply my experience in a new province. I had been in Iraq seven months. The car was loaded with my clothes, a clay fish-skin drum from Gordon, a picture from the Czech NGO, and a box kite Molly had given me for Christmas that I had flown from the roof of our building with the Prince of the Marshes on Boxing Day. We passed the empty swimming pool, which the contractors were finally about to fill, and the Prince's riverfront villa, streets mostly empty for the siesta, a boy on a bicycle waving, and men in boiler suits working on one of our employment projects, and then continued on into the countryside, past the bombed bridges and the suspicious stares of men on the dusty main street of Maimuna.

There had been a lull in the violence since the demonstrations on January 10, although a day before my departure the battle group was caught in a firefight just south of Amara. It seemed to be a squabble between the Prince of the Marshes' tribe and the Iranian-linked militia groups. Three Iraqis were killed; some of the British soldiers were wounded.

After an hour, we came onto a causeway and entered my new province of Dhi Qar through a lake, where I could see reeds, and men standing in boats. From the marshes, we returned to scrub and occasional patches of young wheat, the pale green shoots only slightly taller than the yellow and black stubble of the previous year's harvest.

Different military histories lay across our path: the line of General Gorringe's advance in 1916 and that of the U.S. Marine Corps in 2003. I spoke later to Nate Fick, whose vision of my new province had been from the open top of a speeding, unarmored Humvee belonging to his Marine Recon platoon. Nate had seen the large towns outside Nasiriyah—Gharraf, Qalat Sukkur—largely deserted by the local population and occupied by thousands of Fedayeen militiamen in plain clothes, firing mortars and rocket-propelled grenades. In Nasiriyah he had been pinned on the bank of the Euphrates watching the medivac helicopters extract wounded Marines; a firefight had killed twenty of them. Running the gauntlet of an ambush in al-Gharraf, in the north of the province, his Marines fired heavy rounds and grenades into buildings on both sides of the main street. In Qalat Sukkur, his ambushers turned out to be foreign fighters, each carrying a Syrian passport with an Iraqi entry stamp a week old. But almost a year had passed since those events. The streets, though shabby, were now apparently peaceful.

We reached the cracked walls and fecal allotments that formed the suburbs of Nasiriyah and took a detour toward the Euhprates. There were two main bridges—one, larger on the highway, running through the town center, the other, smaller, ran next to the building where a suicide bomber had killed eighteen Italian carabinieri. The building was still an empty shell. We passed the main government building, which Nate had seen demolished by rockets; only a fragile façade of colored tiles remained, and a sculpture commemorating the Iraqis' 1920 uprising against the British. It depicted a British officer being shot in the back of the head. The ground beside the river and the highway was a moribund expanse of damp sand and villainous pools oozing soiled plastic. In Amara many roads were adequate; most buildings were intact; there were avenues of mature trees and parks along the river; people no longer had to wait in line for gas; and since the employment program had begun the streets were mostly clean. But Nasiriyah was a mess, and hundreds of cars queued at each gas station.

We passed a statue of the Sumerian Queen Puabi—the beech or poplar leaves had fallen from her crown—and a cracked sculpture of the harp of Ur and reached a dark patch of pale water beside the main hospital. We stopped at a barrier manned by Iraqi policemen who lifted the drop bar, allowing us to clatter down a dirt track beneath a tall concrete T-wall. In the sunken ground on our left, enclosed by a chain-link fence and overlooked by rickety illegal housing, was the courtyard that served as our office. We stopped once more at an inner gate and alighted in a sprawling trailer park that contained some shipping containers, a line of armored vehicles, and two Italian tanks. I was shown to a trailer and a shower that I was to share with an Italian doctor. I unloaded my belongings. The clay drum and the picture had broken on the journey.

I looked out through the diamond latticework of the razor wire at the casual filth and the jerry-built houses of sagging brick. After a few minutes the ditches reflected what an earlier generation might have called "the faint flush of a watery sunset." The halogen lights kicked on, driven by rattling generators, and the sand turned orange. For a moment I had an image of people in Britain living like this: in barren compounds, eating pre-packaged food in trailers, with all their wealth invested in body-guard teams, armored vehicles, razor wire, and watchtowers to protect against the malignant wasteland outside the fence. Then I heard the sound of a gun battle somewhere to the south of the compound, the halogen lamps went off, and I walked to the office.

Cast on the inner walls of the courtyard were the shadows of figures in stiff bulletproof jackets and round helmets. The bodyguard team circled like collies, barking into their radios and shepherding the civilians to cover. All the lights had been extinguished; it was hot in our body armor; and the offices were standing-room only. Everyone was too preoccupied to have a decent conversation; I felt irritated. A group of refugees from the American NGO RTI—overweight men, half-dressed, dragging kit bags—piled into the office, looking very nervous. The firefight had started at their compound wall and one of their guards had been injured.

I finally persuaded the bodyguard team that I was needed to "stop the firefight." This was untrue, as I had just arrived and knew no one in Nasiriyah, but I preferred to be in the open. I walked across the courtyard to the main telephone room with Toby, the political officer. In Amara, we would have immediately called the Prince of the Marshes, the Islamist party leaders, and the Sadrists; brought as many as possible into the office; told them to stop; and deployed a British Quick Reaction Force. I asked Toby why we were not doing the same. He shrugged. That was not the way things were done in Nasiriyah. They had too poor a relationship with the Italian military to be able to call them in, and they did not have a close enough relationship with local political leaders to put pressure on them—Toby did not even have most of their cell-phone numbers. So, really, we could only wait for the firefight to finish. It finally stopped four hours later when an Italian carabinieri patrol rolled up to investigate. The Italians reported that the fight had been started by an organization called the Citizens' Security Group.

I found it difficult to sleep that night. Dhi Qar, like Maysan, was Shia, oppressed by Saddam, Marsh Arab in the south, and influenced by large Sadrist and Iranian-linked militias. But it was twice the size of Maysan; almost no development had been done; the Italian forces rarely left their base; the provincial council had not yet been formed; and although Dhi Qar had many of the same political parties as Maysan, they had different leaders and often different programs. Dhi

Qar had a stronger urban working class and a longer political tradition—it was the birthplace of the Baath and Iraqi communist parties
and the source of most of the enlisted men in the old army. It had
fought much harder against the Coalition. The hospital on the other
side of the marshy wasteland from our building was where U.S. Private Jessica Lynch had been rescued by U.S. Special Forces during
the invasion (although the doctors kept telling us that she had been
protected and well-treated). The Euphrates was less liable to flood
than the Tigris and the irrigated farmland around it was richer: This
was why the first cities in the world had been built on its banks five
thousand years before, and why the tribal landlords of Dhi Qar were
among the wealthiest in Iraq. There were a dozen major tribes com-
parable to the two main tribes of Maysan, and their sheikhs often
lived in ancient palaces of considerable grandeur.

I wanted to achieve as much as I had in Maysan. And be more
generous to the Islamists and more supportive of the governor. I
wanted a powerful provincial council, popular development projects,
and a strong police. We had spent six months in Maysan with a
strong military civil affairs team in support. Here we had no civil affairs team and only three and a half months till the handover.

MORNING MEETING

One city does not greet another, but one man greets another.
        —Sumerian proverb from Ur, c. 2000 B.C.

WEDNESDAY, MARCH 10, 2004

There was no half-hour commute between bed and the office in Nasiriyah, so it was necessary on my first morning only to roll out of the trailer and run upstairs for the eight-thirty meeting. In the courtyard I passed a group of Filipino security guards, who smiled. Unlike the British soldiers who manned the gate in Amara, these guards were civilian employees. It was the first time many of them had been outside the Philippines.

In Amara, I had begun as the only civilian in a military base, facing in the morning meetings the British military uniform of the civil affairs team. Here everyone was in civilian dress. At the head of the table was the new governorate coordinator, John's successor Barbara Contini, and around her John's old team. In addition to the Italian doctor, there were three engineers; Barbara's deputy, Jeremy; a facilities manager; administration, political, press, and projects officers; and the security and police advisers—all of whom were American, British, or Italian civilians. Beside them was a young female Danish lawyer, visiting from Basra.

As I entered the room, Harry Boyle, a sixty-year-old Glaswegian facilities manager in a Celtic top and tight soccer shorts, was explaining what he had achieved as coach of the Nasiriyah soccer squad to Jay, a big Cornishman who, having been a submariner, a white-water rafting guide, and an NGO worker in Albania, was now the project officer. It took some time to begin the morning meeting, with various people arriving late.

Brian, the U.S. Air Force intelligence officer, who was lounging in a tan flack jacket, his long legs stretched out in front of him, described the previous night's gun fight between the Citizens' Security Group and the police. He explained that after the big bombings in Nasiriyah a number of Islamist groups had placed militias on the street. The Coalition had decided it was impossible to disband or ignore these militias, so had formed a body called the Citizens' Security Group (CSG) to regularize and control them. Nine representatives from each of the nine leading Islamist militia groups in the province were placed in the CSG and we gave the new organization an office and some basic equipment. Its role was to support the police: CSG members were not allowed to shoot anyone, but they could provide information to the police and make a kind of citizen's arrest. This solution had been approved and financed by senior figures in the Coalition. At the pinnacle of this organization they had placed Abu Jasim, an ex-resistance fighter who was—after a ten-year exile in Holland—also a Dutch citizen.[9]

The police understandably hated the existence of this paramilitary organization. The CSG in turn thought the police were incompetent Baathists. Two days before I arrived in Nasiriyah, Brian had visited the CSG and found in the basement of their building a prisoner who had been tortured. Brian had recommended that the CSG be disbanded.

---

[9] Abu Jasim was related to Sheikh Muhammad Baqr Al-Nasiri, an elderly distinguished cleric who had been the coalition's main partner in the province since the invasion—a sort of religious equivalent of the Prince of the Marshes—and who like the Prince appeared to be very powerful but was, in fact, increasingly discredited among the public, in part because of his proximity to the Coalition.

On the evening of my arrival, a CSG man had argued with a policeman at a checkpoint, the Iraqi police had marched on the CSG
building, and the gun battle started. Over the next four hours, the
CSG killed five policemen and wounded many more. The police
killed no one from the CSG, but when the carabinieri arrived the
CSG surrendered and some of their members were arrested and then
tortured by the angry policemen. The CSG men were still in custody
and both the police and the CSG were shouting for revenge: the
CSG because of the "unprovoked attack" and torture, the police for
their dead comrades.

The timing could not have been worse: Ambassador Bremer had
just told a large press conference that the Coalition had nothing to do
with militia groups and that all militia groups had been disbanded.
Suddenly the press had learned that in Nasiriyah we had financed a
militia group that was killing policemen. Barbara asked me to reassure Baghdad.

I came downstairs to find the courtyard outside my office filled
with widows, unemployed laborers, and builders looking for contracts.
No one had an appointment. In Maysan the gate procedures of the
British Battle Group ensured only senior visitors could enter without
appointments. I was learning that in Nasiriyah the gate guards either
refused to let the governor through the door or allowed everyone in.

I stole some bread from the canteen and slipped into the TV
room to make some toast and coffee. Toast finished, I moved to my
new office—a cramped room half the size of my place in Amara with
a faded purple velvet sofa. My e-mail opened with a message from
Baghdad, marked "importance high," demanding to know whether
we had backed the militia, when we would disband it, and whether
we had any "defensive press lines." I wrote back obsequiously that
"the events of March 9 clarified for everyone the need to integrate
the political parties into the democratic polity and strengthen the police." "Polity" was a word I thought they'd like in Baghdad.

As I finished the e-mail, a slight, bearded Iraqi man in a shiny Rumanian suit entered my office. He seemed surprised to see an unfamiliar face. I guessed everyone else had refused to see him so he had been passed on to me. But he glanced around my shabby room without reproach. He was not surprised that the Coalition administration operated out of cramped concrete rooms with peeling walls and cheap furniture. He looked nervous.

"Seyyed Rory, you must reopen the office of the Citizens' Security Group," he said after introducing himself as Abu Jasim, the commander of the CSG.

"I am afraid after last night that will not be possible," I replied.

Abu Jasim insisted that the CSG had unrivaled intelligence networks and was the only hope for security in the province. "But most important," he added, "I need fifteen thousand dollars."

"Why?"

"To pay blood money to the dead policemen's families. If we pay, they will release the CSG men from prison."

"But the CSG men have killed five policemen—they should be tried," I said.

"They committed no crime. If someone attacked your house would you not shoot back? Everyone has a right to defend their property with guns."

"Not if the people trying to enter it are the police," I said.

"But we are police too."

"No. You are not," I insisted.

"Anyway, this is off the point. The blame is probably equal. But the problem is that the dead policemen's tribal sheikhs have taken out *gauma* on me—their entire tribe will be against me and no one will defend me if I don't pay immediately. If the money is not paid the province will go up in flames. So you must give me the money."

"Me? Why is this my responsibility?" I asked. "You shot the policemen. And now you want me to pay compensation?"

"Yes."

He left without the money.

The canteen, where I went for coffee, was run by a subsidiary of Halliburton. It was in a single metal trailer that could only seat half the office at any time and served cardboard hamburgers on plastic plates. The South Asian kitchen staff worked in cramped conditions, did not get the opportunity to cook the food they liked, and seemed unhappy.

The first visitor after coffee was a middle-aged representative of Hizbollah-Iraq, the Nasiriyah branch of the Prince of the Marshes party. He said he had been in Iran for a decade and was committed to Sharia law. In Maysan, the Prince's party distanced itself from both Iran and the Islamists. I would have to rewrite my chart of the political parties to describe Dhi Qar. He told me to reopen the CSG; his group had been part of it.

I reminded him that the CSG had tortured a prisoner.

He leaned forward before I had finished speaking and said with a smile, "Seyyed Rory, the Coalition tortures people."

"No, we do not," I answered angrily, convincing myself.

"Seyyed Rory, you do not understand. How do you make a prisoner talk without torturing them?" He raised his hands and looked at the interpreter, who nodded sympathetically. "Do you think they will just tell you what you need to know out of the goodness of their heart?"

This was too much for me. I told him torture was illegal and he could leave my office. The interpreter apparently failed to convey my disgust, because the party leader gave an amiable and patronizing smile, said he hoped I would remember his words and he looked forward to meeting me again, and swaggered to the door.

That evening, Toby and I met the Islamist parties that wanted to be included in the new provincial council. I felt I was back in Amara, four months earlier. We met in the assistant governor's office because the parties refused to come to the CPA building and sat opposite an unsmiling engineer from the more moderate wing of the Sadrist party and two younger men from the more extreme faction.

Toby had tried to find many of the candidates through mini-elections with female NGOs, a gathering of tribes, and their unions. But the political parties refused to agree on a division of power and Toby was now compelled to decide how many seats to give to the Sadrists, the Iranian-linked Islamist parties, and the secular parties.

When the Sadrists insisted that they should have the most seats on the provincial council, Toby replied in his quick colloquial Arabic, clarifying their reasons and, when their demands became too extreme, gently teasing them. When they said they would resign, he flattered them into dropping the threat. When they became unreasonable, he let them see his anger and disappointment. I—and I think they—were impressed by his combination of Jordanian Arabic, Californian charm, and sincerity.

My role was to explain our choices. Amara had taught me to be as clear and firm as possible. I said the council was supposed to represent as many groups as possible, rather than mimic a national election. I would allow two Sadrist factions but not a further sub-division between Fodala and Fadhile—the virtue party and the virtuous party; nor was I prepared to see the clerics as separate from the political parties. They threw the names of twenty parties at me and I explained why only three factions mattered. When they accused us of being prejudiced against the Sadrists, I agreed. They gave me two reasons to believe that SCIRI was associated with Iran; I gave a further ten. Then Toby reminded them of how far we had come and asked for a compromise. We left with an agreement. There would be more Islamists and Trade Union Representatives on the council than in Amara and this seemed good.

A SECOND GOVERNOR

Win and keep the confidence of your leader. Strengthen his prestige at your expense before others when you can. Never refuse or quash schemes he may put forward; but ensure that they are put forward in the first instance privately to you. Always approve them and after praise modify them insensibly, causing the suggestions to come from him, until they are in accord with your opinion. When you attain this point, hold him to it, keep a tight grip of his ideas, and push him forward as firmly as possibly, but secretly, so that no one but himself (and he not too clearly) is aware of your pressure.

—*T. E. Lawrence*, Article 4 of 27 Articles,
first published in the Arab Bulletin, *1917*

THURSDAY, MARCH 11, 2004

When I walked into Toby's office on my second day in Nasiriyah, Toby was leaning on his desk with his sleeves rolled up, surrounded by papers and shouting at a man in a tightly cut brown suit. The man was shouting back.

Toby introduced me. This man was the governor of Dhi Qar. Since it seemed the energy had gone out of the conversation, I suggested the governor lunch with me in the canteen.

As I arrived with the governor and his two bodyguards, the canteen trailer was about to close. We received a number of aggressive looks from people who apparently did not think I should be taking an Iraqi into the canteen. I spoke a little Nepali and was able to ask the kitchen staff not to lock the canteen door, but there seemed no way to get hot food. Instead, the governor's bodyguards gathered a selection of fruits, soft drinks, and cheese-flavored crackers.

The bodyguards sat at the other end of the room and the governor spoke good English, so we could talk freely. The governor's grandfather, Badr Rumaiath, had been a great guerrilla leader known as the Lord of the Marshes. When he fought the British, he rode into battle with twenty-five of his sons.

Determined not to repeat the mistakes of Amara and conscious of how little time remained, I told the governor that we would immediately give him a budget for his office expenses, a private secretary, and a secretariat for the ministries and the provincial councils. I felt that if he did not have political and financial power he wouldn't be able to secure the province.

I picked up the remnants of the lunch—the banana skins and orange peel and cracker wrappers and soda cans—and, balancing them on the tray, began to walk toward the door, wondering how I was going to fund all this.

"Thank you," said the governor, embracing and kissing me.

That afternoon, Toby and I visited a district council. We drove for an hour and a half, across flat ground and on causeways through marshes, into a cluster of shabby concrete buildings beside a tributary of the Euphrates. Although it was only mid-March, it was very hot and the dust, the harsh light on white-washed walls, and the streets empty for siesta hinted at the coming summer. We parked on the street and walked though a courtyard that shimmered with flies, into a dark room with heavy furniture. There we were given smeared glasses of tap water and, in Arabic, Toby launched into a long and detailed discussion of election procedures.

There had been no free elections in Iraq in fifty years, no proper census or voter registration, no agreement on electoral procedures, and no voter education. The CPA had prevented us from holding early elections—because "in Bosnia early elections produced bad parties and a sectarian split." Baghdad had written an e-mail saying that "we agreed from the moment of the invasion that there were to be no elections in Iraq in the foreseeable future." So long as we appointed the councils—and, indirectly, the governors—we could limit their powers and interfere if we found their policies too authoritarian, too Islamist, or too confrontational. If councils were elected, we would lose control.

Toby had agreed to appoint the provincial council, much as we had in Maysan, but he had disobeyed Baghdad over the district councils and held elections in fifteen districts. He was planning to hold one more in this district. His elections were rough and ready affairs, with the voter rolls drawn from lists of ration-card holders (lists that were not perfect and led to arguments about places of residence).

I thought the elections were dangerous and unnecessary at a time when Dhi Qar seemed to lag behind Maysan. Whereas in Amara we had undertaken hundreds of projects with budgets of millions of dollars, almost nothing of the sort had been attempted in Nasiriyah—or at least nothing that had been recorded and run through the CPA accounting system. The Italian military did far fewer patrols than their British counterparts, and whole areas of the province rarely saw anyone from the Coalition. There was no weekly coordination meeting with the ministry directors; the police were badly led, incompetent, and disliked. The office needed to resolve its relationship with the police-murdering Citizens' Security Group. There was no database of local tribal structures or political parties; the gate system hardly functioned; translators were often unavailable; transport had to be booked twenty-four hours in advance; it was difficult to persuade many local figures to visit the office. I thought we needed to solve all these problems before we considered more elections. But both Toby and I agreed that we needed to give more power to the local bodies.

———

Baghdad had still not confirmed the powers of the local governments. The central budget of the Iraqi government remained dwarfed by the money directly controlled by the CPA—billions of dollars, confiscated from Saddam or from the UN oil-for-food program, were spent by CPA officials and Coalition generals, and the further 18.3 billion for development was administered and allocated by the U.S., rather than the Iraqi, government. Coalition forces frequently overruled local police chiefs and refused to give them heavy weapons.

There were good reasons for all of this—the Iraqi government lacked capacity and was corrupt, and the 18.3 billion was from U.S. taxpayers; the Iraqi police would use the heavy weapons for crime and intimidation or simply sell them to the insurgents. Local politicians were often violent, criminal, and fanatic. But we were transferring sovereignty in three months. We were not proposing to run a colonial government. So long as we refused to give our successors credibility through elections, money, and a powerful security force, they would be unable to create a functioning state. This was why, against instructions from Baghdad, Toby was holding elections and I was giving a large independent budget to the governor and his colleagues. The Iraqis needed to have status and money and the power to make legal decisions and appointments. How else could they secure the province?

SAGE OF THE ASSEMBLY

These rushes, these old reeds—when set on fire, they come down from the sky.

—Sumerian proverb from Ur, c. 2000 B.C.

FRIDAY, MARCH 12, 2004

My first morning visitor was the archaeological director, a tall man in his forties with sunken cheeks. He had brought as a welcome gift a book on Sumerian religion.

"Now that you are with us," he said, "you can help to pay for the archaeological guards. Mr. John Bourne has been supporting them for months. The police chiefs are weak. Thousands of policemen do not come to work. The Sadrist leader Ali Zeidi has taken control of the northern towns. All the Sumerian sites are being looted, Seyyed Rory, right up the route of Gilgamesh, from Larsa to Umma. Twelve thousand dollars a month would be enough to employ two hundred guards."

I said I thought we could find the money and agreed to chase up the vehicles and weapons that were apparently waiting for him in Baghdad. It seemed a pity that this gentle historian should now have to become a paramilitary commander.

He talked a little about the third dynasty of Ur, whose heartland had been the twin modern provinces around Nasiriyah and Amara. He continued to come across administrative correspondence that had survived on shattered cuneiform tablets; the letters were four thousand years old but some of the problems with provincial administration seemed unchanged. Sulgi, the King of Ur, had written advising an official to give full power and authority to a ruler of the marsh region and cease trying to overrule him:

The man to whom I have sent you is not your subordinate—he will not take orders from you. How can you ignore what he has achieved in his own right?

If I do not make my Sage of the Assembly feel just as important as I am, if he is not allowed both to appoint and then to remove a governor, if he does not kill or blind anyone, if he does not elevate his favorite over others—how else can he secure the provinces?

If you truly love me, you will not bear him a grudge; come to an understanding, you two; secure the foundations of the provinces: it is urgent!

Sulgi's attempt had failed. He relied heavily on one of his senior commanders, Isbi-Erra, to secure his borders with modern Iran. This commander seems to have had close connections to the enemy and to have turned against the king. And in the subsequent invasion the government of Ur was toppled, its treasures looted.

Then I went upstairs to see Barbara Contini, the governorate coordinator. She looked up as I entered, said "Amore, at last you come to visit," and patted the seat beside her. As I sat, she laid her well-rounded arm and perfect red nails on my forearm. She was one of the few officials who managed to be glamorous in a war zone. Later, when we were thrown out of our bunks by mortar fire, she emerged with precise eyeliner and a loosely wrapped kimono, like a mature Madame Butterfly. The kimono—along with her fluent Japanese—was a legacy from her many years working for an aerospace agency in Japan. From there through the mysterious channels of Italian politics—she was rumored to be close to the right-wing party—she had been appointed to run an international office in Bosnia.

"Amore" was her favorite word. She used it to greet everyone from her project staff to Iraqi clerics. She was adored by her body-guard team and by the British military and disliked by other women in the CPA and the men who had worked for her predecessor in Nasiriyah. The Iraqis appeared to like her and enjoy her emotional outbursts and her maternal bearing.

I explained what we were trying to do with the CSG and pro-posed we set up a more innocuous body—an advisory council or something—so the ex-militia commanders would feel they had not been entirely excluded.

"I trust you. As far as I am concerned, you are me—I don't need to know the detail."

We discussed how to spend ten million dollars. Barbara and I had been brought in to ensure that many official projects were completed before the handover. She wanted to make sure the projects were prop-erly publicized by the media; she mentioned extra donations she had received from companies in Italy, and sketched out four million dol-lars of water projects she was keen to complete. I began arguing for the money to run the three-thousand-person employment scheme and she said, "Listen, Amore, if you think this is worth doing we will do it. You have total independence to design and implement your own programs."

I was delighted. I wanted to use this opportunity to transfer pro-grams immediately to the Iraqis. I did not want us to run things six-teen hours a day right through to the last day and then switch off the lights. In any case, in Nasiriyah, unlike Amara, we had neither the re-sources nor the manpower to run things ourselves. I said I was deter-mined to build the kind of trust with the Dhi Qar Iraqi governor that I had failed to build in Amara. Barbara nodded and then asked an Italian soldier to bring us some espresso. It took twenty minutes to make and came with a rich top like caramel.

In the evening I played Ping-Pong with the Iraqi Deputy Governor. He praised Toby for all his efforts in holding elections. Earlier, I had heard the same from some of the translators. I was discovering that Toby's elections had been very popular. They had generally resulted in the election of men in their mid-thirties—non-political technocrats with engineering degrees from good universities. Whereas in Maysan people perpetually criticized us for selecting councils, here the process was transparent and the councils seemed more legitimate.

The deputy governor asked me if it was true that Danish citizens were being evacuated. I said it probably was. "In which case, I would like to be evacuated. I am a Danish citizen." I told him he was the deputy governor and he could not leave. He beat me at Ping-Pong.

Then I had a beer with Franco Corbani, a sixty-year-old Italian engineer. Franco had been in the office for longer than anyone else— so long that no one could remember what he had been hired to do. His card said "Special Projects." Franco wanted to interest me in funding a three-mile tree-lined Haussman boulevard through the center of Nasiriyah, ending with a "Palazzo Italia" on the river bank. He told me he had been a young communist in Cuba:

"When Castro was forming a cabinet, he gathered everyone and said, 'Who knows about education?' One man replied, 'I was a teacher, comrade,' and Castro said, 'You are the minister of education. Who is an economist?' Che raised his hand. 'You, Che, are the governor of the central bank.' Later we asked Che, 'Why did you say you were an economist?' 'Economist?' says Che. 'I thought he asked, "Who is a communist?"'" He was governor of the Central Bank of Cuba for eighteen months."

Some others joined us and Jay, the Cornish projects officer, described how Franco had come into the morning meeting a month earlier to describe a strange tap he had found between the shower-head and the soap dish when washing his hair in his trailer.

"We all went down to have a look," said Jay, "and fuck me if there wasn't an unexploded mortar shell stuck in his shower wall, three feet from where he was sleeping. Someone had dropped it straight through the roof."

Everyone had heard the story before but they still laughed—they liked the idea of Franco, with his eyes full of shampoo, trying to adjust the hot water by turning the tail fin on a mortar shell. That was the end of my third day in Nasiriyah.

MUDHIF

SATURDAY, MARCH 13, 2004

I introduced some of the things that had seemed to work well in Maysan. I established the foundations of a three-thousand-person employment scheme, met and documented all the political parties, wrote a forty-page paper on the tribes of Dhi Qar, organized the selection of a new police chief, managed staff inside the office, helped Toby select the provincial council, dealt with riots and large demonstrations outside the door, went on leave. The carabinieri and the Iraqi police were late for the first day of the employment registration and I walked out of the labor office to find an unruly crowd at the gates. I spent two hours shepherding them into three lines, pleading with them to be patient, reassuring old men, joking, wrestling people out of the lines. After months locked in a compound, surrounded by bodyguards, I enjoyed the physical contact with the crowd. A small British military civil affairs team joined us and took responsibility for the reconstruction projects. Two of them in particular—Ginnie and Sam—were systematic, quick, and efficient and enabled us to keep our attention on the politics. I was able to do some things I hadn't done in Maysan: fund the archaeological protection service to guard the Sumerian sites, and write a visitor's sign explaining the history of the Ziggurat of Ur.

I also commissioned Abu Mthenna, the man who had built the Beni Hashim mudhifs, to build two mudhifs in Nasiriyah. I placed a small one at the gate so visitors could wait in private, not humiliatingly in the sun. For the larger one, by the Euphrates, I asked him to copy the now long-vanished mudhif of the Albu Muhammad chief Majid Bin Khalife from a 1953 photograph and then enlarge it. The result was a hundred feet long and had twenty-five columns on each side. It was, I think, the largest mudhif ever built.

I went out with Ginnie, a British Engineer Lieutenant, to see it constructed. Abu Mthenna and four relatives had cut and bound a high pile of reeds into fifty bundles, each thirty feet long and just too broad for a man to wrap his arms around; two rows of twenty-five holes had been dug and the bundles driven into the earth as pillars, the sharp blades of the tallest water grass standing up in a ragged spike; each column was ribbed with horizontal bands binding the sheaf together.

Ginnie found an unexploded mortar shell in the foundations and we had to wait until the Italian bomb disposal team could clear the mortar. Then Abu Mthenna continued. From the top of reed ladders he bent the two rows and wove them into each other so they appeared as single hoops, making a barrel vault. The space between was enclosed with solid reed mats; two entrance columns stood at the front of the building; and two shorter, conical stumps formed the corners. The façade was broken by the shadows of the diagonal supporting struts. It took him a week to build a hall that would last for twenty years and could accommodate hundreds of people. We placed it on the edge of a public park as a symbol of traditional culture and invited tenders for someone to create a teahouse inside.

I continued to help Toby design the provincial council and we became much closer friends. I had now met a number of his elected councils. Some were corrupt, many were dominated by particular tribes—but they had a legitimacy none of the appointed councils could hope for. I was beginning to realize that delaying elections would not produce more moderate councils. In fact, by delaying we would only undermine the transitional government and strengthen the hands of the Islamist parties. We should have held elections all over Iraq. I agreed to hold an election for Toby in one of the remaining districts. Even Baghdad seemed to be coming round to his side: they had begun to boast of his elections in press conferences and he had been profiled on the front cover of the *Washington Post*.

I also helped form a public safety committee, modeled on the one in Maysan. It included Abu Jasim, the controversial leader of the now-disbanded Citizens' Security Group militia, who claimed he was an invaluable intelligence source. "Not a leaf drops in the province without my knowing it." The committee was presided over by Seyyed Faris, a formidable tribal and religious leader from the south. And it included a man who was deep in the carjacking and looting rings but was reputed to have unrivalled insights into the criminal world. The committee's role was to oversee the police and to agree with the police chief on a policing plan.

Its members saw themselves, however, as super-policemen. They wanted to carry weapons and fancy permits and be able to give orders to policemen at will.

"You are not policemen," I explained. "You are not supposed to give orders to police officers. You are only an oversight committee providing accountability to the public."

"You will see," replied Seyyed Faris, "how much you need us. This is a small place. We know everything that happens here."

I asked them to keep an eye out for insurgents and terrorists.

"Of course we will. Why do you think there have been no attacks here since November? Because of us."

ALI ZEIDI

In the city with no dogs, the fox is boss.
                    —Sumerian proverb from Ur, c. 2000 B.C.

In my first three weeks in Nasiriyah we held three municipal elections, appointed a new police chief, disbanded the CSG militia, dealt successfully with a flood on the Euphrates, completed the registration of fifty thousand people for our jobs program—nearly five times as many as in Amara, and spent a million dollars on a new road and nearly two million on new council buildings. But the councils remained at the mercy of the Sadrist militia—particularly in al-Rafai, a town of 150,000 people in the north of the province. Its council had been elected the previous September. Toby thought the election was valid and was determined that this new body be supported. But the Sadrist militia in the town had boycotted the elections and now resented their exclusion from power. When the council funded an Internet café, the Sadrists complained that the café was being used to surf porn sites and that the councilors had skimmed money from the contract.

The Sadrist leader had walked with some armed friends into the council office and forced the council chairman to resign at gunpoint. Toby had persuaded the chairman to resume office. Then the

Sadrists bombed the Internet café; raided the city council warehouse, apparently stealing humanitarian aid; and sent all council members letters saying they would be killed.

This was a test case not just for Toby's elections but for political order in the south. Were we going to be able to transfer power to an authoritative Iraqi government, or were we going to leave a handful of fanatical militias controlling provincial towns?

The Iraqi police refused to act although there were nearly four hundred policemen in the town and the militia rarely numbered more than six. The Italians sent a patrol to investigate; the young Sadrist militia commander and his friends fired two rocket-propelled grenades at the patrol; the Italians left quickly and from then on the Coalition rarely visited. The neighboring Sumerian archeological site of Umma was looted. The city was now out of control. There were rumors that the militia would use this base to mount attacks on the Coalition elsewhere. Toby was furious with the Italians for not arresting the militia commander.

"I'm sure we can get around this," I said. "Why don't we call a meeting of local notables and sheikhs and get them to agree to hand over the militia leaders and support the council?"

"Sheikhs? I didn't come here to set up a feudal state."

"We need to work for a political solution."

"I can work for a political solution," he exploded, "but I am completely bored of having to do this. This is not my job. Why will the Italians never do anything? Why has it always got to be me who goes out there and sorts it out? All they need to do is send a patrol."

"That's true, Toby. But we're going to find a way round it together."

"Whatever," he said. "But please don't talk to me about it now. I have slept about three hours in the last three days. I cannot handle this now. I am trying to set up a new council or the province is going down."

———

I went to al-Rafai the following week. I learned there had been flaws in the election; the elected council probably was corrupt; and council members had themselves thrown bombs at the houses of two Sadrists and attacked the Sadr office. Nevertheless, our reputation was pinned to supporting them and this test was vital for the future of councils throughout the province.

The attacks were blamed on "the Co-ordination Committee of Political Parties in al-Rafai." I had never heard of this committee. "Khazeh Hamid and Turkey Lahmoud" were rumored to be key players. I had never heard of them either. But everyone agreed that at the center of the trouble was a young Sadr cleric called Sheikh Ali Zeidi. It was he who had attacked the council office and fired the RPGs at the Italians. And I hoped to use the two largest tribes in al-Rafai—the Shweilat and the Beni Rikaab—to deal with him.

I traveled to al-Rafai with Barbara and a burly translator whose father was a farmer in al-Rafai. The translator claimed, as a local, to be an expert on the tribes of al-Rafai, but he seemed to know little about them. He had been the first of his family to graduate from high school, but his previous career as an English teacher in a secondary school had been interrupted when he was arrested by the Baath and tortured in the building opposite our office. They had burned him with electric wires and he had cursed them. They had warned him that if he did not shut up they would kill him and he had cursed them again. Eventually they released him but translating for us was his first job for years. His colleagues said the worst damage had been to his mind. He made little attempt to conceal his rage against British and American imperialism.

On the outskirts of al-Rafai, where the Marine officer Nate Fick had called down an air-strike on a building locals assured him was a Baath headquarters, traffic and people were moving in the streets. We could see no sign of the recent fighting. We drove out of town through an expanse of flat, dry, empty fields and then turned toward a compound. A tractor, a threshing machine, and a large black Mercedes were parked outside a long, low one-story cement structure that resembled the office on a construction site. We entered a narrow and dark hall with a bare cement floor and there took off our shoes. There was the sound of children running and a clatter as though of two pans brought sharply together. The bodyguards were ahead of us as usual, weapons out. They went through the main door, then stopped suddenly.

When we entered behind them we found a room a hundred feet long with a high ceiling and long windows. A hundred imitation Louis XV chairs with carved and painted arms and powder-blue silk covers lined the sides. The silk carpets were soft under our stockinged feet, and small black-and-white photographs showed Arab men in riding jodhpurs, standing on podiums, or in gardens beside British officers and Iraqi royals. The photographs stopped in 1956 with the revolution. But this was a new room, the family was still wealthy, and the translator whispered that the sheikh had continued to entertain Saddam in this room and been rewarded accordingly. If so, those photographs had been removed.

A small dark man in a *dishdasha* gestured us to seats at the top of the room, left, and returned with a tray of drinks. We sat in silence. Then another door opened and Sheikh Arkan Hairullah entered the room. He moved very slowly in his robes, one careful pace at a time, and his small eyes were a startling blue. We stood to greet him.

He spoke in a half whisper. "Ahlan wa sahlan bikum," welcome, honorable one. "Welcome, honorable one, thank you," we said. "Welcome, honorable ones," he repeated. Then we sat down and said it a few more times. His head, neck, and shoulders were unnaturally still, but his hands were trembling. It seemed he had Parkinson's disease.

I began by saying that we came to introduce ourselves, having heard so much about him and his distinguished family. He nodded. The translator began to light up a cigarette. Barbara thought it was rude to smoke during meetings. She glowered at him; he glowered back. I reached out and patted his arm and he put down the packet and returned to translating.

The sheikh pointed to a painting of his grandfather, who had fought the British in the First World War. The slightly primitive painting of this man in ringlets with a cloak never seen today suggested a quite different era when the Shweilat had still been both landlords and bedouin, masters of many horses. As one of the two largest tribes in al-Rafai, the Shweilat had played a prominent role during the First World War, swapping sides between the Ottomans and the British.

He talked of his relatives who were doctors in London. He described their old castle, which still stood in the center of al-Rafai. He showed me a picture of his relatives standing with the crown prince on one of the castle balconies in the 1930s. He feared he would eventually have to demolish it. I suggested that we could co-operate to restore it and turn it into a museum; it was the only piece of nineteenth-century secular architecture left in the province. He was doubtful whether craftsman who could repair the carved wooden balconies and the plasterwork still existed.

The interpreter again took out his packet of cigarettes, put one in his mouth, and reached to light it. Again, Barbara motioned to him to put it away. The translator looked at her for a moment, then violently tore the entire packet in half, held up the stumps of the broken cigarettes, and threw them into the ashtray. The sheikh looked away.

We assured the sheikh that we would build a clinic in his area. Barbara and I then explained that the elected council in al-Rafai was being threatened by the Sadr office and that we needed his support. We asked him what he thought of the council. He said he had been surprised that no one had informed him about the election when it occurred. Nevertheless, he would do his best.

"Can we tell this to the head of the council?"

"Yes. Tell him he can come to me and I will give him the protection of my tribe."

Business over, we moved through to lunch at a table laid end to end with flat fish two and a half feet long, bowls of sweet grilled eggplant, mounds of saffron rice, lumps of mutton, and whole roast chickens. Everyone had to eat at least some fish, some fowl, some meat.

The paramount sheikh of a tribe is not simply the eldest son of the previous sheikh; rather, his tribe chooses him in accordance with lineage, wealth, and character. Cousins can, therefore, succeed instead of sons. There was little doubt that Sheikh Arkan Hairullah was the paramount sheikh of the Shweilat. He was clearly wealthier and more powerful than anyone else and only the most genealogy-soaked impoverished cousins muttered that his great-great grandfather had illegitimately displaced their great-great grandfather, that most of his land had been acquired by blackmailing and legal trickery that had shocked even the British, and that the Shweilat was technically only a clan of the Humeid confederation.

But the Beni Rikaab, the next tribe I visited, had no clear paramount sheikh. Ismail—the eldest son of the last great sheikh—had visited me earlier to ask for his lands back. He had lived with his son in London for the last decade and had brought his eighteen-year-old son with him. The son was tall with bright red lips, very good-looking, and apparently aware of it. Although he was wearing tribal robes, he looked as though he was wearing them over six hundred dollar jeans. Taleb, Ismail's younger brother, was unwilling to concede the leadership and, being more Machiavellian, had succeeded in carving out a position for himself. Meanwhile their uncle Shlage, though frail, was still alive and perceived by the majority of people in al-Rafai as the paramount sheikh with his son Yunus serving as his heir and representative. Time, the performance and wealth of the sheikhs, and the preference of the tribe theoretically would determine which of these cousins emerged as paramount. But tribal structures were no longer what they had once been, and I guessed that the issue would never be resolved.

I had seen Ismail in the office, and been to Shlage and Yunus' house the week before. Now we wanted to visit Taleb. Taleb was much better known among the party crowd in Baghdad than any of his brothers or cousins. The Italian ambassador who had been in Baghdad for five years particularly recommended him to me as a civilized, powerful man well-disposed to the Coalition. We had asked for his assistance and he had promised to mobilize the town in support of the council. He also offered to keep security in the whole district if we would just give him the money and the weapons.

Taleb lived in a narrow street, in a house much smaller than his cousin's, in the center of al-Rafai, a city essentially under Sadrist control. We, therefore, took an extra bodyguard team and the Italian military moved tanks into the square to support us. Taleb, a thin man in Polaroid glasses, kissed Barbara when we alighted—the first time in the south I had seen an Iraqi kiss a woman. Thirty middle-aged Iraqis were sitting in a cramped room. These, he whispered, were the people he had invited to resolve the problem with Ali Zeidi, the Sadrist leader.

Barbara began by saying how grateful she was to everyone. She reminded them of the election of the council and said she was counting on everyone to support the council and not be intimidated by Ali Zeidi.

But to our surprise, man after man replied that the council was no longer acceptable and that they would form their own council. We objected. Then Ali Zeidi, the man we wanted to arrest, entered the room. He was in his late twenties and, like many of the Sadr clerics, wore a robe of rich dark cloth. Everyone stood to greet him. He sat down and told us the current council was composed of criminals and he was delighted that we had agreed on Sheikh Taleb's advice to abolish it.

"Sheikh Ali Zeidi, we have agreed nothing of the sort," I said angrily. "We are supporting the elected council. And we will continue to support it against anyone who threatens it."

Sheikh Taleb intervened. "Barbara, I am sorry I did not have time to prepare you properly, but really the current council is no good. In any case its term has expired. We will form another council and I am prepared to serve as chairman. We have already chosen the members of the council from this room. When you leave today, there will be a new council, supported by Ali Zeidi. But please let us wait for a moment until the food comes, because we have prepared a special banquet for you. Then we can talk more."

Sheikh Ali Zeidi turned to the room and talked about the iniquities of the Coalition and the importance of remaining separate from Coalition structures.

I stood up, signaling Barbara. I said we were not prepared to listen to this from a man such as Sheikh Ali Zeidi, who had attacked unarmed civilians and fired rocket-propelled grenades at Coalition troops, and we walked out. The entire room rose to their feet. To refuse a meal is a serious insult. At the door, I told Sheikh Taleb that we did not appreciate being invited into a trap and did not expect to meet with him again. We drove out on back-streets half-expecting to confront an angry Sadrist mob. But the city was quiet and I hoped that Ali Zeidi would not dare to attack us in Nasiriyah.

Back at the office, Barbara sacked the translator because of the argument over the cigarettes. He left shouting, "We are coming for you. We will not rest until you are driven from this province screaming." I walked with him to the door and there he stopped, took my hand, and said, "Rory, you must study E. M. Forster. It is the only way to understand our cultures. 'Only connect.'" He walked out onto the street, turned, and shouted again, "Only connect."

POLICE

Be sure you perform your oath for if you fail, I myself swear by the same oath to return and find you out, and punish you though you should hide yourself as close as a lizard . . . I am the valorous Don Quixote Da La Mancha, the righter of wrongers, the revenger and redresser of grievances.
—*Cervantes,* The Threat of Don Quixote, *Book 1, Chapter 4*

MARCH 2004

Ali Zeidi was still at large and the council was still in hiding. I decided to try again to use the police. They were failing not only in al-Rafai but throughout the province: the Sadrists frequently ambushed Coalition forces; fuel trucks were attacked on the main highway; kidnapping was widespread. Iraqis wanted us to quadruple the size of the police force, erect checkpoints every hundred yards, give the police grenade launchers, and set up more intelligence networks. We had so far refused to establish what seemed to us a "Saddam State" and our police advisers continued to insist the solution was not numbers but training. But they were yet to produce the "light, intelligent police service" of which they dreamed.

I encouraged the governor to call a televised meeting of all the police chiefs in the province and I sat with him. We had the names of more than a hundred policemen who were corrupt, had collaborated with Sadr, or were senior Baathists. Another fifteen hundred policemen were overaged or failing to perform their duties. But the

Ministry of Interior had so far failed to provide any mechanism for dismissing policemen and there were no redundancy or pension arrangements.

The governor began by haranguing the officers for their useless-ness. "The Chiefs of Police of al-Gharraf, al-Rafai, and Suq-ash-Shuyukh and his assistant Rahim Abu Ali have entirely failed to keep security in their towns. You, Captain Basem, have stolen a truck trailer on the road in front of ten witnesses."

A man stood up to defend these men.

"Ah, Captain Qusay," said the governor, "the head of internal af-fairs. So there are no problems in the police?"

"I didn't say there were no problems," replied the captain.

"Well, if there are problems, why have you failed to provide any complaints or reports to either the CPA or the provincial council about bad behavior of the police over the last three months? Does this have anything to do with your past position in the Baath party or perhaps your business connections?"

The captain sat down angrily. The governor told them that in Al Isla he had driven a radical Sadrist cleric out of town simply by gath-ering the tribal sheikhs. He concluded his speech by telling the offi-cers that they should not worry about dying in the pursuit of their duties because a policeman who died on duty was a *shahid,* or martyr, guaranteed to go straight to heaven. They did not seem very excited by this idea.

The police chiefs stood up one after another. The police chief of al-Rafai made a particularly bold speech boasting of his courage and achievement. The governor interrupted, "How many people are in your force?"

"Three hundred and twenty."

"Then why when I visited al-Rafai last week was there no one at all in the police station?"

"That is a lie."

"Are you calling me a liar?" asked the governor.

"Why," I interrupted, "if you are such a hero, is the Sadrist Ali Zeidi with six men capable of toppling the council, running your entire town, and you do nothing to stop him?"

"We will stop him," roared the police chief, "and if anyone suggests I am a coward I will fight him with my bare hands. It is not my fault that things are a mess. It is your fault, Seyyed Rory, that we police are poorly trained and poorly equipped."

"Okay," I said, "I'm going to say something serious." I asked for the television cameras to be turned off. Then I said, "Yes, I'm sure you're right; it is mostly my fault and the Coalition's fault. We have made a lot of mistakes. We have not given you enough weapons, or enough training; we have failed to deliver equipment that we have promised and we have failed to keep security ourselves. All that is true." It was not traditional to make this kind of admission and people were staring at me. "But the question is what are you going to do about it? It is too late now. We are leaving in weeks. If you don't have what you want now you are probably never going to get it. So it is up to you. To be honest, I am not very optimistic about this place. You can talk and complain all you want. But I'm leaving. The question is what kind of society is going to be left after June?

"I have seen this all before in the Balkans. This month we have had elected council members attacked and tortured in their offices, fuel trucks hijacked on the main road, kidnappings, RPGs fired in the streets of Rafai, archaeological looting across Umma, mortar attacks on the CPA compound, and now criminals attacking the police station in al-Gharraf and freeing all the prisoners. At this rate, I will return in six months time and find not a big civil war but a collapse into fighting sub-district by sub-district, a mess of different militia groups, political parties, religious factions, tribes, criminals, all killing each other; the central government collapsed; services no longer delivered to the people. You are the only people who can prevent this. You must take the monopoly of violence. You must assert your authority." I found my voice trembling slightly. "There is no point arguing about who is at fault anymore or making excuses. I am leaving. You need to work together with the governor and take control."

ECHOES FROM THE FRONTIERS

The deprivation of the privilege of sharing the defense and administration of their country is galling to the educated Mesopotamians. It is true that we have increased prosperity but who cares when liberty is at the other end of the scale? They waited and welcomed the news of our mandate, because they thought it meant Dominion, self-government for themselves. They are now losing hope in our good intentions.
—*T. E. Lawrence, letter to the* Times *(London), July 22, 1920*

MARCH 28–APRIL 4, 2004

At the beginning of April, we heard in a Basra meeting that the situation was becoming less stable across the south. Speaking on behalf of Nasiriyah, I described the problems with the CSG militia, and Ali Zeidi's attack on the council of al-Rafai. Nevertheless, I added, we had finally managed to get the development projects running smoothly, had held more successful elections, and had appointed an apparently effective provincial council.

Molly, speaking for Amara, had more disturbing news. Since I left, Dr. Kifiyah, the head of the women's center from Baghdad, had continued to ignore threatening letters from the Islamist parties. A vehicle had pulled up one morning when she was walking to work. Two gunmen had got out and asked the colleague with her to step aside. They had murdered Dr. Kifiyah on the sidewalk. The culprits had not been caught. Three of the Islamist parties claimed credit. There had been mortar attacks on the compound in Amara, and

Molly seemed increasingly dissatisfied with the Prince of the Marshes. But the moderate clerics such as Abu Mustafa and even Sheikh Rahim continued to be supportive and other aspects of life appeared to be manageable.

Molly was continuing to undertake hundreds of development projects. She had funded Haider's magazine and a library for the public intellectual Abu Muslim, and her new deputy had begun to re-form the district councils. The swimming pool had finally been filled—though it had been drained again after a visiting U.S. soldier came the day after it opened, dived into the shallow end, and para-lyzed himself. A successful Marsh Arab meeting had been held in the giant *mudhif* we had commissioned across the river from the office.

Things were much worse in Kut, on the northern border of Amara and Nasiriyah, where Mark Etherington, who had flown into Iraq with me, was the Coalition governor. His compound had been attacked by militia from the Sadr movement. The Ukrainian soldiers protecting him tried to run away and he had to order his bodyguard team to drive their armored vehicles across the exit to stop the Ukrainians from escaping. His bodyguards kept up steady defensive fire for hours while Baghdad struggled to respond. When a helicop-ter gunship arrived, Mark was able to extract his team to the military base. The next day, when he decided to drive to Baghdad, he was at-tacked on the outskirts of town. The armor of his vehicle held off the bullets and the team managed to get back to the base. Elsewhere in Iraq, six foreigners were taken hostage and a British civilian was killed near Baghdad.

After the meeting, the regional coordinator warned us that the decision had been made and confrontation with the Sadrists was now inevitable. The U.S. in particular thought that we had allowed the Sadrists to get away with far too much. But he did not know when Bremer would act. Bremer had been talking about action for six months.

———

On March 29 there had been a demonstration of three thousand
people outside the Nasiriyah compound. The leaders who came in to
talk to me were men I had met a number of times before. They were
prominent Sadrists: a lawyer called Jawad, with a beard and a plain
white *dishdasha,* and a man called Sheikh Muwayad. Although we
were pressing to arrest Ali Zeidi, we still wanted to include these
Sadrists on the provincial council. Jawad sat down and handed me a
flyer I could not read. I asked him to read it aloud and listened to the
translation. He read in a monotone from a text three pages long:

"At last the mask has fallen from the scaly face of America the
great Satan and its partners in the triad, Britain the little Satan and
Israel. Now we see the true nature of that imbecile Bremer and the
donkey Rory Stewart—"

I laughed. "I don't think I need to need to hear the rest," I said.

They looked up at me a little anxiously.

"What can I do for you?" I continued.

"We have come to protest the closing of our newspaper in Baghdad. You talk about freedom of speech and then you close our newspaper. That would never happen in your country."

I did not know the Sadr newspaper had been closed. And I had
no idea what reason had been given. But I defended the decision
anyway. "Freedom of speech does not mean you can write libel or in-
cite religious hatred." Judging by the statement they had just read, I
guessed they were doing both. "We close newspapers in Britain too,"
I said, not sure that we did. "But I will look into it. What is it you actually want us to do?"

"You are the agent of an evil occupation. You are here to steal
from us."

"What do you want us to do?" I repeated. "We are leaving in
twelve weeks and transferring all power to the Iraqi government.
Would you prefer us to leave tomorrow? We are doing development
projects. Do you want us to stop them? What is it you want?"

I was quite enjoying the dialectic but perhaps I should have seen it more from their perspective. They had walked into a Coalition base—taking the risk of being arrested. They were young men, younger than me, dealing with an unfamiliar authority. One was a cleric and one was a lawyer and this normally entitled them to quiet deference. I had not allowed them to read out the manifesto they had written with such care. And now I insisted on knowing what they wanted.

What did they want exactly? They did not know. They did not want us to leave immediately or stop our projects. No, their grievances were longer standing: an opposition to imperialism and to infidels in a Muslim land; a sense that they and not a foreigner should be running things; a belief that the west often acted in bad faith; a suspicion that oil played a part in it all—valid complaints. But to whom could they address them? How should they articulate them? They had organized a demonstration; they were spokesmen for thousands of people standing outside, expecting some result. But what? We talked a little longer. I told them how much I liked them and how much I enjoyed the meeting. They returned the compliment. We parted with smiles. I thought it was over.

Two days later, four American civilian contractors were dragged from their cars by a mob and two of their charred, mutilated bodies were hung up in Fallujah.

I went on my week's leave on a Saturday. The same day, Yakubi, one of Muqtada Sadr's main spokesmen, was arrested in Baghdad. On April 5 the CPA compound in Kut was attacked and closed. In Najaf, in the Spanish sector, an attack killed twenty Iraqis and four Salvadoran soldiers and injured two hundred.[10] Seven U.S. soldiers were

----

[10]The Spanish were already due to leave Iraq afer losing nearly two hundred people in Madrid commuter-train bombings the previous month.

killed trying to re-establish order in the "Sadr city" suburb of Baghdad. And the Director of Health in al-Amara—a man I had known
well—told the news agency AFP that the British Battle Group had
killed twelve and injured twenty-five in Amara when they opened fire
on a Sadr crowd the same day. The beautiful *mudhif* we had commissioned in Amara had been burned to the ground.

Muqtada Sadr's statement ran, "I am accused by one of the leaders of evil, Bremer, of being an outlaw. If that means breaking the law
of the American tyranny and its filthy constitution for Iraq, I am
proud of that, and that is why I am in revolt." By Tuesday morning,
when I was in Scotland, I read news reports that claimed that fifteen
Iraqis had been killed and twelve Italians wounded close to our office
in Nasiriyah. Sheikh Muwayad and Jawad—who had visited me in
the office—were among the leaders of this attack. A British businessman in Nasiriyah had been kidnapped.

I cut short my leave in Britain and returned with some apprehen-
sion to what I believed had become a war zone. My bodyguard detail
was increased from four to six people and I traveled with two support
vehicles in case we were ambushed. As we drove through the province,
I was surprised to see that shops were open, children were returning
from school, and there was little sign of the fighting. But the compound had changed a great deal in five days. There was now a sand-
bag wall across our courtyard entrance and boxes of ammunition and
water piled outside my office. The staff looked shattered and some
immediately told me that they were going to resign. The Sadrists had
captured the two main bridges across the Tigris and the Italians had
failed to prevent them; anyone with any military experience—including our female Danish legal adviser—had been on the roof with
weapons, waiting for the onslaught of the militia.

Toby was particularly angry. He said that the Italian military had
had no support plan, that the office was in danger.

"On Thursday morning," he said, "we were told to be ready for
'evacuation' from the compound. I don't know why they wanted to

do it. I think because we told Baghdad that the Italians had abandoned the city. We were driven in armored vehicles a mile to the Italian base. And then they abandoned us. For an hour and a half none of the promised Italian vehicles turned up. We were in this nearly empty base, totally exposed to the public, crawling under the barbed wire fence in our body armor. It was a miracle we were not killed. That's it. We're going. We are not staying in this place. These people are simply not in control of the situation. It is a waste of time."

For many of the staff, this was their first direct exposure to war and insurgency. I had missed it and I struggled to understand what exactly had happened when the Sadrists "took" the town. The Coalition participants were generally locked in their compounds, peering at events from their roofs—or, on the rare occasions that they went out, from the narrow windows of their armored vehicles. Our Iraqi staff—like most Iraqis in Nasiriyah—had stayed at home. And the situation had become so dangerous that the media largely stayed away. Then and later, the world press were unaware that we were losing control of a city of 600,000 people. John's old team—Jeremy, Jay, and Toby—left within a fortnight.

Meanwhile Bremer and the Green Zone were furious with the Italians. The Italian press reported that Barbara Contini had held a meeting with the Sadr leader Aws al-Khafagi and had made sympathetic comments about the Sadr movement. And the Americans were horrified by reports that the Italians had agreed to abandon Nasiriyah and not pursue the Sadr office. The Italians hotly denied this. They said they were diplomatic but could be aggressive when needed. But they were under pressure to prove to the Coalition that they were capable of taking action.

KIDNAPPED

The foreigner and Christian is not a popular person in Arabia.
—T. E. Lawrence, Article 11 of 27,
first published in the Arab Bulletin, *1917*

APRIL 11–13, 2004

My priority on my return was to find a British businessman who had been kidnapped at the start of the disturbances. Gary Michael Teeley lived in Nasiriyah but had very little to do with us. He said, improbably, that he had come to Iraq to start a "laundry business." Kidnapping had become common: the same week two German hostages were killed in the Sunni triangle and three Japanese were taken, as were four Italians.

We called everyone we could think of to try to get Teeley back: the governor, the police chief, many of the local tribal sheikhs, and the political leaders. We had no reliable information on where he was being held but it was reasonable to assume the Sadrists had something to do with it. I, therefore, focused on Sheikh Aws al-Khafagi, the Sadr cleric in Nasiriyah—a young contemporary of Muqtada's, one of his close friends, and Minister of Defense in his "alternative government." Aws was now on an arrest list issued in Baghdad. But through intermediaries Aws denied any connection with the kidnapping, though he added some of his followers had formed splinter groups that were no longer under his control. The only way I could

see to put pressure on Aws was through the tribal route and in particular through his uncle, Sheikh Amer, the paramount sheikh of his
tribe. But how was I to put pressure on Sheikh Amer?

We called in the leading figures in the province, emphasized how
much Nasiriyah's economic development depended on security, and
raised the threat of American troops coming into the city. The governor and the leading sheikhs of al-Amara told me they had called a
meeting to make Sheikh Amer pressure his nephew. They hinted but
did not state that they might turn their tribes against his if he did not
cooperate. Meanwhile, our contacts in the Sadr office were saying it
was all under control. By Saturday, I was more optimistic.

That night, the Italian military entered the headquarters of the
Sadr organization in the center of town. During the operation, an explosion destroyed the office. The Italians had not informed us of their
plans, but they immediately briefed the press, saying they had been
trying to seize weapons. I guessed they were trying to show the U.S.
command in Baghdad that they were capable of acting against the
Sadrists. But it was a curious gesture. The Sadrists had been warned
in advance and their office was empty.

The next morning, my office was filled with angry local leaders.
They claimed the Sadrists had only withdrawn from Nasiriyah because the Italians had promised they would not attack. And now this.
The Italians, they said, had laid the explosion and then detonated it
after they left the building. The Sadr leaders threatened to occupy the
city again. They demanded the Italians issue a public apology and repair their offices. They said the British businessman might not be released. I apologized, although I was unaware of any agreements
between the Sadrists and the Italians. I explained that we were under
pressure from Baghdad.

An hour later the governor called and said, "Be in your office in
half an hour; I have a surprise for you." An hour later, there were
twenty Iraqis at the gate and with them a white man: pale with a
week-old beard, stinking clothes, and blood-shot eyes, looking fifty. "A

present for you, Seyyed Rory," said the sheikh of the Abude. "We wouldn't give him to anyone else." I wanted to get Teeley inside immediately but everyone in the crowd wanted to be thanked in person. I tried to do it but missed some. I could hear the Italian soldiers gathering round Teeley saying, "Hey, did they torture you?"; "Hey, did they rape you?" I cut off the thanks, greatly offending some of the tribal sheikhs, and took Teeley to my office.

He sat on the velvet sofa and asked for a beer and some cigarettes. He said he had been held in the Sadr office and then delivered to the sheikh of the Abude, from him to the governor, and from the governor to me. He had seen no sign of Coalition troops. He said he was pleased to see the British Foreign Office finally doing its job. He said how grateful he was to his captors for releasing him. He had sworn to remember them, he said, but he had forgotten the names—Ali, he thought, and Hussein. If I ever saw them I was to thank them. I said we would do our best. He was safe now and we would get him to the military hospital and then back to Britain.

After another beer he began to talk about the captivity. "They ripped the blindfold from my face and there were two of them with keffiyahs. One put his weapon to my head and said he would kill me. I remember feeling in my pockets—you know, just for the junk you carry—as a bit of comfort, a sort of lucky charm. Then the man cocked his weapon. You hear that sound—that noise of a weapon cocked at your head—at a much deeper level than any other sound, somehow lower down in the brain."

I gave him a satellite telephone, and he called home. His first words were, "Hello, did West Ham win?" He was referring to his favorite soccer team.

Another beer and he was telling more stories. He was clearly shattered and having difficulty being coherent but he was also beginning to turn the bleak and bewildering experience, piece by piece, into anecdotes. He asked how much he had been in the news, and wondered whether he would be giving interviews. And then he talked more about the imprisonment. We spent about an hour together.

I had called for an ambulance to take him to the Italian military hospital for a checkup. The ambulance arrived, and he clambered into the back and gave me a last grateful wave. I wrote an e-mail to London, imagining they would be pleased to hear that he was safe. I then drove to the base.

The Italians were for some reason reluctant to let me into the camp; at the hospital I was assured by the Italian doctor that Teeley was doing fine but I was not allowed to see him.

As I left the hospital I passed a frantic British woman in military uniform. She shouted at me. She was a hostage expert. She had been on standby at Tallil for three days. Why had I not contacted her? I explained that no one had told me she existed. Why had I handed Teeley to the Italians? He was not supposed to be with the Italians. He should be flying directly to the British base at Basra. I said I thought he had been through enough and I had just wanted to get him to a hospital. She turned and walked off, furious.

I looked into the Italian general's office: he was telling his adjutant to phone all the major news channels to set up television interviews for him to announce Teeley's liberation. One of his staff officers put his hand on my shoulder and said the general was too busy to see me now. An Italian soldier told me the general had given explicit orders to stop me or anyone in the CPA from being seen with Teeley. That is why I had trouble getting into the base and the hospital. Back at the compound I received a call from the British saying that for public relations purposes it was essential Teeley be moved to Basra that night. I told them it was out of my hands.

REWARDING FRIENDS

He who always lies is a messenger from distant places.
—Sumerian proverb from Ur, c. 2000 B.C.

When I drove up to Shatra to thank the great sheikh of the Abude, Ali Hussein al-Khayun, for his part in the release, we parked in a walled garden beside some gnarled trees. The sheikh's house was famous in the province. It was known as a "traditional British palace." In fact, it was a sprawling, single-story plastered brick building with polished stone floors and high ceilings and no decoration. The high stone skirting board and the curved lines suggested it had been built in the 1920s. It resembled the government rest houses the British built across India, and I guessed it he been designed by a British engineer from the Public Works Department.

At the time this building was constructed, Shatra was the headquarters of a British political officer, Bertram Thomas. He went on to become one of the great explorers of the Arabian Desert, winning the gold medal of the Royal Geographical Society for a book dedicated in part to recording the skull sizes of various Arabian peoples and using the measurements to speculate on their racial inheritance. He had been posted to Shatra when he was twenty-four, in 1919, and spent much of his days hunting with sight hounds and conducting amateur archaeological digs. In the Shia uprising of 1920 he had found himself surrounded by hundreds of angry tribesman demonstrating at his door, and had only been saved by the intervention of Sheikh Ali's grandfather, who had smuggled him to safety. He had returned, chastened, six months later, saying that "to win the respect of the Arab, the administrator must show power, the will to use that power, and a genuine respect for the welfare of the people."

Sheikh Ali entered the anteroom after keeping me waiting for a half hour on a stiff-backed and slightly faded armchair. He was probably expressing his displeasure that I had not treated him with proper respect at the gate of the compound when he delivered Teeley. The noble magnate was four foot ten, with a large and wrinkled head and a frail, hunched body. He wore a splendid black band around his headdress. But in the picture on the wall his grandfather wore a gold band three times as broad. He invited me to lunch but without any of the normal smiles and pleasantries. He seemed conscious of being one of the leading sheikhs of Iraq and, unlike most sheikhs of his generation, he was an educated man—a lawyer, in fact.

He showed me a gold British fob watch, inscribed "to Sheikh al-Khayun with great respect General Wilson, 1922." Gifts are an important part of Iraqi culture but financial procedures no longer allowed us to reward loyalty with gold objects. I admired the watch and said how much we remembered the service his family had done for Bertram Thomas and how grateful the British government was still to his family. He nodded, glancing around the room as though he were bored from having heard all this a hundred times before. I thanked him for the release of Teeley.

"I had worked," said the sheikh in his precise legal voice, "with the governor to pressure the Sadr leader Sheikh Aws through his tribal chief. Sheikh Aws is from this town; I know his father and grandfather. Then I found out where Teeley was being held—just to the east of Shatra—and I found out who held him. I called the kidnappers in to see me and I told them to release him on Saturday.

They said they had already sold him onward to another syndicate and they had no idea where he was.

"I told them," he drawled, "here in this room—they were sitting where you are sitting—that I would bury them up to their necks in sand if they did not return him. The next morning they brought Teeley here to my house. I called the governor and we took him to the governor's office and then the governor suggested we bring him on to you."

"Thank you so much, Sheikh."

"You did not thank me at the time. You did not bring me into the compound."

"Sheikh, I am so sorry. I was very worried for Teeley and wanted to get him in as soon as possible."

"Teeley was fine," said the Sheikh dismissively. "No one harmed him."

When I returned to the compound, the Sadr office called claiming their pressure had been the key to getting Teeley released to the sheikhs. I believed they had kidnapped him in the first place. But I thanked them anyway. I was called by the cousin and tribal sheikh of the Sadrist leader, who claimed credit for putting pressure on his cousin. I thanked him too. And two Iraqis who had worked with Teeley. The Italian Ambassador sent a message saying it had all been arranged by his old friend Sheikh Taleb of the Beni Rikaab—who had tricked us a week earlier. Then I called the governor to thank him and to tell him I had managed to get him the money for a budget and secretarial assistance. He said, "You are welcome, Seyyed Rory. I hope you were congratulated—he was a present to you." It was not at all clear to me whose pressure had been decisive in getting Teeley released; there seemed to have been about five hundred people involved. All I knew was that he had been brought by the sheikhs and the governor to my office, not rescued by Coalition troops.

The next morning, the front page of the *Daily Telegraph* ran a large picture of the Italian general shaking hands with Teeley. The *Sun* led with: "Gary, 37, was suffering severe shock when dramatically freed from a rebel stronghold by Italian special forces in Iraq on Sunday . . . Patrolling Italian choppers spotted rebels fleeing the building and noted their direction as they sped off in cars. After gleaning other intelligence, they swooped on a flat in the north of Nasiriyah and found Gary there, bound by his legs. His captors had fled."

The next day a letter printed in the *Sun* congratulated the Italians for "doing a great job in Iraq." I was glad Toby was gone. This would have been bad for his blood pressure.

By the weekend (when Gary was reportedly negotiating to sell the rights to his story) there was a new twist. "ITALIAN troops were given the credit for freeing Gary Teeley," wrote Christopher Leake of the *Mail on Sunday*, "but the *Mail on Sunday* has learned his rescue was masterminded by elite [British] SAS officers wearing borrowed Italian army uniforms to disguise their involvement . . . four officers from the 22 SAS regiment were secretly flown at night by helicopter to Nasiriyah. Carrying M16 assault rifles and computer equipment to eavesdrop on phone conversations, the team studied aerial photographs taken by an unmanned U.S. Predator spy plane. They narrowed Mr. Teeley's location down to a building guarded by rebels. An Arab-speaking officer made the breakthrough which led to his release after six days in captivity . . . The SAS team had borrowed uniforms from their Italian counterparts to melt into the local scene because Italian forces are in charge of the area. However, local leaders who met the officers were in no doubt that they were SAS. The SAS team knew they were in a race against time to save Mr. Teeley and that he would be killed within 72 hours."

Someone called with congratulations, believing me to be the "Arab-speaking officer," and asked if it was true that Delta Force had disguised themselves as Iraqi sheikhs.

In the same newspaper Gary's ex-partner, Sharon, appeared under the headline: "Gary Is an Arrogant, Selfish, Violent Cheat Who Has Abandoned Me and His Children." Paragraph four ended: "What I didn't know was that Gary was having an affair with a teenage girl, Lisa, who ended up going out to Dubai with him." Lisa, the article explained, is now mother to Gary's fifth child while Sharon is seeing her former brother-in-law after his split from Gary's sister.

On the night of Gary's release, the Italians had given him tranquilizers and, in celebration of his successful press conference with the general, the *bersaglieri* in their ostrich feather plumes and pressed uniforms took the disheveled hostage to their canteen. They let him drink four beers on top of their tranquilizers and the four beers I had given him. He then got a little aggressive and had to be restrained by the military police. I would have liked to see Gary staging an English pub brawl in the Italian canteen. But I did not get to see him again. He was flown in haste back to London the next day.

FOREIGN ELEMENTS

Let the snake find its deep hole, the scorpion its crevice, and the hyena its exit.

—Sumerian proverb from Ur, c. 2000 B.C.

SUNDAY, APRIL 25, 2004

Ten days after Teeley's release, when I was still in sole charge of the office (Barbara was in Italy), I was woken by an explosion at three in the morning. Once I realized that I was not in Indonesia being woken by an earthquake but in Iraq under mortar fire, I was more disturbed by the gap between the explosions than by the explosions themselves. Another member of the staff came running into my room and crouched next to me. He was talking calmly and seemed in control but he had shit himself and I was keen to get out of the room. As we ran toward the main building, the sentries on the roof fired at us, and missed, apparently mistaking us in the dark for insurgents. Lieutenant Burti, our Italian liaison officer, led some men out into the mortar fire to investigate the screaming at the gate and returned carrying two wounded Italian soldiers who had been hit. One of them had his legs nearly swept off. A thick slurry of blood marked his trail from the front door to the improvized first-aid room, where Dr. Pedrale, having torn off the soldier's trousers, worked on him with morphine. Pedrale was quick and efficient. He stopped the blood loss. I shouted for an ambulance. The mortar fire ceased and we were able to evacuate the sentries. Neither died; one was paralyzed from the waist down. As the ambulance left, I received a call from a colleague who was traveling abroad and who asked how things were going. I explained and returned the question.

"I am exhausted," my colleague said. "It is terrible. I can't tell you how tough it is here in Europe. I have barely slept, meetings every hour of the day, breakfast television appearances. I am shattered."

I sympathized.

"Thank you Rory, it is terrible. But we shall survive, eh, we shall survive. Well, I wanted to ask you a favor. I want you to make sure I am booked on this flight from Baghdad, do you have a pen? And then I want you to arrange my transport for the airport."

For a moment I felt like describing how the compound looked with blood coagulating on the front step. But I remembered that Europe was far away, so I took down the flight details and said goodbye.

I decided that the staff should sleep on the office floors rather than in the trailers. There was unexploded ordinance in the compound and I did not want anyone more injured. This was an unpopular decision. I went to sleep beside my desk and was woken four hours later to be told that three suicide truck bombers had driven their vehicles into Basrah police stations. A busload of female students was caught up in one of the blasts. An hour later another suicide truck drove into the Police Academy at Zubayr. Early reports suggested at least forty dead (thirty in one hospital alone) and many (one report said two hundred) injured in Basrah.

That week, the Italian troops had been ambushed in five district towns and we had been attacked twice in the compound with rocket-propelled grenades, though there had been no casualties. Elsewhere, Najaf was under the control of Sadr insurgents and Kerbala was under siege. One of the other governorate coordinators, an American, had written saying that any negotiation with the Sadrists might make our lives easier but was a betrayal of the Iraqi people. If, he said, we rolled tanks into the center of Najaf, we would be greeted with flowers in the streets: none but a tiny minority supported Muqtada.

I drove the following morning, much against the wishes of the bodyguard team to the provincial council. As I walked in, one of the Sadr representatives was making a speech criticizing the Coalition for its brutality. I interrupted that these attacks against the CPA helped no one and I wanted assistance from the provincial council in finding the perpetrators. There was an embarrassed silence and then they continued with procedural issues. I asked the security committee to stay behind after the meeting.

"You must give us resources, Mr. Rory," said Seyyed Faris. "We are the only ones able to control security in the province. We know this city. No one can enter or leave without our knowledge. This is a small place. We know everything that happens here."

"Indeed," echoed Abu Jasim with his favorite phrase, "they say not a leaf drops in the province without us knowing it."

I had not slept well and my patience was not what it ought to have been. "Really?" I said, "A leaf? How about a mortar? One of my staff lost his legs at the waist last night from a mortar shell. Any idea who fired it?"

"Someone from outside the province, Mr. Rory, I'm sure of it."

"How very helpful," I said.

"We are not policemen," said one of them, reciting portentously, "we are not supposed to give orders to police officers, we are only an oversight committee providing accountability to the public."

"Thank you so much," I said and stood up to leave. As I reached the top of the stairs there was a gunshot inside the building. My bodyguard dived on the ground; I looked around bewildered and then lay down next to him, at which point he tried to get on top of me. The Arabs, who had made no attempt to take cover, looked on pityingly. I stood up and dusted myself off. Someone explained that one of the governor's bodyguards had pulled his trigger, forgetting there was a round in the chamber.

I found Adnan, an experienced lawyer, waiting in my office. He denied any Sadr role in the recent attacks. He said the Sadr office had no reason to attack the Coalition when the negotiations in Najaf were going well. Sheikh aws Al-Khafagi, the Sadr leader, was anxious to meet the CPA. He had pressed his men to withdraw from the center of Nasiriyah despite considerable opposition and they had not attacked when the Italians destroyed their office with explosive. The attack on the CPA had not been sophisticated and that the use of automatic weapons after the RPGs was "a pointless piece of showing off" that was too amateur for the Sadr office.

"So who did it?" I asked. "Sheikh Ali Zeidi?"

"No. No. Of course Sheikh Ali Zeidi may have attacked the Coalition in Rafai but not here. Anyway he is not part of the Sadr office anymore. He has resigned after his brother was killed fighting the Coalition on the Nasiriyah Bridge. He has called al-Khafagi 'a coward.'"

"So who then?"

"It is just part of the national terrorist campaign, like the attacks in the Sunni areas. It is made to look as though Sadr did it, to force you to confront the Sadrists. But in fact it was done by Baathist fedayeen. [Pause] Or by al Qaeda. [Pause] Or by Syria. [Silence] Or Iran."

RETURN TO THE GREEN ZONE

The palace is a slippery place which catches those who do not know it.
—Sumerian proverb from Ur, c. 2000 B.C.

APRIL–MAY, 2004

Throughout this the normal cycle of meetings continued in Baghdad and Basra. On my April visit to Baghdad, the British Embassy office greeted me politely but ironically. One of the staff said, "Ah, the Lord of the Marshes—from Amara to Nasiriyah," and everyone laughed. They were focused on the governing council and the UN and they were not comfortable with the idea of British diplomats administering provinces. I asked what they thought of our policies and a senior diplomat replied, "When we look back on what we're doing in two years' time, we will see a history of counterintuitive experiments going wrong."

In a meeting with Bremer, the colonel from strategic planning said, "What we are hoping to do is lay out some philosophical underpinnings of a plan . . . to begin a journey of discovery for building a more cohesive implementation of plans and policies across the five core areas."

An American Arabist governor who favored broad-brimmed hats and was rumored to carry a pair of revolvers said, "This is not just a military struggle. This is an ideological struggle. We need to engage

with Islamicization and Arab socialism, otherwise we might just produce a well-furnished dictatorship."

Strategic Planning replied with a speech about "best practice
gaps analysis" and privatization.

And one of the American governors from a Sunni region said, "If
we wanted to destabilize the country we couldn't have done a better
job. We are hemorrhaging out there: abolishing the army, opening
the borders, destroying industry."

In a coffee break, a young staffer told me he would be instructing
the development agencies to stop working in Amara and Nasiriyah
and focus instead on our neighbor Samawah.

"But that is nonsense," I exploded. "We are much poorer than
Samawah. Have you ever seen our province?"

"I don't need to. I have figures."

"Figures?" I told him all figures were unreliable and our provinces
were very poor.

"They are not. Unemployment is twice as bad in Samawah."

I told him three out of four people were unemployed in Nasiriyah;
we were on the edge of civil war; and some of our slums looked like
rural India.

"I'm not going to listen to you. I know about you. You are a powerful advocate for your province and you have your reasons for want-
ing money in your province. Maybe the man in Samawah is less good
as an advocate. So I am just going to have rely on my numbers. Some
numbers are better than no numbers."

I told him that was nonsense.

"How do you propose I allocate money, then?"

I suggested he gather us all at a table, ask tough questions, let us
justify our requests, listen to us argue, get to know our personalities,
correct for those who seemed more forceful, and come to a decision.
I said, "You can't get around problems with numbers. It doesn't matter how many people died; it matters how they died and why and
who killed them, and for that you need political officers. There is no

exact relationship between your indexes and policy. You may want to put more money into a richer place if it is about to collapse into civil war; you may—"

"What you suggest is very messy, imprecise, and imperfect," he interrupted. "There will be biases. That is why we use metrics." Fortunately, however, we continued to receive our money.

Bremer asked us to "communicate and sell the transitional administrative law." His central political team in Baghdad seemed to have been putting most of its energy into dealing with the twenty people on the governing council, placating Washington, and drafting this Transitional Administrative Law (TAL), which was to be the interim constitution. It was supposed to be a document provided by Iraqis, but there had been little Iraqi control of the process, which provided no real opportunity for public debate or participation. The TAL had been drafted primarily by Americans and then forced through the governing council in an all-night session.

Bremer believed the TAL would become an important part of the new Iraq—a proud part of the nation's identity, just as the U.S. constitution had become central to U.S. identity. Perhaps because I came from a country without a written constitution, I was less convinced. Iraq's 1968 constitution had been fine on paper. The problem was implementation. It did not matter what human rights were enshrined in documents if your local sheikh, party leader, or policeman could still beat you up on the street corner.

When we called a meeting of the town councils to explain the TAL, they objected to the statement that Sharia law would be "a" but not "the" source of legislation. They were angry that three provinces would be able to veto the future constitution and called it a "Kurdish veto." They wanted more power for provincial councils. These were common objections in other provinces. Ayatollah Sistani, the supreme Shia leader in Najaf, had made many of these points. But there was no way of responding to them since the document was finished and could not be altered.

I attended a meeting with one of the senior Iraqi politicians who had been working on the TAL. He had been in the United States since he was a young man and was wearing a gray suit and a pair of large jade cufflinks. He began in an astonishing upper-class transatlantic drawl that made him sound like a Boston Brahmin in the 1950s, "We have no history like Yugoslavia, no history of person-to-person conflict." I had heard Yugoslavs say the same. "Iraq has been a nation since the first century. Despite the 'caprice and whim'"—he pronounced it "h-whim"—"of Saddam, our history is a history of liberalism. We are neither non-integral, nor sectarian, nor illiberal. We must reclaim and reconnect with our liberal past." The other foreigners around the table nodded approvingly.

He talked about his particular interest in gender equality, asylum seekers, and the protection of civil society organizations, concluding with a large smile, "It is not the devil but God who is in the detail."

"Thank you," said the female State Department Officer who had introduced him. "And I hope the audience listened to this impressive debate. This is why I am so optimistic about Iraq. Is it not ironic, now that we have heard this, to think that we are lecturing *Iraqis* on democracy?"

THE RULE OF LAW

Brotherhood is founded on the words of a quarrel. At the witness box,
friendship becomes known.

—Sumerian proverb from Ur, c. 2000 B.C.

MONDAY, MAY 10, 2004

In Nasiriyah, in early May, I was reading a telegram from Baghdad about "civil society programs" when Ali Abdullah Salman, one of the elected councilors of al-Rafai, came to tell me he had been abducted and tortured. He had fallen asleep in the library of al-Rafai waiting for a meeting. He was woken by thirty armed men. Only four wore masks and he recognized the others. They were led by the Sadrist Ali Zeidi. They took him to the former Baath headquarters on the main street of Shatra, which was now occupied by the Sadr office. He was put in a dark cell, blindfolded, and burned with live electric wires. He was finally released at five the following morning. I called in Pauline, our Danish legal adviser, who led the questioning. Ali was a very good witness, precise and clear.

"And you want to push for criminal proceedings?" I asked.

"Why do you think I am here? People have tried to convince me not to report this. My brother was threatened by three armed men. My family and the tribal sheikhs tried to persuade me to withdraw my complaint. But I want to build a society based on the rule of law."

I looked at him, trying to understand what was driving him to do this. The police did nothing in al-Rafai. No one would protect him if the Sadr office came after him.

"And do you have the details?"

"All and everything. The people who abducted me were Sheikh Sattar al-Jaber and Said Haider Makhtouf—they were armed with pistols—Salman al-Ghadwan, Mohammed Khadum Mohi, Sayed Aziz Mohsen—they carried rifles and grenades—and Ali Zeidi, who was in charge of the men and carrying a pistol. They were from the Sadr office and 15th Shabaan. They dragged me off in a black Caprice with a gray rear hood and the license plate Thi Qar 7116."

"Have you reported this to the police?"

"Yes. They did not want to take the complaint but I insisted and eventually an officer wrote it down. I was then sent to get a medical examination. The doctor's report confirms that I was tortured. Then I went to the investigating magistrate. He was also reluctant to take the statement but in the end he wrote summons for the people who arrested me and I brought it back to the police. Since then nothing has happened. Neither the police nor the judiciary of al-Rafai will act because they are scared of the Sadrists or support them. I will show you the marks."

I asked Pauline to leave the room and he showed me some small bruises on his shoulder that I had no way of interpreting. By his account they were three weeks old. I sympathized and thanked him.

According to Pauline, all the correct steps had been followed. She recommended I transfer the case to a different jurisdiction—either to the Baghdad court or the Central Criminal Court of Iraq—"using your powers under CPA Order 13, Section 18, 2, d and f, 'actions intended to destabilize democratic institutions or processes [and] instances in which a criminal defendant may not be able to obtain a fair trial in a local court.'" At least the councilor and the legal adviser still had faith in the legal system.

When I saw on television that Iraqi prisoners had been tortured in Abu Ghraib, I almost resigned. I had always seen myself as a realist. But I had believed that we were in a position to set an example and lecture Iraqis about democracy and human rights. I would have taken the news better if I had thought it an isolated incident. But I realized that I had always known, without admitting it to myself, that such things were going on. For a moment, I wondered if this was only an American phenomenon, but I knew the British could have done the same; any army might when not aggressively monitored. Military culture was often about bending the rules to get results; a certain ruthlessness was admired; many of these things happened in hazing rituals.

I recognized the attitudes and sense of humor of the people who had taken the photographs. I remembered sitting with groups of men who had laughed at pictures of dead Iraqis and films of Apache helicopters shooting crowds. And I felt ashamed. But I loved my work and could see no purpose in leaving with only two months remaining, so I did not resign. The Iraqis hardly commented on it and I saw for the first time that they had always assumed we were doing these things and had never believed my statements about human rights and the rule of law.

It was, for us, a surprisingly quiet week, but the situation reports were full of news of attacks on other provincial CPA teams. On Monday, a Dutch soldier was killed in Samawah and in Baqubah the governor's motorcade was hit by a roadside bomb; on Tuesday, fighting broke out in the center of Kerbala and an Italian patrol was attacked in the southern town of Suq-Ash-Shuyukh; on Wednesday, the Sadr militia seized the main police station in Najaf and fired fifteen mortar rounds at the Coalition base. On Thursday, there was an explosion at the German Embassy in Baghdad, more fighting in Kerbala, and the ambush of a CPA civilian in his vehicle in Anbar.

My concerns were more mundane. My last e-mail on Thursday asked for advice on paying people per kilo of garbage dropped at the dump. Nonetheless, things were clearly heating up, so when Barbara went to the coordinators' conference in Baghdad on Friday, I stayed in Nasiriyah. Our troubles began that evening.

PART FIVE

BESIEGED

O city, your rites have been alienated from you, your powers have been changed into alien powers.

—The lament for Urim, c. 2000 B.C.

THE QUICK REACTION FORCE

Mercenaries and auxiliaries are useless and dangerous . . . for they are disunited, ambitious, undisciplined and treacherous . . . weak and cowardly when they are met by determined enemies; they have no fear of God and do not maintain commitments with men.

—Machiavelli, The Prince, *Chapter 12*

TUESDAY, MAY 11, 2004

I was on top of the Ziggurat of Ur with the Minister for Archaeology when someone from the office called to say the Sadrist militia had seized the main bridge. I asked the bodyguard team to take us on the back road over the smaller bridge. When I reached the office, I found the governor in the conference room. He grasped my hand as soon as I entered, speaking fast:

"I was in my office. A few of them came into the forecourt with PKCs and AK-47s. I was sitting with the chief of police." The police chief had called for backup and the governor had gone down to try to talk to the Sadr militiamen, but they had hit his bodyguard. He gestured to the man, whose hand was wrapped in a bloody bandage. "There are fifteen policemen and their cars at my office. But the police have run away. And the Mehdi army have taken the five police cars and are driving around town. When no one from the police came to rescue us we left by the back way. They fired at us on the bridge. But they did not hit us and now I am here and the Sadr militia are occupying my office."

I offered the governor a bed for the night but he was in a great hurry to leave us and get home to his tribal area. I walked him to the gate. When I returned, one of the translators told me Sadrists had now gathered outside police stations and seized all the bridges across the Tigris. This meant we were cut off from the Italian military, whose barracks were on the south side of the river. There were no Coalition troops in the province north of us. Over the last few weeks, we had tried to plan for this kind of situation. We had checked the number of soldiers. I had asked for regular updates on our supplies of food, ammunition, water, and fuel. The staff reported that we had ample stocks to hold out for three or four days. The Italians had promised they could get a Quick Reaction Force to us in twenty minutes. I called them and asked for the Quick Reaction Force immediately.

I then called anyone I could think of connected with the Sadr office, including all the sheikhs and officials who had helped with the Teeley kidnapping. Very few answered their phones and those who did were evasive. I called in the leaders of the security details. In the compound were my six-person bodyguard team led by Geoff, recently retired after twenty-two years in the British infantry, and Paul, a New Zealand policeman; six Americans in charge of perimeter security and their Filipino support staff; and a platoon of Italian soldiers—in all, about sixty armed men from three organizations.

There were fourteen civilians including an Italian television crew in for the day; Pauline, the twenty-eight-year-old Danish legal adviser; Charlie Morris, the twenty-six-year-old social affairs adviser who had worked with me in Amara; and John Layfield, the acting political officer now that Toby had left. I called the civilians into my office and the adjoining office as protection from mortar fire since we had no underground bunker, put mattresses and pillows over the windows, told them the Italian Quick Reaction Force was on its way, opened a bottle of wine, handed out some oatcakes and marmalade from my desk drawer, and, opening my computer, turned on some music. The only music saved on my laptop was *Cosi Fan Tutte;* everyone laughed as though they were having a picnic at an open-air opera. I would have preferred bagpipes.

At twenty past six, two columns of black smoke appeared to the south-southwest of the CPA building. They appeared to be close to one of the main police stations and a watertower.

"There goes your *mudhif,*" said Joe, the U.S. security commander.

I laughed. A little uncomfortably.

At half past six, the sentries saw two pickup trucks drive up and drop off men a block to the east of us. Just before dusk there were two loud explosions inside the compound, a burst of small-arms fire, and, ten minutes later, another loud explosion. From then on the firing was almost continual. The first mortar rounds that landed inside our fence wounded two of the Filipino guards. We brought them in and laid them in my office. Geoff called me outside and shouted over the noise of gunfire that the Italians had abandoned the guns on the roof because they were worried about the mortar fire. I told the British and American bodyguards that they should take over the guns while I talked to the Italian commander. When I found him, the commander insisted it had been "just a tactical withdrawal" and ordered his troops back to the roof.

I asked one of the civilian CPA staff to go outside with me to repair our server, which had been hit by a mortar, but he refused. He wasn't a soldier and he didn't see why he should leave the room. I found I was able to reboot the server on my own. Over the next couple of hours the attackers became more accurate. At ten they were able to walk three mortars up our front path quite elegantly, culminating in a large explosion five meters from our front door that blew over the sentries in the courtyard and smashed into the registry/computer room. That was the end of my e-mail connection with Baghdad. By midnight the Quick Reaction Force had still not arrived. The mortars were apparently being fired from a school and guided in by someone from the nearby hospital roof. I continued to walk between the guard force and the civilians. Understandably, the civilian staff no longer

believed my promises that the Quick Reaction Force was "on its way."
I assured them that the Italians would compensate for their late deliv-
ery with free garlic bread. At two o'clock the Italian soldiers inside the
compound fired an anti-tank weapon at a nearby building. There was
a brief lull, then the attack began again.

The Quick Reaction Force finally arrived, seven hours after we
had called them, but they did not drive out to engage the mortar positions. Instead they evacuated the wounded Filipino sentries and
drove straight back to the Italian camp. The Sadr office concluded
that we had now fled the site and, ten minutes later, began firing
more RPGs and mortars. The Italian armed personnel carriers
(APCs) in our compound did not deploy against them. The most
dangerous spot was the roof, where the machine gunners and sentries
had very little protection from incoming missiles. Much of one sentry
box was blown away but, fortunately, it was unoccupied at the time.
The attackers didn't succeed in dropping a mortar into the central
courtyard, which would have killed many of us. By first light Geoff
calculated we had been hit with thirty-four mortar shells and fifty-
nine rocket-propelled grenades. But only two people in the compound had been wounded and no one had been killed.

I asked someone to make coffee while I tried to deal with the mess
in the computer room. To my astonishment the server had survived the
explosion. This meant that, with power, we could get the e-mail system
going again. I went out with some of the others to start the emergency
generator. It was wonderful to be out in the cool early morning air but
we walked carefully, avoiding unexploded ordinance. The streets were
very quiet except for the occasional sound of an Iraqi ambulance arriving outside the perimeter to pick up casualties. The machine gunners
on the roof had, it seemed, killed or injured a number of people during the attack. I counted the bottles of water with our bodyguard team
provided by the private security company Control Risks (CRG). The
small plastic bottles, each containing a third of a liter, made an impressive pile. But in fact we had only two liters per person—not really

enough for a day in a climate like Iraq. Either we had been consuming our supplies very quickly or I had been misinformed. The Italians promised they would drive in extra water in the next hour or so.

Most of the civilians were now trying to sleep. I went to my trailer, showered, shaved, and put on a suit jacket, hoping that in the chaos and filth of the compound the suit jacket would give the impression it was business as usual. I sent an e-mail chasing up a missing contract on a water plant and did not mention the attack. I climbed onto the roof and saw no cars or people on the streets. There, I received a call from the assistant governor saying the Sadr militia (the Jeish-el-Mehdi) were roaming free and armed in large numbers in the center of the town. All the shops were closed, along with the schools. My *mudhifs* had been burned to the ground.

In the security meeting, the teams reminded me that the compound was very difficult to defend because it lay in a hollow surrounded by taller buildings that protected the insurgents as they fired on us. Unless we were reinforced, the insurgents would eventually be able to pin us in the corner of the building with mortar fire and then come over the razor-wire fence and kill us at close quarters. They emphasized that after the farce of the previous night, the Sadr office would be inviting people from all over the country to join in the fun. I told the security team leaders that I would put political pressure on the Sadr office and evacuate the other civilians.

When I telephoned them, the Sadr leaders claimed they had no control over the crowd. The gunmen, they said, were from outside town and were defying the Nasiriyah leadership.

I called Asad, the goateed Ghuzzi playboy at whose house I had eaten a week before. He was rumored to have a senior position in the Sadr office.

"Seyyed Rory, you must leave your compound. All of you, tonight," he said.

I replied that there was no way that I was abandoning the headquarters of the CPA: We were in charge of the province and the city.

I asked him to tell his friends not to attack us, "otherwise people will be killed." I hoped I was convincing.

"Seyyed Rory, I like you. Believe me. You must leave now."

"Asad—"

The connection was cut off and I could not reach him on the phone again.

A translator called to apologize for not coming to the office. He said one of the mortar positions was in a building next to his own. He gave us the exact address and we worked out the grid coordinates. He assured us that if the Italians raided the building they would catch many of the Sadr leaders who were organizing the attack. We briefed the Italians on the site, distinguishing features of the building, and the routes in and out. They nodded earnestly and took notes. I hoped for the best. But they did nothing.

I sent an e-mail to Baghdad:

> *To remain safe in this building we need aggressive patrols dominating the ground and deterring the mortars. The so-called Quick Reaction Force arrived seven hours after we were told they were setting off . . . We need air assets to counter the mortars (including thermal imagery and drones) and most importantly a genuine QRF based in this compound but patrolling aggressively out of it. We were very lucky that our attackers had so few mortar rounds.*

Shortly thereafter, this e-mail came to the attention of the Italians, who viewed it as a gross insult to their national honor. I received three e-mails from Baghdad criticizing me for insulting a Coalition partner. The Italian guard commander came in to say the general wanted an apology. The guard commander was a good man. He had been brave and calm during the attack. He had wanted to mount patrols and take a more aggressive stance but was stopped from doing so. Berlusconi apparently believed that the loss of any more lives would force Italy to withdraw from the Coalition. But the commander said all the rules had been changed; they would be much more proactive in the future. He begged me to give them another chance. I agreed to write a note saying the QRF had been late because they were delayed on the bridge. I had no way of telling whether this was true, but I had to act as though it were.

I then received an e-mail from Baghdad instructing me to evacuate the compound and close the office immediately. I decided I could not leave the compound but I agreed to evacuate the rest of the civilian staff. My bureaucratic prose was even more pompous from a night without sleep:

> *It would send a worrying political signal if we were compelled to shut completely by a small group of extremists. And I think it is politically (and even morally) important for us to keep this site operating.*

Aleem volunteered to take a truck to get the kerosene we needed to keep the generator working and the sewage drained. This was a very brave act. Aleem was driving into a city controlled by Sadr militiamen, any of whom might kill him for being a collaborator. But without power we would be unable to recharge out satellite phones, our last source of communication. I gave him cash from my wallet and told him we would pay the generator man, who normally earned a hundred dollars a month, a hundred dollars just for coming in. We could not find the keys to the truck so I broke a window and Aleem hot-wired it. Aleem then opened the glove compartment and found the keys inside. He wrapped a *keiffyah* around his face, put a pistol beside him, and drove out the gate.

Meanwhile, the Iraqis we phoned took a very bleak view of the situation. Usually, there was no shortage of volunteers to mediate and people were quick, perhaps too quick, to propose settlements. But in this case the tribal leaders said they were powerless and the governor, who was usually the first to seek a compromise, said negotiation was impossible. The assistant governor was hardly even polite, as if we were no longer worth his time.

KABUL

I certainly think it is better to be impetuous than cautious.
                    —*Machiavelli,* The Prince, *Chapter 25*

WEDNESDAY, MAY 12, 2004

The few RPGs fired at us that morning did not injure anyone. Two hours later, Aleem returned with the kerosene and the generator man. He said people in the street believed the Sadr militia were bringing in heavier weapons and more people and planned to have a better go at the CPA that night. This seemed plausible. I called the governor and the police chief. They refused to come to the compound because, they said, they would be killed en route. The translators and cleaners also refused to come.

But Salman Duffar from the small Dhi Qar party 15th Shaaban did. I met him and Seyyed Ibadi, the mayor of Nasiriyah, at the gate. It was a very hot afternoon. They entered, shook hands, accepted the gate search with grace, and looked around at what remained of the familiar compound. The mortars had gouged khaki scars into the white walls; there were craters in the pavement; and the window glass lay in shards. The small *mudhif* had been burned away.

We picked our way over the sandbags at the entrance and past a dozen soldiers curled over their guns, asleep in the courtyard. In every drawn unshaven face, the visitors could see the effects of the previous night.

We stopped at the door to my office and I waved them through, saying, *"Enta daifi."* You are the guest.

"Enta awalin." You first.

I slipped to their left-hand side. *"Allah Yamin."* God is on the right, I said and they laughed and walked through.

I had tried to pull the room back to something approaching normality but it was clear that it had recently been a dormitory. I did, however, manage to get my guests some tea.

The Italian guard commander sat with us, as did John Layfield, the new political officer. Salman Sherif Duffar had grown up in Shatra, the hometown of the diminutive sheikh Ali Hussein al-Khayun. In the early nineties he had joined 15th Shabaan, then a secret Iranian-backed insurgency cell, which later claimed credit for the assassination attempt on Saddam's son Uday in which a bomb tore apart half of one the wealthiest streets in Baghdad and left Uday very badly wounded. Some said Salman had triggered the bomb. Others denied this and said that the central figures in the plot had been killed by Saddam's agents. No one denied that when Salman escaped to Iran, Saddam tortured and killed six of his brothers, apparently in an attempt to find him.

I had no idea what he had been like before his family was killed. Now he was reserved and favored long and slightly pedantic speeches, occasionally enlivened by a shy smile. His beard was neatly trimmed, and he always wore large glasses and a neat suit that was slightly large for his thin shoulders. He had the mannerisms more of an Edinburgh school-master than a famous Iraqi guerrilla. Only his shirt—buttoned to the neck and worn without a tie—and the theological words in his speeches revealed the time he had spent in Iran.

"We have talked to the Sadr office," said Salman Duffar. "They propose a settlement. If the Italians agree to withdraw all their troops from this compound and never return to the city of Nasiriyah, the attacks will stop. If you attempt to remain, they will attack in force tonight and I am afraid that will be the end."

I laughed. I looked at Seyyed Ibadi, who smiled nervously, then looked away.

"We are serious," said Salman. "You know we are not with them. But we have spoken to them. This is the only option." I knew that members of his party were close to the Sadr office and that he was speaking with the authority of the Sadr office.

"I am disappointed in you," I said. "We have worked together for months. How can you come and represent the views of these people? You know that we are trying to bring investment here, that we are handing over to the Iraqi government in five weeks time. What is this? People are being killed, the city is being wrecked. How can you stand by?"

"There is nothing we can do. No one can control these men. It is out of our hands," said Seyyed Ibadi.

"We are not saying that you have to withdraw," said Salman. "Your civilians can stay in the office and keep doing your work. There must just be no Italian troops anywhere. They must withdraw to Tallil and never enter the city again."

"This is unacceptable," I said. "No agreement with the Sadr office can be relied upon. Let me remind you of this week's events. Last Sunday the Sadr office said that if the Italians released Sheikh Muwayad it would be peace forever, so the Italians released Sheikh Muwayad. Then on Tuesday they attacked an Italian convoy outside Suq-Ash-Shuyukh and said that if the Italians left Suq-Ash-Shuyukh it would be peace forever, so the Italians abandoned Suq-Ash-Shuyukh. Yesterday, Friday, they attacked us in Nasiriyah and they tell us that if the Italians leave Nasiriyah it will be peace forever. How can we trust them? They will not stop until we are dead."

"Wait a second, Rory," said the Italian commander. "Let us try to listen to these men. Is there a compromise? Could we perhaps withdraw from Nasiriyah for two or three days?"

"*Mish mumkin.* Impossible. You must leave the city for good and then there will be peace forever," said Salman.

"Excuse me," I said. "My Italian colleague and I need to talk outside for a moment." I smiled at the Iraqis and said we would be back soon.

I took the guard commander into the sun and leaned on the balcony. "They think we are weak and on the run. They make a 'final demand,' promise peace if we accept it, and then attack us again and make a new demand. This," I said, feeling increasingly pompous, "is what happened to us in Kabul in 1842. First, the Afghans said if we would just move down from the citadel to the camp it would be peace forever. So we did. Then they said if we would just hand over our heavy weapons it would be peace forever. So we did. Then if we just agreed to leave the country, they would allow us safe passage and not attack us. And so we set off and they massacred the whole army—fourteen thousand soldiers—one by one in the retreat. That is what will happen here. They will keep making demands until we are entirely isolated in this compound with no protection force and then they will come over the walls and kill us all. That is the bottom line. If we accept this, we are all dead."

I felt ridiculous conjuring Kabul and talking about last stands. But I believed what I was saying and the Italian took this with a straight face. We walked back inside.

"So?" said Salman Duffar.

"As I said before," I replied, "we are the legitimate government of this province. I am here to serve the interests of the Iraqi people and we are not going anywhere. What you propose is humiliating because we have three and a half thousand Italian troops and you have a hundred militiamen at most out there. It is dangerous because we cannot keep my staff safe here without a guard force. And it is worthless because the Sadr office cannot be trusted."

"Then it is war," said Salman Duffar.

"Damn right it is war," I said. "And this meeting is over. Thank you."

They stood up, looked at me carefully, shook my hand, and made for the door. As they walked down the path to the gate, I saw the Italian commander trotting after them, saying, "Wait a second."

While he was following them, I called Baghdad and told them that the Italians were on no account to be allowed to agree to leave Nasiriyah. I repeated that I was prepared to stay and give the Italians a final chance to defend the compound but I would be evacuating my civilian staff.

I received an e-mail reporting the conclusions of the conference Molly and Barbara were attending in Baghdad, where Mark was lecturing on the lessons learned from the attack on his compound in Kut. Bremer's final speech was circulated to us all. He said:

> We welcome ideas during the next two weeks on how to get broader public buy-in to the interim government . . . we are starting to build serious momentum despite the security problems we are faced with. I am personally optimistic about Iraq. It is a very rich country in people skills and pride in their country. It has the makings of a great country. Let's run the race all the way to the tape, and meet again in June.

In our particular version of the race to the tape, I was gathering the civilians to prepare them for evacuation. Geoff, the bodyguard team commander, took me aside and said, "Listen, Rory, if the Italians don't control the city, the evacuation will be too dangerous. Those vehicles are not proof against RPGs. I'm not letting the civilians be evacuated unless we have an undertaking that the Italians control the city." I nodded.

The Italian APCs arrived mid-afternoon. To my fury the Italians had forgotten to bring any water. We were now down to a liter a person. The commander sprang out shouting, "*Andiamo*. Let's go. We get the people in. We are leaving." I asked for a minute to discuss things. He said there was no time.

I held him by the arm. "Do you control the city now?" I asked.

"Yes, yes. We control the city. All the city. No problem."

"There are no Sadrists on the streets?"

"None at all. We control it. They must hurry."

"Look, you understand, if you don't, these people will be killed in the APCs."

"No problem, we are taking the small bridge. It is safe. We have just driven through the city. We go now." He shook me off.

Geoff asked, "Do you believe him?"

I told Geoff we had no good options. The Sadr office had seen that we were not able to defend the place. Tonight would be twice as bad as the night before. We had to get people out. I didn't think they would make it through another night.

"As long as you understand I have my reservations. I have done what I can to try to establish the security situation. You witnessed it. I've got an answer from the Italians. This is your call."

I repeated that I had chosen the best option.

The CPA staff looked strangely vulnerable lined up in the court-yard holding their heavy bags with ugly helmets crammed on their heads. We were all over-tired. One person was crying. Three made a last offer to stay. Franco, the sixty-five-year-old ex-communist, said, "I know I am an old man but I would rather be here with you, my friend, if there is anything I can do. I have handled a gun before and I can remind myself how quickly." I thanked him. Franco shook my hand. "Yes, I thought as much. And from us all, our love—and thank you." He embraced me. I prayed they were right to thank me for sending them through a city full of RPGs. I did not say this to them.

I helped carry the bags to the back of the APCs and loaded them.

The Italian commander repeated that the road was safe. I didn't believe him. The staff crammed in five to each APC, their backs against the metal walls, suitcases on their laps.

My last sight of them was Charlie Morris in her blue helmet with a long strand of blonde hair over her face, smiling vaguely and waving, and then the ramp came up. Now only the heads of the commander and his driver were visible, poking out of their turrets. The commander shouted an order and the APC was thrown into reverse. Geoff and I stood back and the vehicle slammed into our compound wall, knocking down about three foot of it. The commander swore, *"Che Cazzo,"* leaned down, and cuffed the driver around the ear, striking his helmet. The vehicle leapt forward, wrapping a ball of barbed wire round its tracks, and ground to a halt. Geoff and I ran forward, signaling wildly, and did our best to unwrap the barbed wire.

The APC charged out of the first compound gate, followed by four others. We saw them drive down the track beneath the T-wall in a cloud of dust, pause at the outer compound barrier, and then they were round the corner and out of sight. Suddenly there was the sound of bullets. Geoff ran up to the roof. The Italians had driven straight into a militia ambush. Machine guns were firing from all sides. The civilians, packed like sardines in the backs of the APCs, could see nothing. Bullets were clattering off the metal walls of their vehicles, the Italian machine gunner firing belt after belt of ammunition in return. One of the vehicles was suddenly hit hard. The side of the APC buckled but did not break. It had been an RPG. The vehicle stopped and then miraculously moved again. The convoy turned another corner and we could not see them anymore. But for twenty minutes we followed their progress by the sound of the machine guns. I was thinking about having made a decision that might have sent fifteen of the staff to their deaths. Then the gunfire stopped. A phone call came from one of the civilians. They had arrived in the heavily defended Tallil airbase. It had been the worst twenty-five minutes any of them had experienced but they were uninjured and safe.

Whatever happened that night, there were only soldiers and ex-soldiers left in the compound.

A number of the Filipino guards stopped me to ask if they could borrow my satellite telephone to call home and tell their families they were all right. I was only able to allow five to do so because the battery was going and I was not sure we would be able to recharge it.

The e-mail waiting for me in my office, I could have done without. It was from the chief of staff in Basra. He implied I had exaggerated the danger of the previous night and caused unnecessary concern in Baghdad:

> *My very real concern is tinged with not a small degree of annoyance . . . The Italians kept us informed of their intentions throughout and in their own measured way appeared to us to deal with the situation effectively . . . I fully understand that from your perspective this was a very uncomfortable and frightening few hours . . . Also, from your perspective, help seemed a long time in coming. I hope you understand, however, that the Italian response, just like ours, must be measured by balancing risk and effect.*

I sent a report updating Baghdad on our staff and supply situation. I then wrote to the chief of staff, in a friendly tone, re-emphasizing that I had no wish to insult the Italians but encouraging him to send air support that night. And then I wrote a situation report intended to mollify the Italians, to be sent to all the provincial capitals in Iraq.

REPRISE

For the people were crying out against the senate and the senate against the people; the population was running wildly through the streets, closing their shops and leaving the cities in droves.
                          —*Machiavelli,* Discourses, *Book I, Chapter 4*

MAY 12–14, 2004

Dusk came. Three hours passed. Shortly after nine I received another breezy e-mail from the chief of staff in Basra telling me the Italians were keeping him fully informed. He was delighted to discover from the Italians that things were "calm" and "quiet" across the province that night and hoped I was getting some rest. Things, he said, were much worse in Amara. I replied immediately that things were not particularly "calm" or "quiet." We had received twenty incoming mortar rounds at the CPA in the last two hours, six detonating within the perimeter. The last two had fallen within twenty meters of our building beside the cookhouse. The Quick Reaction Force had not moved yet. I concluded that I was sure, however, "the Italians are keeping you fully informed of the situation and their response to the threat."

The bodyguard team had been on the roof for two hours, firing hundreds of rounds at the insurgents. I did not receive a reply from the chief of staff. Someone handed me a weapon, but I handed it back because I wanted to focus on getting support from Baghdad. I gathered the team leaders for another briefing in the courtyard.

Geoff read from a pad: "In the last thirty minutes we have had one eighty-one-millimeter mortar round on the northeast corner, two outside the compound, three RPGs on the rim of the roof, then more sixty-millimeter mortars up the front path—which makes me think they still have a spotter on the hospital roof."

"Is the gate guard alright?" I asked.

"Minor injuries."

"And what hit the computer room?" I asked.

"Probably an eighty-two-millimeter mortar, I'd guess."

"Can you come with me?" I said. We walked into the room. It was a little quieter inside than outside, but not much. The room was still a jumble of splintered plastic and wood. "Looks like it too came through the air conditioner."

"I'd guess then it was an RPG, not a mortar. We'll see if we can find the projectile tomorrow."

We walked back outside into the courtyard. And then there was a distinctive thud, someone shouted "incoming," and we took cover. Geoff continued briefing us. "That sounded bigger than an eighty-two-millimeter. But they've lost the range again. They're trying to pin us down in here, get us stuck in a corner of the building, and then they will come over the wire. That's why we need to keep the fifty caliber on the roof."

"Sir, we need air support now," said one of the Americans. "A gunship could clear them in no time. We're not taking this shit. It's easy to take out a mortar position. I'm tempted to lead the fucking assault myself if the Italians won't do it."

I laughed. "Anything else?"

"No."

"Okay," I concluded, "so since 2300 we have had a large mortar shell landing in the northeast; sixty-millimeters walked up the path, which implies spotters; four RPGs, including the one through the computer room. One gate guard injured. No dead. Everyone else accounted for. Action: we need a patrol or air support immediately to take out the mortar base-plates. I will focus on getting help from the U.S. military now."

The mobile phone network was down and we had not managed to repair the Internet connection, so I could now only communicate with Baghdad via a Thuraya satellite phone. This required "direct line of sight to the sky"—in other words, standing outside. So I called in my reports in my helmet and body armor. Tash, Andy Bearpark's deputy, on the other end of the line in Baghdad was probably having a worse night than me. She was dealing simultaneously with calls about smaller attacks in Amara, Samawah, Kerbala, and Najaf while I called in accounts of mortar fire and pushed for a promise of air support.

I was failing again to persuade the Italians to deploy from the compound. The Italian commander who had promised "this time we will respond, we will not be sitting ducks," became more and more frantic. He could not quite explain to me why the QRF still refused to take out the mortar position. At about midnight, Barbara Contini came through on the military phone from the conference in Baghdad. She promised to go through Berlusconi if necessary to make the Italian general order the deployment of the QRF.

I strode upstairs into the middle of an argument between the Italian commander and the American security team leader. They were standing in a room where a circular hole in the window glass and a mark on the wall showed that one of the CRG guys had just had a lucky miss. The Italian had finally agreed to drive his armored unit into the streets to engage the mortar position but he wanted the Filipino guard force to open the drop gates at the outer entrance.

"No way," said the American. "My guys have got no body armor. Look at where that gate is. It's a hundred-and-fifty-meter run down a lit passage from our compound. We are overlooked on every side. The guys will be running into a wall of fire and they will just be mown down by the insurgents if they try it."

"Someone has to open the gate," said the Italian, "and I don't want my soldiers getting out of their vehicles. I want them rolling smoothly all the way from here without stopping."

"You will have to open the gate yourselves."

"That is not our job," said the Italian. "That is the job of you and the Filipinos. That is what you are employed to do."

"This is suicide," said the American.

Perhaps because I hadn't slept for two nights or because I felt I wasn't doing enough, I thought of offering to open the drop bar myself. But I realized how ridiculous that would sound. I thanked everyone and suggested the Italians lend some body armor to the Filipino sentries. The Filipinos could take cover behind the armored vehicles as they rolled through, so they would only be exposed for a few seconds.

The American argued, but I said for once I was on the Italians' side. This was the security team's job. I talked to him privately for a minute. He agreed. I told the Italians and we waited for the armored group to roll out and end it all. The objective was to drive around behind the mortar positions, attack them from the rear, and drive off the insurgents. We guessed only a few dozen Sadrists were manning the mortars and they would be entirely outgunned by the Italian armor. This was standard procedure elsewhere. In Amara, if mortars came in the British immediately deployed a fighting patrol. As a result it was rare for the insurgents to get off more than four rounds in a night, or ever really perfect their range, since as soon as they fired they had to run for it. We, on the other hand, were sitting ducks. We had been hit with almost a hundred shells and rocket-propelled grenades the night before and were already approaching those numbers again.

When the Italian armored response happened, we watched it from the roof. First one of the Filipino sentries in Italian body armor sprinted out of the compound gate, down the long passage; covering fire exploded from the roof. He levered open the gate as the armored column rolled toward it, then closed the bar and ran back when the vehicles were through. As he reached the concrete sentry hut, the Italian column was racing down the main road, blazing away at both sides. The noise was astonishing and must have terrified anyone in the streets. The column reached the roundabout five hundred meters away; there was a sudden squawk from the radio, a hurried message. Then the column turned round the roundabout and began racing back to the compound. The Filipino ran down the path to reopen the bar. The Sadrists fired at him from the hospital roof. He crouched behind the line of vehicles as they rolled past. Then he leapt up, closed the bar, and—half-crouched, weaving as he went—sprinted back to the compound. He reached it shortly after the Italians, who were now pouring back into the building. The American and British guards looked at each other.

Then one of them said, "You fucking believe it?" He glanced at his watch. "They drive up to the roundabout giving it all they've got, shooting at nothing, turn around again, and come back. Thirty seconds. They were outside for thirty seconds."

It was the last time the Italians left the compound that night. And the mortars started falling again after their return.

By now any respect the American and British security contractors had for their Italian counterparts was gone. Some of the Italian soldiers were brave: we had seen them run out into mortar fire to bring back injured comrades, and many of them wanted to attack the insurgents. But their leadership was not prepared to engage the mortar base plates.

A huge, black-bearded American contractor who went by the nickname "Euro" came to see me just after midnight and laughed and laughed. He had been on the roof, exposed to direct fire, for hours. I asked what was up.

"Well, Rory," he said, "it's fucking great up there on the roof. Either the Italians shoot at anyone they can see—I just saw them shoot up a car that was trying to drive down the road—or they do nothing. It's mayhem. I was just up there and this Sadr asshole runs toward us with an RPG and I shout at the Italian on the fifty cal, 'shoot him.' And the Italian does nothing. So the asshole shoots the tube. Wham. Smack into the Hesco blast wall. Fucking huge explosion. The Iraqi runs back round the corner and then he reappears with another RPG, about a hundred yards from us. I shout again at the Italian, 'Shoot him.' Again the machine gunner does nothing. The Iraqi releases another rocket, the grenade hits one of our vehicles. Bang. Vehicle up in flames. I run across the roof and I just fucking push the Italian off his gun. He's like, 'hey, hey.' And I just like shout 'Navy Seal' and grab it. And then I see the problem. The guy had stacked the sandbags so high around himself that his gun can only fire at a forty-five degree angle in the air."

In the cacophony of the battle, each caliber of weapon had its own voice: the vicious yap, the snap, the continual growl, and an occasional giant roar, which represented the 7.62 of the attackers, the 5.56 of the guards, the fifty cal on the roof, the rocket-propelled grenades, the panzerfaust, the three different calibers of mortar. None of us had ever heard anything so loud. But no one seemed paralyzed by the experience. Debriefs of the sentries and the bodyguards and orders went smoothly. The situation reports were clear.

The mortars and RPGs came with little interruption and from three directions. Most enraging was that the insurgents had now established a position on a rooftop only three hundred yards from our building and were dropping mortars in with impunity.

It was unusual in a modern Western army to be under mortar fire for hours on end because usually you could expect a patrol or a plane or counter-battery fire to deal with the mortar position. None of us—even soldiers who had been in the army twenty-two years—had had to sit passively under this kind of bombardment before. In historical terms this was nothing—a few hundred rounds and two nights without sleep was hardly enough to constitute shell shock. Still, I was glad not to have to worry any longer about reassuring civilian staff in my office.

The men on the roof held the attackers back; no one came over the razor wire; and none of us were killed by incoming fire. Many Iraqis died, though. Toward the end of the night, it became clear that our own incompetence was being exceeded by that of the insurgents. They were beginning to fire in mortars with time delay fuses and strange aluminium cases—anything they could get their hands on— and when the attack stopped around dawn, we guessed they had run out of ammunition. They had apparently not believed they would be allowed to keep firing at us indefinitely. So instead of bringing in a thousand rounds and some heavier mortars—which the Sadr movement had in neighboring provinces—and burying us in rubble, they had apparently assembled a rag bag and used it up.

A round landed in full daylight at about 7:15 in the morning, the first for more than half an hour, then there was silence again. I walked out to look around the compound and then called a meeting to assess the damage. We needed the sewage truck to come in. Our shallow cess pits were starting to overflow and we were going to get sick. Heads of rocket-propelled grenades were scattered across the gravel. Mortars had gone through the roof of the dining hall, and into bedrooms. Two bodyguards found shrapnel deep in the mattresses on their beds. One of the mortar rounds had destroyed for good any chance of getting main power. The water was no longer coming out of the taps because it depended on an electric pump and the generator had stopped working during the night. Since there was no way to flush, the toilets were looking terrible. We fixed the generator, but since we were low on fuel, I banned the use of fans, air conditioners, or lights during the day. The Italians had still not arrived with the water and I regretted not having told Aleem to buy some.

I could only conclude, after a second night of their failure to defend the compound, that the Italians were under orders not to deploy.

Nasiriyah was a ghost town. Everyone was locked in their houses, except for the Sadr militia—who were parading openly, dancing in the streets—and some policemen, who were apparently walking hand in hand with the Sadrists. We needed an immediate promise of continual air support or troops prepared to take offensive action. I wanted a company of American or British troops. Otherwise we would have to close the compound because we were unable to do any work. Normally on a Sunday we would have had a crowd of petitioners; we would be signing contracts, preparing elections, pushing ahead with new development projects. But for the last two days, no one had come to see us. Even our translators were boycotting the office. There was no point keeping the office open, with overflowing sewage and incoming mortar fire, if the city was closed and we were unable to work. I tried to explain to Baghdad that we needed enough military support to drive off the attackers and restore normal life in the city:

> *If we can get this support this site can continue to complete 12 million dollars of development programs, run our 5,000-job scheme, continue with our badly needed reform of the police, and establish a dignified and constructive transition from us to the Iraqi government in seven weeks' time.*

Meanwhile Barbara had arrived by helicopter at the Italian base. I sent a number of messages telling her not to come to the compound. At 10:15 there was a burst of fifty-caliber machine-gun fire from the bridge and then the carabinieri rolled in and emerged running from their vehicles. Everyone was very hyped up by the firefight that they had just experienced, crossing the bridge. One of the carabinieri had been injured. Then, one of the armored personnel carriers opened, and out walked Barbara. One of the senior bodyguards was so horrified to see another civilian come into the compound after we had just evacuated them through such danger that, to my astonishment, he began to cry.

The afternoon was quiet. We were again assured of air support. The evening attack started with the militia mortaring not us but the Italian base. Their aim had improved and with the first bombardment they killed an Italian soldier. The Italians abandoned the base. The Sadr militia were now traveling with a cameraman, who filmed them gleefully rushing inside, finding vehicles, rations, and even some ammunition. Then they set up their mortar plate in the Italian base and began mortaring us again. With two nights of range practice they landed their first five rounds very elegantly in the northeast corner of the compound. I had by now not slept in sixty-five hours, so I did a final check with the perimeter commanders, called in a situation report to Baghdad, asked to be woken in half an hour, and lay down.

As I closed my eyes, I heard someone kick a soccer ball against my door. I tried to ignore it but it came again, the sound of a leather ball hitting the concrete and then bouncing up against a wooden door: th-thump, th-thump. I thought this was the last straw: the Italians do nothing and then as soon as I am trying to get some sleep, they start playing soccer against my door. Really enraged for the first time in three days, I stormed outside. But the courtyard was deserted. I could hear nothing. I was not, however, awake enough to realize how strange it was to hear total silence after hours of bombardment. I lay down again and as soon as I closed my eyes, I heard the soccer ball. Again I flung open the door. This time I could still hear it. I ran up to the roof. And there I saw the source of the noise—an AC-130 Specter gunship: a circling Hercules airplane filled with imaging equipment enabling its crew to see all the insurgents at their mortars and a forty-millimeter cannon able to shoot them one by one from ten thousand feet in the air.

There was no more mortar fire. The gunship stayed in the air all night, and I went to sleep to the th-thump of its cannon. It killed people at their mortar positions and as they fled. A translator recognized one of the Sadr clerics lying dead on his street. The next morning I woke to a bustling city, all the shops and schools open, the translators and cleaners again at the door. The insurgency, such as it had been, had been solved with a single plane. I called Baghdad to tell them that if they could guarantee air support we could keep the city functioning and the office open.

After avoiding us for days, the senior leadership of the province came en masse. They were quick to express their outrage now that the militia, tired from three days of fighting and with many killed and fourteen seriously wounded by the gunship, had withdrawn—many to their homes outside the city. They complained that the Science College and part of the museum had been looted, along with private houses on Zeitun Street. Five thousand books had been burned in the museum library. The schools had been forced to close during the vital pre-exam period.

Barbara proposed a march for peace. The chairman of the provincial council refused. He said no one would come and SCIRI would use the opportunity to make a violent attack on Sadr. Barbara talked of Dhi Qar's reputation for courage and resistance, and offered funds to support the demonstration.

The council said they would hold a demonstration the next morning and offered to issue a statement condemning the Sadrists. For a moment it looked as though we were taking control again and Barbara hoped this would be enough to convince the Green Zone to leave the site open. But it was too late; a final order came from Baghdad: the site was closing.

I spent the morning with the CRG teams destroying all the paperwork and piling up the computer equipment and putting incendiary grenades next to it, ready for the moment when the site was finally abandoned. Then we began breaking into the accommodation trailers to get the most valuable items out of the staff rooms. We had no keys so we kicked in doors, smashed windows with fire extinguishers, and had quite a good time of it. I then pulled what I could of my own stuff into a duffel bag, had a final look at my bedroom, and added my bag to the pile waiting for evacuation.

Just before the truck arrived, one of the British CRG bodyguard team came up to me and thanked me for "real leadership," but they were the heroes. They had manned the machine guns on the roof, kept the enemy heads down, monitored the incoming fire, and made suggestions about patrols and air support. Through all of this they had been in their element: considered, rational, matter of fact. Between them they had a couple hundred years of military experience and they knew far more than I did. I had only to smile, look calm, gather them every half hour, and listen, clarify, summarize, and send their views to Baghdad. A little later, I heard a Canadian general say military contractors were mercenaries whose loyalty could not be relied on. I told him these contractors had risked their lives manning guns that soldiers had abandoned. A hundred of them could have brought order back to the province.

There was—predictably, perhaps—no sign of the promised evacuation convoy at eight that evening. Or at ten. It finally arrived at 11:15. We loaded the remaining staff, drove out—this time with no incoming fire clattering off the vehicles—and, just after midnight, I phoned Baghdad to say we were safely in Tallil.

FINAL DAYS

Many still think that the affairs of the world are so ruled by fortune and by God that it is beyond the ability of man to control them.
                                   —*Machiavelli,* The Prince, *Chapter 25*

MAY 15–30, 2004

My final days in Iraq were chaos. The British military company that had been on standby to take over Nasiriyah from the Italians was prevented from coming. Berlusconi had apparently said it was too humiliating for him to hand over the provincial capital to another country. It would be an admission that the Italians could not perform their role, in which case they would leave the Coalition. No one was prepared to lose the third largest force in the Coalition. We were, therefore, not allowed to return to our office. My superiors said that whatever my work had been, it wasn't worth getting killed for. That seemed a pretty depressing statement of how serious we were about the occupation. I protested that I was supposed be running a province of two million people, but received no reply.

We opened, instead, a shabby temporary base in an old Iraqi training camp in the desert between Nasiriyah and the Ziggurat of Ur. Meanwhile, our old compound was thoroughly looted. I had wanted to turn over the site to the provincial council and this was agreed to. But instead of getting a well-furnished site with computer equipment and kitchens, they received a bombed out, empty shell.

The assistant governor who had refused to help during the attack came in to see me. I arranged what he wanted—a training program for his staff—but I told him I thought he had behaved disgracefully.

Much of the paperwork had been destroyed in the evacuation. We had lost at least a week of progress on the programs, and Ginnie and Sam, two British women in our military civil affairs team, worked seventeen hours a day to finalize the accounts on ten million dollars' worth of projects. A British colonel in Basra said this should have been work for civilians and ordered them to stop. I said that I had no staff left and they were our only chance of wrapping up things in the province. He replied that this was my problem and the military was not there to pick up the pieces. I was forced to appeal to the general to keep them. I wanted to pay the final month's salary to the local translators and cleaners but Basra refused to release funds until the end of the month, by which time we would all be gone. I was worried that if I followed their guidelines the local staff would never get paid, so I again had to force through my request at a senior level.

Over the next few weeks our staff left one by one until, from our large civilian office, only Barbara and I remained. An Iraqi contractor came to see me, claiming he was owed a hundred thousand dollars for a water unit. He had certainly received the first installment four months before I reached Nasiriyah, and had built the plant, but there was no proper documentation. I tried to track down someone who had been there when the agreement was made, but everyone was evasive. I eventually found myself filling out a form on which I signed for the hundred thousand dollars as "the officer responsible for the unauthorized commitment." Initially, I could find no one who would counter-sign.

We then withdrew to the Italian section of the Tallil base. I spent some evenings with the carabinieri paracadutisti and the Italian Special Forces and grew to like them. They had built their own pizza ovens. Otherwise, I ate in the dining hall. Breakfast was a disappointment for a Briton—dried biscuits and a plastic-wrapped croissant. Lunch and dinner were magnificent.

In my last week I was standing trying to decide whether to have trout poached in foil or veal with my pasta when I—and all the Italian soldiers—noticed a beautiful blond in civilian clothes walk into the dining hall. I had to walk past her to get my plastic fork. To my astonishment, she smiled at me. I smiled foolishly back. And then she said, "Rory," and I realized who she was.

I had met Marie-Helene in Uzbekistan when I was twenty-five. We had spent a week traveling together, and I had spent most of the flight home writing poems about her. But she hadn't answered my e-mails and finally I had stopped writing to her. Beside her was her boyfriend, Micah Garen, whom I had never met. They were making a documentary about archaeological looting, focused on my friend Abdul Amir al-Hamdani, the cuneiform-quoting archaeological director with the sunken cheeks. Unlike me, or even most of the journalists in Iraq, they traveled entirely unprotected up and down the country, trying to pass as Arabs though neither spoke much Arabic. They did not seem to see that the risks they were taking far exceeded the likely impact of their documentary.

On the street in Baghdad Micah had bought a new DVD made by the Sadr office. It was called "The Attack on the CPA in Nasiriyah." It had taken the Sadr office a week to edit and distribute the film. It opened with long religious sermons by Sadr II and then showed Sadrists swarming down the side streets around our compound, waving Kalashnikovs. Few of them made any attempt to cover their faces and I recognized many of the people who had come to my office. Then the film showed them setting up their mortar plates and firing shells into our compound. One of the mortarmen almost blew his own head off trying to look down the tube after he had dropped in the shell. But otherwise they seemed to be having a great time. The cameraman kept zooming in on our roof and its limp Iraqi flag. The film finished with the Sadrists overrunning the Italian base, working their way through the abandoned supplies, and mortaring us again from there. It was clearly more fun being an insurgent than an Iraqi policeman. Micah, Marie-Helene, and I had dinner together, interrupted only when one of the Italian tents caught fire.

Outside the compound we had lost authority. Politicians insisted that the current police leadership had cooperated with the Sadr attack. On the days we were under siege, Major Dakhil, north Nasiriyah commander, was seen patrolling with the Sadr militia dressed in a black *dishdasha,* having discarded his uniform. Major Ali of the Crime Control Center spent the last two days drinking tea with the Sadrists and gave them his patrol cars.

I wrote a speech for television in which I said, "People of Nasiriyah, choose. This is your country. Do you want to be run by a group of illiterate gunmen who mock your policemen, close your shops and schools, and destroy your economy, or do you want to take advantage of the future? The choice is yours." The director of the state television company, which was funded by the CPA, refused to show the speech. I ordered him to do so. He refused again. I told the Italians to arrest him. They refused. By now it was clear we no longer had the power to enforce our will. And since the Coalition could not establish order, I wanted to install Iraqis who could.

I encouraged the provincial council and the governor to choose fifty new officers for the police. The chairman of the provincial council agreed to remove the current police chief and appoint the commander of the Iranian-linked SCIRI/Badr brigades in his place. This man was a large, two-hundred-pound, ex-Special Forces officer from the old army.

Although I was sympathetic to the Iranian-linked groups, I saw the danger of putting too many in positions of authority. The governor of Samawah was now from Badr and so was the acting governor of Basra and the police chief of Amara. If we made a Badr officer the police chief of Nasiriyah, this Iranian-linked group and its armed militia would have a stranglehold on the four southern provinces. But in the case of Dhi Qar, I felt this man was now the only one who could assert control of the police. So I sent his name to the provincial council. And then to my surprise, having apparently supported his appointment, they rejected him under pressure from the Sadr office.

I wrote a letter full of the grand verbiage of UN resolutions and covered in seals, saying that, pursuant to my authority, etc., he was the chief. The council refused him again. I told the new chief just to walk into the office and take control. He led this coup reluctantly and the provincial council blocked formal confirmation from Baghdad. I wondered how long he would last.

LEADERS

My house founded by the righteous was pushed over on its side like a garden fence.

—The lament for Urim, c. 2000 B.C.

Meanwhile, I had to pick up the various matters that had been dropped during the mortar attack. Most important was the continuing problem with Sheikh Ali Zeidi in al-Rafai and in particular the case of the council member he had tortured. I asked the governor to chair a meeting of all the leaders of al-Rafai: tribal sheikhs, headmasters, government ministers, the police chief, the preachers from the mosques. Sheikh Taleb, the Machiavellian sheikh of the Beni Rikaab, was among them.

We met in the governor's large office. I began, "This is a humiliating embarrassment for al-Rafai. You are a city of one hundred thirty thousand people with a democratically elected council—elected by your citizens. But Sheikh Ali Zeidi is able with a handful of young friends to walk into your council building, throw out the council members, abduct and torture one of them, hang flags out of the office, and then walk off. The local police—of whom there are nearly four hundred—do nothing."

There was a pause. "I propose," said one of the senior clerics, "that we have another election and elect a new council."

378

"That is no good," I replied, "Sheikh Ali Zeidi will just attack the new council and it will happen all over again.

"Come on," I said, "Sheikh Talib, you have been saying for months that if you had the resources you would be able to keep security in al-Rafai. Here is your chance. What do you need—what can I give you?"

"I cannot answer for Sheikh Ali Zeidi. He is not from our tribe."

"Nevertheless, Sheikh Talib," I said, "forty-five percent of the people in al-Rafai belong to your tribe and another forty percent to Sheikh Arkan of the Shweilat. Between you, you have eighty-five percent of the population. Surely together you are strong enough to act against Sheikh Ali Zeidi."

"No. I'm afraid not," said Sheikh Talib. "We can only deal with our own tribes."

I talked about impunity and the rule of law and finished, "Are you going to let a twenty-something-year-old man run your community, fire RPGs in the street, torture council members? And you do nothing?"

"Seyyed Rory," said the headmaster, "Sheikh Ali Zeidi has had a difficult life. His father died when he was young; his brother was killed in the fighting; he is a little unbalanced. Can we not just forget about him?"

It was not that they did not understand my talk of justice and the rule of law. They understood that Sheikh Ali Zeidi had committed a crime. But no one wanted to take responsibility. Although he was young and violent, Ali Zeidi was a cleric and that entitled him to a certain respect. And the Sadr office was dangerous. No one believed in our capacity to protect them. In Afghanistan there was always someone—often three—beating his chest and saying he was the boss. In Nasiriyah at this moment, people did not want political power. Not even Sheikh Ali Zeidi.

I made a last grand speech proposing a deal: first, they would arrest Ali Zeidi, and then I would hold an election. They would show their courage, we our reasonableness, and dignity and order would return to al-Rafai. For a moment, they seemed won over. There were enthusiastic nods and smiles as they considered this new heroic idea. "We will arrest him then, Seyyed Rory," said a sheikh, "and then we will hold elections." But they never did.

Some successes stood out in the last month. One was the arrival of a great deal of municipal equipment—some bought by the CPA and some donated by Italian companies—that Barbara distributed in a large ceremony in the center of town. The second was the employment scheme that had finally taken off, with men in red boiler suits filling the streets. Their first action was to paint the old battle tanks that had been left as souvenirs in parks pink. And, finally, we were able to provide more funding for the guards and the Ziggurat of Ur. I told the archaeological director that the Sadrist leader still said he had nothing to apologize for in relation to the riots. The archaeological director replied: "For a donkey there is no stench, for a donkey there is no washing with soap"—a four-thousand-year-old proverb found on one of the fragments at Ur.

Then there was the "Prince's Trust" vocational educational project at the Labor Union. The Prince of Wales had read an article about my work in Amara and had sent me a letter suggesting we provide training and opportunities for young unemployed men to take them out of the grip of militia groups. We approached the labor union and the Sons of Dhi Qar, an NGO consisting of middle-class professionals. Together we designed a program that took two hundred and fifty boys a month, taught them carpentry, sport, literacy skills, and a little computing, and exposed them to visiting speakers and ideas of civil society. We bought all the heavy carpentry equipment.

It was an expensive project but it was probably the best project I saw. Nasiriyah embraced the idea, the Arab media stations covered it, all the local leaders went to visit it and make speeches, and the

Labor Union, which had been faltering, found a new purpose. When we visited we found a huge sign at the Union reading "Prince Charles Training Institute." The program directors had put it up spontaneously and the head of the Union personally chased out some men protesting the British name. The boys (with "Charles" embroidered on their boiler suits) were cheerful, active, and competent, and already being approached to work in the carpentry and building trades.

Finally, I paid a visit to the site of my largest *mudhif.* It had been one of our first highly visible projects. Parents often took their children to visit it. Many saw it as an important symbol of our respect for traditional culture and a way of rewarding and preserving the unique skills that went into making it.

For this particular building, Abu Mthenna had created windows in the façade using diagonal bundles of canes. From the outside they seemed solid but inside the sun turned them into a lattice of dark diamonds, containing, on the highest pentagonal window, 157 circles of bright white light. One long afternoon I had counted the panels of light in each window—on the lower windows, thirteen rows of twelve topped by an equilateral triangle: eleven, nine, seven, five, three, one. In all, 801 circles of light.[1]

The Sadrists, however, had burned it. All that remained was a black rectangle of burned grass on the edge of the park. It was difficult to believe a cathedral could disappear so completely.

---

[1]Because there were also seven rows of twelve in each of the rectangles and four more where they met the sloping roof.

LAST DAYS IN AMARA

Countless examples in the records of ancient history demonstrate how difficult it is for a people accustomed to living under a prince to preserve its freedom afterward if by chance it acquires it.

—*Machiavelli,* Discourses, *Book I, Chapter 16*

AMARA

We, the Coalition Provisional Authority, transferred sovereignty to the Iraqi government on June 28, 2004. In Amara, there was no formal handover ceremony. Nor in Kut. And even in Baghdad it was a hurried, low-key affair. Chaos had come to Amara while we had been under siege. For weeks, Molly and her team had been mortared nightly, although the rapid response from the British units ensured the insurgents rarely fired more than three or four rounds before being forced to flee. The Prince of the Marshes had allied himself with the Sadr office, having seemingly forgotten his previous desire to exterminate them. Now they were simply nationalist allies against the Iranian-linked Badr brigades. The Prince went on a highly publicized visit to Muqtada in Najaf and when Bremer protested he resigned from the governing council in Baghdad.

On the Friday morning when we were being mortared in Nasiriyah, the British troops in Amara received warning of an ambush in Majar, south of Amara. They led a counter-ambush, killed twenty, seriously wounded nine, and injured eight. They brought the bodies to the British base at Abu Naji.

The next morning Governor Riyadh, the Prince of the Marshes' brother, claimed the British had executed twenty prisoners at the base. The Prince of the Marshes stated publicly that not only had the British forces killed the prisoners at Abu Naji, they had, in his characteristic complaint, plucked out their eyes—he had seen that himself. He threatened to lead a demonstration against the CPA. Doctors at the city hospitals gave interviews to the Arab media saying the bodies had definitely been executed overnight and their hands severed.

The British colonel sent the bodies to the morgue of the Majar hospital. He hoped to be able to show that no executions or mutilation had taken place. The police chief of Majar, who was from Badr, met the Prince at the morgue. The Prince accused the police chief of warning the Coalition of the ambush and held the police chief responsible for the deaths of these men, who were from the Prince's tribe. There was a heated argument that ended when pistols were pulled. The police chief was shot dead in the morgue. Many claimed Governor Riyadh had fired the shot that killed him.

The provincial council split into two factions: one of Iranian-linked Islamists, including the moderate clerics; the second of the Prince of the Marshes and the Sadrists. The CPA pressed for an arrest warrant and Molly announced that Riyadh had been suspended as governor. Then, on June 28, Molly transferred power to the provincial council and closed the CPA office in Amara. The following day, Riyadh walked back into his office and took over again as governor.

I received e-mails from the moderate clerics, Abu Mustafa and Abu Muslim, asking for help. But we had no more legal power to intervene. Riyadh fired the Iranian-linked parties and the moderate clerics from the council, made a deal with the Sadrists, and convinced the interior minister to drop the arrest warrant. The province was now engulfed in a full anti-Coalition insurgency. The British battle group suffered more attacks than any British unit since the Korean War. Many insurgents were killed. I saw photographs of Iraqi corpses laid out beside the still-empty swimming pool. The British said they had shown the Iraqis that the insurgents could be beaten. The next battle group decided there was no point trying to defend our building in the center of town. Tigris the dog was taken to Britain as a regimental mascot. The compound was abandoned, turned over to the Iraqi police, and looted. Some Iraqis saw this as a progressive step. Others said the Sadr militia had driven the British out.

HANDING OVER

My powers have been alienated from me.
—The lament for Urim, c. 2000 B.C.

MONDAY, JUNE 28, 2004

In Nasiriyah we held the handover ceremony at the Ziggurat of Ur. I greeted people, led them to their seats, and then stood in the background. Barbara and three generals were on the podium facing the cameras. I looked for the rest of the team and remembered that everyone had gone. Behind me on the chairs were councilors, police officers, and the archaeological director. He was looking at the new sign we had painted for the Ziggurat. I could see Barbara's back as she began to read, in her slow Italian-English, the speech I had written for her:

> Governor, Members of the Provincial Council, Sheikhs, Leaders, General Stewart, General Spagniolo, General Dalzini, colleagues, successors, friends. Tonight, we stand at the Ziggurat of Ur at the center of the world's first civilization.
>
> Within one hundred meters of us lie cuneiform tablets written in an alphabet invented here five thousand years ago, eighty-five generations before anyone in Italy, Britain, or

America began to write . . . A little further and we come to
the oldest law court in the world and the house where Abra-
ham was born. Here is the birthplace of civilized man, the
foundation of our urban life and of our philosophy.

Through gaps in the front row I could see the musicians and a
line of cavalry troopers facing us. Their formal jackets were tight and
their faces were red and hot over their cravats. The blue pennants on
their lances flapped in the breeze, but their ten-foot poles seemed ce-
mented into the ground.

Saddam too had held ceremonies at Babylon and Ur. He too had
invoked the Sumerian past. We were in the temple forecourt of the
Ziggurat at the bottom of the only set of steps. We were on the cross-
roads between the old port road and the road that led to the law
courts and the palace. Tens of thousands must have passed through
this point, every year from the first building on the Ziggurat site in
3000 B.C. And yet we knew nothing really about the theology of this
temple or the ceremonies that had been performed here.

I turned round and saw the Sadrist assistant governor looking at
me from his seat. He rose slightly, put his hand to his chest, and
bowed to me. I remembered our last argument and was still angry
with him. I put my hand to my chest and bowed back.

Barbara continued slowly and carefully through the unfamiliar
English. Zeid was translating it line for line. I could not hear him well
enough to judge how much the speech was being mistranslated:

This experience of working side by side has changed us all:
each of us, whether Italian, British, Iraqi, or American, will
take home a little bit of this experience, a little bit of this understanding. We will never be the same again.

Here beside the rich-colored brick of the Ziggurat bound
together four thousand years ago by those two potent symbols

of your country, the reeds of the marshes and the bitumen of your oil, I want to thank you.

When they clapped, Barbara turned and called me to podium. The generals shuffled along so that I was standing between her and the governor. She asked if I wanted to say anything; I shook my head. The governor began his speech. He thanked Barbara and me for how much we had done for the province and said it was a great day but also a difficult day.

When he finished, the brass band of the Parachute Regiment struck up, I stood to attention, and the three generals saluted. Through the dust in the air and the fading light, the horns sounded three clear notes and then the rest of the band joined in to the clipped metronome gestures of the band master. I had been in the stadium in Hong Kong for that handover in 1997 and I thought how strange it was that after our short stay, the siege, the flight from the compound, the ragged end to our programs, we should enact the stately transfer of a colony. And yet the Iraqi audience seemed comfortable, as though they too wanted to be the actors in the end of Empire. The military band was playing an eighteenth-century trumpet concerto; it seemed like music for an intermission—neither happy nor sad, neither triumphal nor recessional. The governor reached for my hand; he did not squeeze it—just held it loosely.

The first tune finished. There was a pause. Italian officers came forward to guide us to the steps of the Ziggurat. The governor made way for General Stewart and General Stewart said, "No, this is your day, Governor." In the end they walked side by side up the stairs. The trumpets played again and we fell awkwardly into step with the music. On either side of the staircase all the way to the top were lancers, eyes front, at attention, with their lances facing forward.

I marched beside the head of the Nasiriyah council, Seyyed Ibadi, and asked him how he felt. "Very sad, Seyyed Rory," he said.

"I am worried. It is all going to collapse—watch. You do not realize how dangerous these groups are. Your leaving is a big mistake. It is much too early. There will be civil war in a few weeks and the Italians will be able to do nothing. This is a sad day for all of us." The governor had whispered something similar.

I said goodbye to Marie-Helene and Micah. I told them to be careful traveling without an escort; things were becoming more dangerous. I told Micah I didn't want to turn on CNN and see him saying, "I call on American troops to leave Iraq." I suggested he get a neck brace, to stop them from beheading him. He laughed.

Six weeks later Micah was on television, flanked by armed men in Kaffiyeh, and he was calling for the American troops to withdraw. He had been kidnapped in Nasiriyah by the Sadr militia. And they were threatening to behead him in forty-eight hours. Marie-Helene coordinated a vast campaign to get him released, using every contact and pressure anyone could think of. I called everyone I knew in Nasiriyah. The governor and Adnan, the Sadr representative, swore it would be all right: "He will be out tomorrow." But I assumed this was just Iraqis lying to make me feel happy. The day after Micah was taken, they kidnapped Georges Malbrunot, the Figaro correspondent who had sat with me by the pool in Baghdad. Micah was released after ten days. Georges after nine months. And then Marla, the young Californian who had stayed in my room on the first night in Baghdad, was killed by a roadside bomb.

At that time I did not know what was going to happen to my friends, but I believed that Seyyed Ibadi was right and the province could only sink more deeply into a state of nature. Whatever elections were held, whatever development money was spent, this would be a land without a functioning state. The police would be powerless, officials entirely corrupt, beatings, rape, and assassination commonplace. Services would falter. Security would be non-existent. The influence of foreign intelligence services would grow. Protection rackets would spread. And among the buildings of Nasiriyah, now lit by a few faltering street lamps, and right across the province, I expected a continual civil war—not between grand factions but between small local groups that were simultaneously mafia, tribes, and political parties—a violence that neither the police nor the Italians were in a position to control and that the people were powerless to prevent.

After they had circled the Ziggurat platform, the senior figures walked down the steps again, heading north. I stayed at the top and watched them descending toward the photographers and the television cameras. I turned to the east and saw the pit ring-marked by the biblical flood. I turned again to the south, and saw the American cookhouse and some of Saddam's bunkers; and I turned to my right and saw the red ball of the sun just meeting the horizon of the empty desert.

Adnan Sherife, Abbas the deputy governor, Salman Duffar, and Asad had joined me on the roof and stood silhouetted by the pale sky. Two military helicopters flew close past them, firing flares to mark the handover. They were watching me and they all smiled as I turned and walked toward them. The helicopters flew out of sight and we were alone together on that plateau a hundred feet in the air with the desert far beneath and the sun dropping through the horizon: Salman, whose six brothers had been killed by Saddam and who had been in exile in Iran; Abbas, a Danish citizen, close to the Dawa party; me; Adnan, who had been a civil servant under the old regime; and Asad, who drank and chased girls but was close to the Sadr office that had been fighting the others and me. I assumed few of them would be alive within a year. And yet on the roof we stood together like old friends on a picnic. And then they embraced me and kissed me and laughed as though it was all some great joke that we shared.

They asked how I was and I did the same. They had never been to the top of the Ziggurat before—it was closed both in Saddam's time and now because it was inside the Air Force base. They asked whether there was anything inside the Ziggurat. I said it was solid, not hollow like a pyramid, and I picked up one of the bricks from the top. I pulled a pale gray blade of marsh reed from the mortar. I split it length-wise and gave a sliver to each of them, explaining that it was four thousand years old, from roughly the time of the poet-king Sulgi.

When it was nearly dark, I suggested we walk down. Asad, who had been one of the leaders of the attack on our compound, said, "We will all miss you. Everyone in the province knows you and admires you. We know how hard you have worked. We wish you could stay. You are our hero."

"What are you talking about, Asad—why were you firing mortars and trying to kill me five weeks ago?"

"Ah, Seyyed Rory," he replied with a grin, "that was nothing personal."

AFTERWORD

Nanna, you whose penetrating gaze searches hearts, may its people who suffered that evil storm be pure before you . . . Nanna, in your restored city may you be fittingly praised.

—*The Lament for Urim,* c. 2000 B.C.

2005–2006

On January 30, 2005, the day of the Iraqi election, and seven months after the handover, I saw Abu Mustafa and again he greeted me in Farsi, to remind me that the Prince had accused us both of being Iranian spies. He was not stooping or limping. But he looked pale and his clerical turban was draped over his head, rather than worn in a tight knot. I had never seen him dressed like that before.

"*Shlonak,* Sheikh?" I asked.

"*Al Hamdulillah.*"

"How is security, Sheikh?"

"*Inshallah,* things are good."

"I am so sorry to hear about your accident."

"*Shukran.*"

"Are you feeling recovered?"

"*Al Hamdulillah.*"

"What happened?"

"I was coming out of the mosque in the souk in Amara and two gunmen were waiting. It was dark because there is no electricity," he winked—he still blamed me for the lack of electricity in Amara.

391

"They shot at me. Three bullets hit me, here, here and here." He jabbed at three points close together on the right side of his stomach.

"Do you know who did it?"

"No, I do not know. I have good relations with everyone." Although we had known each other for eighteen months, this was all I was going to get. I was left to guess whether it was part of a gangster fight, revenge for a killing he instigated, something connected with the Iranian secret service, or simply an attack by the Sadrists or the Prince. "Perhaps," he conceded, "it is because of my criticism of the corruption."

The Coalition had given two million directly to the provincial council to spend on local development. The Sheikh said that the council stole it. The council claimed he had stolen tens of thousands of dollars he had received from the Coalition to set up Internet cafés, to buy and distribute clothes to the poor at Ramadan, and to refurbish his mosque. Now he was to be given money by a development agency to run a "political participation project" designed to raise awareness of the constitution in rural areas. I was pleased that it would be funded. He still espoused a popular and moderate Islamic politics, supported a free press, accepted electoral results, and condemned violence.

"Despite the shooting you are still smiling," I said.

"We will always keep smiling, whatever happens," he replied and smiled more broadly. "The future," the Sheikh continued, "will be peaceful, *inshallah.*" And then, as an afterthought, he raised an index finger, its tip dyed purple from voting that morning, and curved it, twice.

In the elections, the Sadrists, Dawa, and the Iranian-linked parties took almost all the votes across the South and the majority of seats in the new national parliaments. In Dhi Qar, my friend the governor was replaced by a man from the Iranian-linked Badr brigades, and a Badr commander was elected in the remaining Southern province of Muthanna. In Basra the governor was a Sadrist from the more moderate Fadhile wing. By the spring of 2005, Southern Iraq was under Coalition occupation but not Coalition control. Iraqis were reluctant to trust us or work with us and because of this lack of co-operation, the Coalition achieved little of what it hoped and it received almost no credit for its efforts. Despite thousands of troops and tens of millions invested in essential services, despite a number of impressive reconstruction projects, despite ambitious programs in police training and in developing "good governance and civil society," the Coalition had only a minimal political impact in southern Iraq.

When I returned to Amara in March 2005 to attend the meeting of the new democratically elected provincial council, which was to elect the new Maysan governor, I found almost no record of our projects and initiatives. No foreigner in Amara had been there with Molly or me. My contemporaries, the Light Infantry, had been succeeded by the Princess of Wales's Royal Regiment and they by the Welsh Guards. Now the Welsh Guards were due to leave to be replaced by the Staffords, and the Royal Scots Dragon Guards were already scheduled to replace them. The provincial leadership would deal with seven different British battle groups in just over two years. Most of the soldiers did not even know there had once been a civilian presence in the province. The new British Battle Group claimed that almost no development had happened before their arrival. They implied they were the first to support the Iraqi ministries, do large-scale reconstruction projects, sort out the lines at the gas stations, and run employment programs.

Apart from the "moderates" Abu Mustafa, Abu Muslim, and Abu Ivan of the Communist party, not a single prominent figure from the old council had been re-elected. There was no Christian, Sabian, or Sunni representative. There were no sheikhs or mayors from rural towns, and the new politicians took little interest in rural affairs. The Prince of the Marshes' faction had been eliminated though the Prince was in the national assembly in Baghdad. Riyadh had not turned up to transfer power to his successor. The new rules had ensured that a quarter of the members were women, but every woman was in a full black *abaya* and they did not speak. Some of the members shouted at my British colleague for not covering her head. People seemed less willing to associate with the Coalition. I approached Seyyed Issa, the young mayor from the Marsh Arab village of Beni Hashim, but he looked straight through me.

A party supported by the Sadr militia had received three times as many votes as the next largest party. The man who had called me Hitler and had led many of the attacks on British troops was now a member of the council. The Iranian-linked SCIRI/Badr groups had come in second and the Badr commander Abu Maytham, who was still the police chief, continued to import thousands of his supporters into the police. The head of the Sadr office—a young educated politician from the political wing of the Sadrist movement in the bandit town of Majar, where the Royal Military Police had been executed and where the ambush had occurred—was elected governor with 90 percent of the vote. The other candidates had been eccentric unknown men off the street; none of the serious candidates in the province put their name forward.

In his acceptance speech the new Sadrist governor of Maysan deliberately avoided greeting either me or the colonel. Within a month he had fired old ministry directors, calling them Baathists, and replaced them with his own men. He announced he would no longer allow the Iraqi police to patrol with Coalition forces. He called the Badr commander and Police Chief Abu Maytham an infidel and tried to have him replaced. The number of attacks on the Coalition increased.

As we left the Maysan election, the new British colonel asked me what I thought. We stood in the forecourt between the governor's office and our old office where the new members of the council had led riots a year earlier. I replied that it was a stitch-up. I assumed the Sadrists had intimidated all the credible leaders and convinced them not to stand.

"Stitch-up?" he said angrily. "That was not a stitch-up. The governor is a moderate, reasonable, intelligent technocrat. He campaigns against corruption." I was surprised to find the military that had previously portrayed me as too close to the Sadrists now implying I was prejudiced against them. The colonel's officers, standing beside him, seemed as angry as the colonel. They believed in this new governor and had supported him.

"Everyone campaigns against corruption before they get elected," I replied.

"He is sincere," said the colonel. His Iraqi interpreter nodded emphatically. "I know why you are being critical. It is because your council has gone—a council of decrepit sheikhs and clerics who stole hundreds of thousands of dollars, like Sheikh Rahim."

"Sheikh Rahim defended us against the crowd when this group and this new governor were firing mortars at us. This party wants to drive us out."

"And we are quite happy to go if they want us to leave. You are just embarrassed about your council, and rightly so. Everyone knows that the council you chose in Amara was corrupt. Useless. Utterly discredited."

My predictions at the handover ceremony had not come true. Inchoate gangster groups were not fighting it out town by town. The police had quadrupled in size, acquired heavier weapons, and, by establishing checkpoints every five hundred yards up the highway, had brought some security. The large tribal gangster groups had lost power. There was much less carjacking, kidnapping, and smuggling, and no protection rackets in Basra shops. The state functioned. The only two forces that remained outside the law were the Iranian-linked Badr militias and the Sadrists. But then they were now the elected government. And the leadership controlled its followers.

The new administrations in the South were authoritarian, supported by militia, and in favor of strict Islamic social codes. When the

Sadr militia attacked a picnic of the Basra University engineering faculty, abducted some students, and executed a female student in the street for wearing jeans, the Governor of Basra defended the actions of the militia. He said the picnic had been "decadent" because men and women were sitting together. In many ways the new state resembled the administration in provincial Iran at its most conservative, although clerics were not in government.

This was not the kind of state the Coalition had hoped to create. During more than fourteen months of direct rule, until the handover, it had tried to prevent such a state from emerging. The Coalition refused to allow Sharia law to be "the source of legislation" in the constitution. It had invested in religious minorities and women's centers; supported rural areas and Marsh Arab groups; funded civil society organizations; and created "representative bodies" that were intended to reflect a vision of Iraq as a tolerant, "modern" society. We hoped that we had created the opportunity for progressive groups to organize and govern. The U.S.-led administration had refused to deal with the Sadr militia, fought a prolonged insurgency campaign against them, and tried to limit the number of Badr seats in the provincial councils. But it was these groups with their dark histories and dubious allies that had won in the election. Their new state was reactionary, violent, intolerant toward women and religious minorities, and uncooperative with the Coalition.

Some Iraqis were horrified by their new leaders, many of whom had spent twenty years as Iranian secret agents or had no education outside a theological seminary. Some were so afraid that they were leaving Iraq. But in the December 2005 elections they again voted for the conservative Islamist parties in overwhelming numbers.

ACKNOWLEDGMENTS

This book began at the Carr Center for Human Rights at the John F. Kennedy School of Government, Harvard University, and I am grateful to the director, Michael Ignatieff, for his generosity, patience, and wise advice on the book; to all the staff at the center, in particular Tiawan Gongloe, Samantha Power, Imran Qureshi, Fernande Raine, Matthias Risse, and Sarah Sewall, from whom I learned a great deal; and to Greg Carr. In the wider Cambridge community, I was fortunate in being able to discuss ideas with Nassim Assefi, Noah Feldman, Emily Finer, Catherine Lu, Roy Mottahedeh, Jacqueline Newmyer, Jessica Olin, Roger Owen and Indrani Sen, and in having the indefatigable and intelligent research assistance of Katie Paintin and Amy Rogers.

When I returned to Scotland, Stephen Brown, Joy de Menil, and Patrick Mackie, through patient hours and with different drafts, transformed the sprawling manuscript into a book, and Leo Carey and Naomi Goulder inspired me to continue. For comments on the Coalition, I am grateful to Catherine Day and Charlotte Morris, and for insightful comments on the text, to James Astill, Gillie Green, Fred Robarts, Jennifer Scott, and Kate Steuart-Fothringham. Clare Alexander, my agent, Flip Brophy, Nicholas Blake, and Jason Cooper at Picador, and Stacia Decker and Becky Saletan at Harcourt were patient with my delays and revisions and greatly improved the text. Colin Thubron provided a last tactful and wise review.